Luminos is the Open Access monograph publishing program from UC Press. Luminos provides a framework for preserving and reinvigorating monograph publishing for the future and increases the reach and visibility of important scholarly work. Titles published in the UC Press Luminos model are published with the same high standards for selection, peer review, production, and marketing as those in our traditional program. www.luminosoa.org

Documenting Death

> Definitions of care & how they manifest

↳ concepts later learned

↳ expertise

How Biobuerocracy of western and conception of care expectations effect structural violence on a day-to-day basis

Documenting Death

Maternal Mortality and the Ethics of Care in Tanzania

Adrienne E. Strong

UNIVERSITY OF CALIFORNIA PRESS

University of California Press
Oakland, California

Suggested citation: Strong, A. E. *Documenting death: Maternal Mortality and the Ethics of Care in Tanzania.* Oakland: University of California Press, 2020. DOI: https://doi.org/10.1525/luminos.93

Names: Strong, Adrienne E., 1988– author.
Title: Documenting death : maternal mortality and the ethics of care in Tanzania / Adrienne E. Strong
Description: Oakland, California : University of California Press, [2020] |
Identifiers: LCCN 2020014517 (print) | LCCN 2020014518 (ebook) | ISBN 9780520310704 (paperback) | ISBN 9780520973916 (epub)
Subjects: LCSH: Mawingu Regional Hospital (Rukwa Region, Tanzania) | Mothers—Mortality—Moral and ethical aspects—Tanzania
Classification: LCC RG966.T34 S77 2020 (print) | LCC RG966.T34 (ebook) | DDC 362.1982009678—dc23
LC record available at https://lccn.loc.gov/2020014517
LC ebook record available at https://lccn.loc.gov/2020014518 Strong_CIP

29 28 27 26 25 24 23 22 21 20
10 9 8 7 6 5 4 3 2 1

To all the health care workers of the world in this, 2020,
the first Year of the Nurse and Midwife

CONTENTS

ILLUSTRATIONS

FIGURES

MAPS

TABLES

ACKNOWLEDGMENTS

While so many people made this book, and the research on which it is based, possible, I must certainly first acknowledge my lasting thanks and debt of gratitude to the hospital staff at Mawingu Regional Hospital, as well as to the health administrators of Rukwa region who courageously and, probably, without knowing exactly what they were in for, granted me access and permission to the region and its health facilities. I learned so much from all those who were involved in this project in all ways, large and small. Special thanks go to my dear friend Dr. Samwel Marwa for his lasting support and interest in this work and all my work that has come after it. Likewise, I must thank Dr. John Gurisha for his assistance, support, insights, and interest as I conducted fieldwork. Ester Sanjala and her household have become family since she first picked me up at the Sumbawanga bus stand in 2012. Her hospitality, friendship, and gossip have sustained me during my work. Tumaini Mdapo, Edward Mwakasege, and their family have added so much both to my research and my life. From the fateful nighttime motorcycle ride when Mwakasege and I first met, he and his family have buoyed me up in countless ways, helping with logistics as well as laughter, shared food, and endless stories. Last, but certainly not least, I am grateful to Rebeca Matiku for her work as my research assistant through months of trips to remote villages on treacherous roads and in questionable guesthouses, as well as for her transcription help. Thanks, too, to Hussein Kandoro for his support, friendship, and connections throughout the fieldwork period and to Alida Fernhout, who arrived in my life in Tanzania at just the right moment.

In my intellectual life, I want to thank, first and foremost, Carolyn Sargent for her unflagging support and confidence in my ideas and research direction, even when it took some unanticipated deviations. Her guidance and friendship have led me to where I am currently in my career, and I am forever grateful. Many thanks to John Bowen, who helped to guide the ship home and facilitated and encouraged my connections with the University of Amsterdam and the Health, Care, and the Body group. Priscilla Song was always an enthusiastic cheerleader with incisive and stimulating comments and suggestions. To Shanti Parikh and Brad Stoner, my deepest thanks for support, encouragement, and feedback as committee members. Also from my time at Washington University in St. Louis, I especially thank Lauren Cubellis, Elyse Singer, Dick Powis, Anita Chary, Oğuz Alyanak, and Colleen Walsh-Lang. At the University of Amsterdam, though my time was short, I am so grateful to Anita Hardon, who first proposed the idea of a joint PhD and offered to be my supervisor. I benefited immensely from my interactions with Trudie Gerrits, Bregje de Kok, and Rene Gerrets. Eileen Moyer and her Becoming Men group have not only kept me company but drawn me into new and delightful conversations. To the beautiful people of room B5.16 who welcomed me into their midst, I am so thankful for the care and fun you all showed me. Yvette Ruzibiza and Linda Chipatiso provided so much companionship and moral support. The Trans-Atlantic Forum program made these connections possible and resulted in lasting friendships. The work for this book was supported by the National Science Foundation through a Graduate Research Fellowship, a Doctoral Dissertation Research Improvement Grant, and a Postdoctoral Research Fellowship. Fulbright-Hays, a PEO Scholar Award, and a Dissertation Writing Fellowship from Washington University in St. Louis also supported the research and writing.

While it might seem as if most of the work was already done before I reached the University of Florida, the Department of Anthropology and the Center for African Studies welcomed me with warmth and enthusiasm and helped me bring this project home. My writing and I have both benefited from weekly writing sessions with Marit Østebo and the support of my other colleagues in the department, as well as wonderful grad students and the Center for the Humanities and the Public Sphere. Thanks to Megan Cogburn for long hours of conversation about Tanzania and mutual research topics of interest and to Rebecca Henderson for her enthusiasm and some assistance preparing the manuscript's last bits and pieces. Through funds from the Center for African Studies, I was able workshop my manuscript with Luise White and Claire Wendland. To all of you, thank you for your time and energy and for engaging seriously with my work. Additional special thanks are due to Claire Wendland, a fellow scholar of maternal mortality, for her support and encouragement from this project's earliest stages. Likewise, many thanks to Emma Varley, who never fails to leave me inspired for the road ahead. I am also most grateful for the thoughtful comments from Ellen Foley, Maggie MacDonald, and an anonymous reviewer who read the manuscript for the University of California

Press. The final product is that much better because of your engagement and the potential you saw in it.

In more recent days, all my thanks to Jyoti, who puts up with my stress and anxieties about this, and all my work, with grace, silliness, and love. Last (because, really, they're first), my family's support, encouragement, and patience have made all of this possible throughout the years.

ABBREVIATIONS

AMO	Assistant medical officer
AMTSL/AMSTL	Active management of the third stage of labor
APGAR	Appearance, pulse, grimace, activity, respiration (also named after Virginia Apgar)
APH	Antepartum hemorrhage
BEmONC	Basic emergency obstetric and neonatal care
CCF	Congestive cardiac failure
CEmONC	Comprehensive emergency obstetric and neonatal care
CHFs	Community Health Funds
CO	Clinical officer
CPD	Cephalopelvic disproportion
DIC	Disseminated intravascular coagulopathy
DMO	District medical officer
DRCHCO	District reproductive and child health coordinator
EN	Enrolled nurse
HBB	Helping Babies Breathe
HIV/AIDS	Human immunodeficiency virus /acquired immunodeficiency syndrome
HMT	Hospital Management Team
ICU	Intensive Care Unit

IMF	International Monetary Fund
IUFD	Intrauterine fetal death
IV	Intravenous, short for intravenous fluids in most instances
MDGs	Millennium Development Goals
MMR	Maternal mortality ratio
MO	Medical officer
MoH	Ministry of Health
MoHSW	Ministry of Health and Social Welfare
MSD	Medical Stores Department
MTUHA	Mfumo wa Taarifa za Uendeshaji wa Huduma za Afya (Health Management Information System or HMIS)
NASG	Nonpneumatic antishock garment
NG	Nasogastric
NGO	Nongovernmental organization
NO	Nursing officer
OPD	Outpatient Department
PPH	Postpartum hemorrhage
PV	Per vagina
QIT	Quality Improvement Team
RAS	Regional administrative secretary
RHMT	Regional Health Management Team
RMO	Regional medical officer
RN	Registered nurse
RRCHCO	Regional reproduction and child health coordinator
SBMR	*Standards-Based Management and Recognition for Improving Quality in Maternal and Newborn Care*
SDGs	Sustainable Development Goals
TB	Tuberculosis
TBA	Traditional birth attendant
UNFPA	United Nations Population Fund, formally United Nations Fund for Population Activities
UNICEF	United Nations International Children's Emergency Relief Fund
USAID	United States Agency for International Development
WHO	World Health Organization

PROLOGUE

Paulina was in her late twenties, and as she sat on the chair opposite the doctor, I took in her shining skin, nice clothes, and plump figure. She looked to be the picture of health now, in her third pregnancy. Dr. Deo was meeting with her because she had already had two Cesarean sections and knew from her last birth that she should report to the hospital early to plan the surgery before her contractions began. In addition to looking in excellent health, Paulina was also what a Tanzanian nurse or doctor might consider to be the ideal patient. She had around her feet all the items health care providers told women to bring with them when they came to the hospital to give birth. In the absence of disposable bed coverings or sheets for the beds in the labor room, women brought brightly colored *vitenge* or *khanga* fabric to lay over the cracked or worn foam mattresses encased in vinyl on the metal frame beds. Paulina's all-purpose plastic basin was also there next to her feet, brightly colored and waiting to function as bed pan, emesis basin, trash can, and dirty laundry basket. Peeking out of her purse were pairs of sterile surgical gloves in the paper packaging; deeper in the bulging bag were neatly folded clothes for the baby. Paulina and Dr. Deo discussed some of the particulars of her present pregnancy and the reasons she had had C-sections previously. They agreed that she would stay overnight and Dr. Deo would perform the operation the first thing the next morning.

I passed by Paulina and Nurse Lucy around 8:30 a.m. the next day as they were on the way to the operating theater for the scheduled C-section. Paulina looked calm, a veteran of the C-section, as Lucy and the ward cleaner wheeled her across the bumpy concrete path between the maternity ward and the operating room on the other side of the hospital. By 1:30 p.m., back on the maternity ward, the nurses and I were still waiting for Paulina's return from the theater. Normally, an uncomplicated C-section would last only a little over one hour, the surgeons working to extract the baby before it was exposed to too much of the mother's general anesthesia. The fact that Paulina had been in the theater for more than five hours suggested something had gone incredibly wrong. Lucy came back to the ward finally, around 1:45 p.m. and reported that Paulina had just died. After Dr. Deo initially finished the operation, Paulina had begun to bleed again and bleed excessively. Staff quickly took her back into the operating room to see what had transpired, only to find that the hospital and Red Cross blood banks had just one unit of O negative blood, a very rare type that would be the only option for Paulina. But as she continued to hemorrhage, the one unit was not enough to begin replacing her lost blood volume, and she descended into hypovolemic shock from which they were unable to save her. Her baby daughter survived and weighed in at an impressive 3.5 kilograms. She lay in the infant warmer, blissfully unaware that her mother had just lost her life as she was only beginning hers.

After Nurse Lucy came back to the ward to tell us that Paulina had died, I witnessed the only time in nearly two years that the nurses would openly discuss their feelings about the deaths of the pregnant women on their ward. Nurse Rukia said to the cluster of gathered nurses that Paulina's death was particularly painful because Paulina was so healthy, so beautiful. She was so unlike some other women whom the nurses might expect to develop complications because of an appearance of poor nutrition, or signs of HIV infection. Rukia also lamented the fact that Paulina had already agreed to have a bilateral tubal ligation, a permanent form of birth control; this was to have been her last pregnancy. Instead of joining her happy, healthy family, Paulina was leaving behind three children, including her newborn daughter left alone in the ward. Later in the afternoon, as the nurses dealt with complication after complication on that particularly busy day, Nurse Peninah said that every time a woman died the way Paulina did it hurt a lot, *inaumia sana.* Peninah told us that some people said, "Pregnancy is not a sickness" (*ujauzito si ugonjwa*), to which Rukia immediately retorted bitterly, "Who says that? Pregnancy is poison!" (*Nani anasema hivi? Mimba ni sumu!*) Peninah admitted that Rukia was right and added that many of the women were so young at the time of their deaths. Paulina was so unlike so many other women whose poverty brought them to the hospital with faded, torn and restitched *khangas,* one rumpled, dirty package of gloves, and a barely legible antenatal card, either snacked on by mice or dirtied by life in a one-room home. Their deaths, too, pained the nurses but were somewhat less unexpected than those of women like Paulina. The nurses clearly recognized that a hard life wore down women. For a pregnant woman, poverty, low levels of education, or being an ethnic minority could mean she was one step closer to death even before any physical obstetric crisis began. Though Paulina was visibly of a slightly higher socioeconomic status, every death was painful for the nurses; young or old, poor or wealthy, unknown to the nurses or a member of their community, every death was an unwelcome event, the afterlife of which trailed along behind those involved in the woman's care for months and years afterward.

Though I was not involved in the clinical care of any of the women who died while I was at Mawingu, their deaths and the countless stillbirths and neonatal deaths affected me as well. Like the feelings of the nurses whose stories I convey here, my own emotions related to witnessing and grappling with maternal and neonatal death are not often visible in the text that follows; they were, nonetheless, a constant companion during the fieldwork. On some days the emotions refused to stay in the background and I had to remove myself from my research setting, leaving the hospital to spend a day doing other things, lest an outburst of feelings, a bubbling over, impinged on the professional setting of the maternity ward. In the local setting of this hospital, the nurses and doctors would have seen such an open demonstration of emotions as unprofessional and inappropriate; such a display would have undermined my credibility and acceptability in their eyes. In light of these norms of professional conduct and the hospital staff members' expectations of me, managing my feelings and engaging in emotion work became important elements of my ethnographer's tool kit during my research. Faced with the events I relate here, I was often deeply saddened, as well as frustrated and enraged. The deaths of pregnant women and their babies *should* provoke these feelings. However, the work of close, nuanced, and full analysis to try to uncover the reasons *why* these deaths continue to occur in health facilities required that I put my feelings (temporarily) on a shelf. While conducting fieldwork, I came back to them in quiet moments at home. Now, five years later, I still return to these emotions. They connect me as an ethnographer, a scholar, and a person not only to the research presented here but also to the first time I witnessed the death of a pregnant woman, when I was just nineteen years old, on my second trip to Tanzania. The emotions evoked by the injustice of these deaths and their profoundly inequitable distribution drive all of my work, even if they do not appear on every page of this text. I invite you to sit with the feelings that might arise for you as you encounter tragic stories of too-short lives and lives not lived. Some of the events and details recounted here will be disturbing. Some of the terms the health care workers use may seem cold or distant, but they offer us clues about the kinds of strategies necessary to cope with work in such a profoundly challenging environment.

Paulina's death illustrates so many of the precarious moments that can arise when a woman is pregnant or in labor and giving birth. In this instance, it was nearly impossible for the hospital staff members to blame Paulina for the events leading to her death. She was a model patient, well-disciplined to arrive early, before the onset of labor, to schedule her Cesarean section. She arrived well dressed and clean, a signal to the nurses and doctors that she was probably of higher socioeconomic status and that either she or her husband probably had attained more than the average level of primary school education. There were no apparent delays in scheduling her surgery, but from there her health and care began to unravel. Structural problems, such as the lack of sufficient blood supplies or cauterizing equipment, contributed to her prolonged hemorrhaging. A small number of present, skilled doctors, and the complete absence of a physician with specialized, advanced training in obstetrics, who might have been equipped with additional knowledge to identify and solve Paulina's complications, also contributed to her death. Poor communication and procedures that had broken down within the hospital because of understaffing meant that the nurses had not sent Paulina's blood samples to the laboratory or received the results before she went to surgery, even though Paulina had been admitted to the ward for nearly twenty-four hours and had a nonemergent C-section.

Paulina's case is but one of thirty-four maternal deaths that transpired in 2014 and 2015 at the Mawingu Regional Referral Hospital in Tanzania. These deaths highlight the need for ethnographic inquiry into hospitals and the lives of health care providers in lower-resource settings to better understand the complicated phenomenon that is maternal death. How is it that skilled (biomedical) assistance during childbirth is the unquestioned hegemonic solution to reducing maternal deaths worldwide, yet the institutions in which these skilled attendants work often operate in ways that not only fail to prevent deaths but can sometimes speed women's decline? From this attempt to understand these facilities and their health care providers' social maneuvers of caretaking, forgetting, and denial as necessitated by their work environments, it becomes clearer that health care workers' strategies ultimately fail to counter the structural conditions, in hospitals, countries, or globally, that lead to pregnant women's deaths.

Introduction

After two long days on the bus, I arrived in Sumbawanga in the beginning of February 2014, the rainy season well underway. The next day, I reported to the Mawingu Regional Hospital and stood up in front of the morning clinical meeting, with nearly one hundred hospital staff members staring back at me, to introduce myself and explain why I was there. I was proposing to research maternal death, a subject often accompanied by resonances of blame and failure on the part of individuals, institutions, and the state. I explained the goals of my research in a way that emphasized the need for the voices and perspectives of health care providers, those who were working hard to provide pregnant women with lifesaving care during emergencies, despite many challenges, and who are so often overlooked as whole people, or are taken for granted, in the reams of protocols and technical guidelines that policy makers and public health practitioners continue to turn out.

In less than three weeks after my arrival, we saw five maternal deaths on the maternity ward, one of whom was Paulina, the woman whose story opens this book. Over the course of the following fifteen months at the hospital, I began to unravel the complex intersections of history, geography, regional identity, state policies, political economics, biomedicine, and institutional and individual goals for providing and receiving care as these factors all influenced maternal health and death in the Rukwa region. Life on the maternity ward of a regional referral hospital is fast-paced and high pressure. Not only are these wards often understaffed and lacking material resources for lifesaving obstetric and neonatal care, but the nurses and doctors must respond to, and implement, a seemingly endless parade of new protocols and procedures, evidence based and Ministry of Health supported. All the while, women's and babies' lives rest in the balance, caught between the moment of what might be—an uncomplicated birth—and what sometimes occurs—a quick, often silent, turn of events that leaves one or both dying.

A flurry of other activity constituted the background to Paulina's care on the day of her death. As she and Dr. Deo were in the operating theater fighting for her life, another woman came to the ward with a retained placenta. Even after a physician surgically removed the placenta, she continued to bleed heavily, still under the effects of the earlier general anesthesia and unable to call for help as blood pooled under her. Not twenty minutes later, another woman, Pascalia, started hemorrhaging after she gave birth. Nurse Rukia improvised a pair of elbow-length gynecology gloves (because the real ones were out of stock) and delved into Pascalia's uterus to manually remove the clots that were leading to the hemorrhaging. After she finished, Nurse Rukia had blood well up her arm, as well as where her makeshift elbow-length protection had given way; she was desperately calling for antiseptic to disinfect herself because of this blood contamination. Later that morning, relatives came to pick up a baby whose mother had died on the ward after giving birth the day before. In the afternoon, an eighteen-year-old woman arrived as a referral case from an outlying health center. She had started having seizures due to eclampsia from pregnancy-induced high blood pressure. Shortly thereafter, Nurse Lucy came back to the ward to deliver the news of Paulina's death in the operating theater.

As all of these emergencies unfolded, the nurses and doctors did their best to save lives and prevent other problems. In the aftermath of the death of any mother or baby, there was also a significant amount of paperwork. However, in the deluge of deaths that occurred during such a short three-week period, files went missing, and providers and administrators forgot details or were unable to follow up on a case as they might have wished. The resulting data that passed through the hospital, to the regional level and up to the Ministry of Health, were partial at best and hardly a reflection of the lives, the professional challenges, and the ethical and moral negotiations that went into each woman's care. Looking at the professional challenges and negotiations in the provision and reception of care that never made it into the reported data serves to pull back the curtain on the professionals who were supposed to prevent maternal deaths. Through these incidents, it is possible to see a workforce that is at once the cornerstone of the political and ideological humanitarian goal of reducing maternal mortality and also the invisible, taken-for-granted element in every facility-based birth—the nurse-midwives and doctors of the maternity service. As Nurse Aneth so aptly stated,

> The maternity ward is the mirror of the hospital. . . . I mean, you will find that in any hospital, a person will ask how is it, how is the language on the maternity ward? How is the care on the maternity ward? How is the drug supply on the maternity ward? How are the deaths on maternity? I mean, it's necessary. A person, if they reach any hospital, the person can be just passing, but they will say they are interested in knowing about the maternity ward. . . . I think it is a sensitive department because it is the workshop, the factory for bringing people into the world after asking God for them.

The negotiations the health care workers lived out on this ward serve, too, as a window not just onto the hospital but onto Tanzania's health care system more generally, as well as onto a global assemblage of institutions, bureaucracies, policies, and power that constitute the regimes of global health. Because of the complicated and unpredictable nature of obstetric emergencies, maternal death is a particularly sensitive indicator that quickly lays bare many health system gaps and weaknesses, making it a useful lens for examining the functioning of health systems but also individual biomedical institutions.[1] Attending to the complexity of this work, especially the moral and ethical complexities that the nurses and doctors navigated each day, holds profound implications for our understanding of how facility-based maternity care is not the straightforward panacea for maternal death the global community imagines it to be.

As much as this book is about complexity—in work, in bodies, in institutions, in realities—it is also, first and foremost, about practices and ethics of care, both technical/clinical care and affective/emotional care. Particularly within health care settings, the word *care* appears in many different contexts. Before moving into a more in-depth discussion of care, we need to differentiate between technical care (which I also refer to as clinical care) and the less bounded affective forms of caring. Technical care is what we are referring to when we say health *care* services. This category includes procedures and tests, medication, surgeries, and monitoring of urine output, blood pressure, or fetal heart rates, among many other indicators. Health care workers have undergone training to be able to conduct these procedures or engage in these processes. Affective care, on the other hand, is a much fuzzier concept encompassing emotional engagement between patients and providers and responses to bodily but also mental and emotional needs; fundamentally, it is an intersubjective relationship.

In the obvious ways one might expect with a hospital ethnography, this book is about how health care providers, working in environments characterized by scarcity, care for their patients or fail to be able to do so. This book also tells how institutions may or may not be capable of caring for patients and for staff members because they are also sites, or conduits, of myriad forms of violence—ranging from the physical to the structural. Too, these pages are about relatives and communities caring for pregnant women and how these groups understand maternal deaths or obstetric emergencies through their interactions with health care at a regional hospital but also closer to home, in village dispensaries. It is about how these people in communities are wounded by their interactions with their health care system through remembered and current incidents of corruption and exclusion. This book is also about how health care providers sought to care for each other through informal modes of accountability that protected them professionally (both within and outside their institution of employment). At the same time, sometimes these affective care acts for colleagues hid clinical mistakes, and the hiding challenged health care workers' personal, private morals and the professional ethics they believed to underpin good care. These ethical and moral challenges, the afterlives of informal accountability or other care acts between colleagues, escaped official documentation and visibility. But these care acts often helped hospital staff members reconcile their clinical and social actions with the burden of deaths that occurred on their watch. Ultimately, in far too many instances, bureaucratic, institutional, and social dynamics of the maternity ward, the hospital generally, and the overall health care system came together in ways that worked against a woman and contributed to the deterioration of her condition and her subsequent death, obstructing individual providers and state efforts to further reduce maternal mortality. The book also tracks maternal deaths and their roots outside hospitals, in communities, but also in historical precedents, in the world of funding and of material and human resources, and in global movements (or the lack thereof). However, "To understand these persistent patterns, one must look back to the period when the path was embarked upon, when the institutions were first constructed."[2] This is the task to which I now turn before coming back to care and this specific hospital.

THE PROBLEM OF MATERNAL MORTALITY

The problem of maternal mortality came of age alongside, and hand in hand with, a global expansion of data collection and disease surveillance. A confluence of contemporary currents of change and much older tides of interest launched the Safe Motherhood Initiative in Nairobi in 1987. Quietly, often in the background, colonial and postcolonial powers throughout Africa, and globally, had been debating the best ways to provide health care services for pregnant women when the time came for them to give birth. In British-controlled Tanganyika, present-day Tanzania, this meant years of memos back and forth arguing for or against institutional (hospital) and domiciliary (home) birth.[3] The ultimate question always was and continues to be: Where is the best place for women to give birth, not only for their own health, but also to accomplish state goals? These state goals have taken various forms, shifting from educating or "modernizing" "Native" women in colonial-era Tanganyika so they might raise a certain, imagined type of ideal colonial subject, to achieving the Millennium Development and now Sustainable Development Goals in the present moment.[4] With each new idea, with each policy oscillation between these poles of home and hospital, came new financial, bureaucratic, and medical implications for infrastructure, human resources, and experiences of caring for and being cared for. Maternal health, and reproduction more generally, can never be extricated from state making and perpetuation.

Throughout the 1970s and early 1980s, as data collection methods improved, and as second-wave feminism in the US and Europe influenced researchers and policy makers to look more closely at so-called women's issues, the global extent of the burden of maternal death began to come into view. Within maternal health, the current focus on data collection and utilization extends back to this period and continues to be both challenge and goal.[5] Systematic definitions of maternal death, as well as greater understanding of the primary causes of these deaths, initially resulted from this time period. On the basis of this work, the World Health Organization (WHO) now defines maternal mortality as "the death of a woman while pregnant or within 42 days of termination of pregnancy, irrespective of the duration and site of the pregnancy, from any cause related to or aggravated by the pregnancy or its management but not from accidental or incidental causes," and it adds, "To facilitate the identification of maternal deaths in circumstances in which cause of death attribution is inadequate, a new category has been introduced: Pregnancy-related death is defined as the death of a woman while pregnant or within 42 days of termination of pregnancy, irrespective of the cause of death."[6] Additionally, the WHO divides the causes of maternal mortality into direct and indirect causes. The direct causes are clinical conditions responsible for the majority of maternal deaths worldwide and include hemorrhage, complications from abortion (or attempted abortion), hypertensive diseases (such as eclampsia and preeclampsia), sepsis/infection, and obstructed labor.[7] Pregnancy exacerbates some underlying health conditions, such as diabetes, HIV, malaria, obesity, or heart problems, leading to indirect maternal deaths.[8]

In 1985, two public health researchers, Allan Rosenfield and Deborah Maine, asked the world why maternal health was being neglected in widespread maternal-child health programs of the period; they reiterated findings from 1979 that more than half a million women were dying every year of pregnancy-related causes.[9] This number, and the lack of attention for maternal health, shocked the global community and catalyzed a host of new organizations and initiatives, as well as a wave of policy priority setting. This historical moment gave birth to the Safe Motherhood Initiative and its Inter-Agency Group, a bricolage of organizations with sometimes-disparate interests, all loosely aligned around the goals of reducing these largely preventable deaths of women.[10] Together, this group of organizations suggested a variety of interventions to reduce maternal deaths, all the while supporting more research into their causes, and into the more removed contributors to the deaths of pregnant women, such as low levels of education or a perceived lack of women's empowerment or low status in their communities. But globally, the complex, radically inclusive and systemic approaches needed to reduce maternal deaths still received less support than child survival programs.[11]

Concurrently, as the global Safe Motherhood Initiative was building momentum, the world was facing economic challenges, most severely felt in lower-income countries. The 1980s were a time of drastic change for many nations in sub-Saharan Africa and globally as they tried to right their economies after the tumultuous 1970s had resulted in the collapse of global markets for the raw goods on which these economies depended.[12] In Tanzania, home to Paulina and the setting of the events to follow, the country's first president, Julius Nyerere, was forced to step down under mounting pressure from within his own party to abandon his unique approach to African socialism, Ujamaa socialism. Tanzania's nine-month military conflict with Uganda resulted in the fall of the brutal dictator Idi Amin but also diverted considerable resources from other national activities. Faced with the realization that *kujitegemea*, or self-reliance, was no longer a viable strategy if he wanted to see his country's economy survive, but too committed to his ideological promises to the country some twenty years before to accept broad outside assistance, Nyerere stepped aside in 1985.[13] The country's second president, Ali Hassan Mwinyi, immediately accepted loans from the International Monetary Fund (IMF) and the World Bank and, as a condition of these loans, implemented broad-sweeping reforms as part of the required Structural Adjustment Program (SAP).[14]

Just as many countries were cutting funds for social programs, including health care services—a move required by the SAPs as a condition for receiving aid—the global community was entreating low-income countries to commit to broad (and vague) campaigns to increase access to primary care and improve maternal health after the 1978 Alma Ata Conference called on governments to ensure citizens' access to health care and health through primary care.[15] Structural adjustment in Tanzania also produced reduced wages for health care providers, exacerbating a general decline in living conditions and social service provision during the 1980s and early 1990s.[16] The longer-term effect was an increase in corruption, which proliferated rapidly and soon took firm root in the health sector in the late 1980s.[17] Structural adjustment only worsened the financing problem for the Tanzanian health sector, which foreign aid had long kept afloat.[18] In 1996, Tanzania decentralized the health care system, shifting the burden to the local level, where inequitable distribution of wealth and resources resulted in growing health rifts between regions.[19] Around the same time, the country implemented user fees, which attempted to transfer some of the financial burden of services onto patients.[20] However, user fees prevented many pregnant women from accessing needed services, and soon they, and select other groups, were exempted from fees thereafter. Where, then, were the funds to accomplish these primary health and Safe Motherhood goals meant to come from? And, crucially for the story that follows, who was imagined to be implementing these new forms of care and expanding services far and wide?

Tanzania's commitment to its socialist experiment meant that the primary care message of Alma Ata neatly aligned with the country's egalitarian socialist goals to ensure that Tanzanian citizens had access to basic health care, provided in Ujamaa villages via small dispensaries, which continue to form the basis of the country's health care system.[21] By this time, Tanzania had been struggling for nearly two decades as an independent nation to provide health care services to the local population. A focus on primary care drew resources and investment away from larger facilities, such as hospitals, and resulted in increasing supply shortages and overcrowding.[22] Despite these challenges, Tanzania was one of the first countries to sign on to the Safe Motherhood Initiative as a show of support for the initiative's direction and goals. This commitment built on the foundation the Ministry of Health had established in 1974 when it launched the first coordinated maternal health services in the country and formed a dedicated maternal health unit in the ministry.[23] In 1988 the Ministry of Health produced Tanzania's inaugural comprehensive national health policy, the first objective of which was to reduce maternal and infant morbidity and mortality.[24]

Initially, faced with a global shortage of funds, infrastructure, and personnel, the Safe Motherhood Initiative advocated increasing access to antenatal care and training so-called traditional birth attendants (TBAs) as two ways to improve maternal health outcomes using already-present resources and in keeping with primary care objectives. Public health experts imagined antenatal care as a low-cost way to identify the women most at risk of developing an obstetric complication. Training TBAs—the name for people (mostly women) already acting as midwives in local communities, providing assistance to women in their homes—was another way to capitalize on existing resources. By training these women to use sanitary methods and recognize complications necessitating referral, public health professionals imagined that TBAs would be able to help reduce maternal deaths due to causes such as infection or obstructed labor. As it so happened, with more training, TBAs maintained, and even improved, their respected status in their communities, and more women utilized their close-to-home services. Particularly when biomedical services were poorly supported or low quality, women and their family members often chose the care of local healers and TBAs instead, reasoning that such care would cost less than the hospital and might be more effective, socially appropriate, and dignified.[25] Conflicts between local beliefs and the practices of biomedicine were also an important factor affecting women's decisions regarding the use of biomedical health care services.[26] Thus the original goal of TBAs referring more women to biomedical care was subverted, and women continued staying at home to give birth. Much like training TBAs, expanding antenatal care did not go as planned; as it turns out, it is an extraordinarily ineffective route for identifying women who will develop obstetric emergencies while giving birth or in the postpartum period.[27] Like Paulina, many healthy women unexpectedly experience complications, and others with a lifetime of health problems can manage to give birth without issue.

If these two approaches—providing TBA care at home and referring women only when home-based care was not an option and increasing antenatal care to identify problems—were failing, what then was the solution to preventing the deaths of pregnant women?[28] As the global policy pendulum once again swung the opposite direction, the undeniable answer seemed to be that all women should give birth with the assistance of a skilled birth attendant in a biomedical health facility equipped with all necessary lifesaving supplies. Yet women's perspectives and ideas about where *they* would like to give birth were often left out of these policy-level debates, historically and in the present day. Giving birth at home has often been about giving birth in a familiar environment surrounded by people deemed socially appropriate. In contrast, biomedical health facilities are unfamiliar, hyperspecialized spaces constrained by the norms and rules of such institutions and facilitated by the knowledge, technology, and tools of their staff members. The unfamiliarity of this environment can, in many cases, amplify women's experiences of uncertainty during this life moment. Pregnancy and birth are already liminal states, marking important social life transitions, solidifying (when all goes well) a woman's place in her marital home, and fulfilling strong pronatalist cultural expectations. This period is also a fraught time, the success of which is threatened by both biomedical and supernatural forces that can steal away a woman, cornerstone of a family and community, and/or a baby, the promise of a new generation.

In the end, skilled attendance at birth came to be the linchpin of programming in the new era.[29] The WHO defines a skilled attendant as "an accredited health professional . . . who has been educated and trained to proficiency in the skills needed to manage normal (uncomplicated) pregnancies, childbirth, and the immediate postnatal period, and in the identification, management, and referral of complications in women and newborns," essentially what is now called basic emergency obstetric and neonatal care (BEmONC).[30] While the WHO makes this definition sound clear-cut, significant gray area exists. If a nurse went to school and was present in classrooms and during clinical rotations related to maternity care but cannot actually describe the signs of eclampsia when asked, is she skilled or unskilled? Technically, she would be grouped with skilled providers because she has a diploma, but functionally she is incompletely capable of providing emergency obstetric care. Alternatively, I have met TBAs, *wakunga wa jadi* in Swahili, who have no formal training but are able to cogently describe procedures for dealing with complications such as retained placenta in a way that many low-level, newly graduated enrolled nurses working in village dispensaries cannot. Who, then, is truly skilled, and do skills or papers (i.e., diplomas and certificates) matter more? This fundamental tension underpins much of what follows in this book. The biomedical institution itself cannot reduce maternal death; something more complex is at play in these places that challenges this clinical reductionism and complicates perceptions and beliefs about how to best prevent the deaths of pregnant women.

It was around this time, 2000, that the global community adopted the Millennium Development Goals (MDGs), a set of eight goals to reduce poverty and improve health. MDG 5 was to reduce maternal deaths by three-quarters from the 1990 level by the year 2015.[31] In addition to structuring health sector priorities in many countries, the Millennium Development Goals helped to usher in an era in which indicators and metrics became a measure for the success, legitimacy, and validity of states and a marker of good governance from the local to the global level. For low- and low-middle-income countries such as Tanzania, evident progress toward meeting the MDGs became an important component of demonstrating deservingness for aid and investment, both from donor countries and from international organizations.

Only nine countries globally were able to achieve MDG 5 by the 2015 endpoint; many others failed to make significant progress.[32] Across sub-Saharan Africa, home to fully two-thirds of these deaths, women still have a 1 in 45 lifetime chance of dying from pregnancy-related causes.[33] In Tanzania, as the country attempted to reach these goals, they accepted support and interventions from numerous outside agencies, governmental and nongovernmental alike, resulting in the unstable "projectification"—reliance on shifting donors and policies—of the health sector,[34] as opposed to comprehensive, synchronized efforts at reform and improvement across various areas of health services. For MDG 5 in the country, there is little evidence to suggest that the millions of dollars and scores of interventions poured into achieving this target have resulted in any sustained change. For example, as of 2016, Tanzania's maternal mortality ratio (MMR) was estimated at 556 per 100,000 live births,[35] lower than the estimate for the period 2000–2005 but higher than estimates from 2010 and 2012. Thus, as the Demographic and Health Survey states, "There is no evidence to conclude that the MMR has changed substantially over the last decade."[36] Likewise, the Ministry of Health's website from 2018 says, "The maternal mortality ratio for births within institutions is not declining."[37] Tanzania has demonstrated strong and consistent political commitment to addressing reproductive and maternal health problems. But unfocused efforts to improve care, lacking consistency and singularity of purpose, not to mention the needed financial and human resources, have long delayed further improvements for maternal health in Tanzania and mirror the troubled trajectory of the Safe Motherhood Initiative itself.[38] After 2015, the Sustainable Development Goals (SDGs) replaced the MDGs, and a human rights framework now unifies seventeen comprehensive target areas, including reducing the global maternal mortality ratio to less than 70 deaths per 100,000 live births by 2030.[39]

With the growth of research, guidelines, policies, and programs designed to help countries achieve lower maternal mortality has come rapid growth of bureaucracy. Anthropologist Matthew Kohrman uses the term *biobureaucracy* to describe the growth of institutions that have emerged with the "conceptual and practical orientation of advancing the health and well-being of people understood to have bodies which are either damaged, sickly, or otherwise different, based on local or translocal norms of existence";[40] biomedicine and its worldview are intrinsically linked to the expansion of bureaucratic institutions.[41] In the case of maternal health, these "otherwise different" bodies are those for which pregnancy, labor, and delivery do not proceed problem-free. Though colonial efforts to increase birthrates and medicalize pregnancy "became enmeshed in the growth of bureaucratic state forms and *la paperasserie* of colonized life," the post–Safe Motherhood era has facilitated the birth of enormous global entities to reduce the most abnormal outcome (death) of one of life's most normal processes (reproduction).[42]

With biobureaucratic expansion has come an increase in modes of accounting for and measuring health.[43] Despite this link with calls for greater (fiscal) accountability, various actors fabricate data for a variety of reasons and manipulate records of care, treatments, or diagnoses to correspond with expected outcomes.[44] In many lower-income countries, the data on MMRs continue to be rough estimates generated through sophisticated statistical analysis.[45] The nurses, doctors, and health administrators at Mawingu Regional Hospital grappled daily with increasing demands for data collection, preservation, and transmission. Their struggles to meet these demands illustrate the unintended effects of this global health fixation on numbers as it draws workers away from person-to-person caring.

Hospitals such as Mawingu are ground zero for the struggle to reduce deaths. Though more and more pregnant women arrive at this hospital with the expectation of receiving high-quality care, the number of deaths at the hospital has not declined, despite years of efforts to increase the number of highly trained providers, improve the availability of supplies, and implement all the Ministry of Health–approved and internationally sanctioned protocols, procedures, and plans. Despite clear evidence about the clinical causes of maternal death (hemorrhage, hypertensive conditions, infections) and the upstream contributors (low levels of education, poverty), why does maternal mortality remain such a seemingly intractable problem in Tanzania, and much of sub-Saharan Africa? What else can help to explain the slow progress toward this goal and all the failed interventions littering the road?

Within the field of medical anthropology, scholars have, since the 1970s, sought to explain why women continue to die during childbirth. Most commonly, these efforts have been based in understanding women's lifeworlds and rooted in explorations of women's perspectives and experiences with care seeking. Researchers have done the important work of aligning themselves with women and communities, often the more marginalized groups. Rarely, however, have these inquiries sought, or been able, to follow women into the very biomedical facilities now positioned by global policy as *the* route to saving women's lives. Yet the central debate about the appropriate place for women to give birth resounds in many of these earlier works.[46] The fact of the matter is that if we examine only communities or only biomedical facilities we will not be able to adequately explain how and why women continue to die during pregnancy and while giving birth. Both anthropologists and public health researchers have thoroughly documented the community-level contributors. Now it is time to turn the anthropological lens on the biomedical facilities, where community meets specialized professionals.

Before reaching the specialized space of Mawingu Regional Referral Hospital, women most often pass through the other levels of the referral chain, starting with the local village dispensaries, which address basic, uncomplicated health needs. From there, a woman might seek more advanced care at a health center, usually

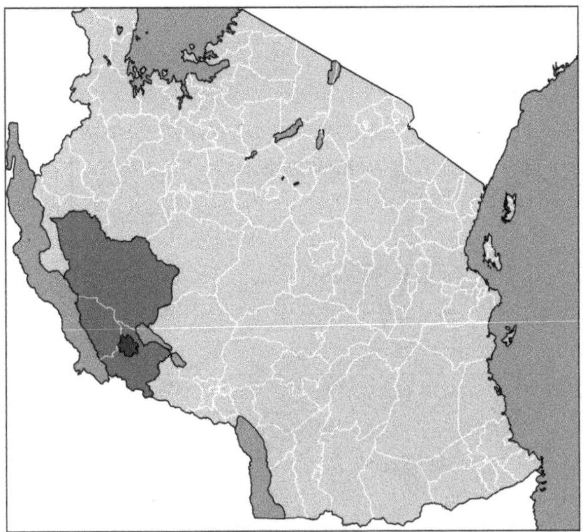

MAP 1. Map highlighting the Rukwa region, with Sumbawanga Urban District in the darkest color. (Available under GNU Free Documentation License, version 1.2, no modifications made. https://commons.wikimedia.org/wiki/File:Tanzania_Sumbawanga_Mjini_location_map.svg)

serving several villages and housing more equipment and additional, and more highly trained, personnel. Then, if health care workers were unable to address a woman's needs, they would send her to a district hospital if available (only two of these existed in the Rukwa region in which Mawingu is located). The regional referral hospital is the end of the regional referral chain. Should someone need more specialized care, regional hospital staff members might refer them to one of Tanzania's four zonal referral hospitals. As of 2013, people in Rukwa had to travel the furthest average distance to a health facility of any region in the country.[47] After the tarmac road was finished in late 2014, the closest zonal referral hospital was four hours away by private car, but patients could undertake the journey only after the lengthy bureaucratic procedure necessary to arrange transport and secure official referral out of the region.

Rukwa is one of Tanzania's twenty-six mainland regions and includes four districts: Sumbawanga Urban, Sumbawanga Rural, Kalambo, and Nkasi (see maps 1 and 2). Despite my arrival at the start of the dry season in 2012, the landscape I encountered was still relatively green, and the tall, lithe eucalyptus trees that clustered in stands just beyond the side of the dirt road surprised me. The climate and feel of the region, high on the Ufipa Plateau some 5,900 feet (1,804 m) above sea level, was uniquely temperate, and I soon learned that dry-season temperatures often dropped into the forties or low fifties (Fahrenheit) at night. With a long rainy season and lower temperatures comes a long growing season on the plateau and, historically, protection from mosquito-borne diseases. However, the region also encompasses communities on the shores of both Lake Tanganyika to the west and the much smaller Lake Rukwa to the east. In these areas, the climate is much more

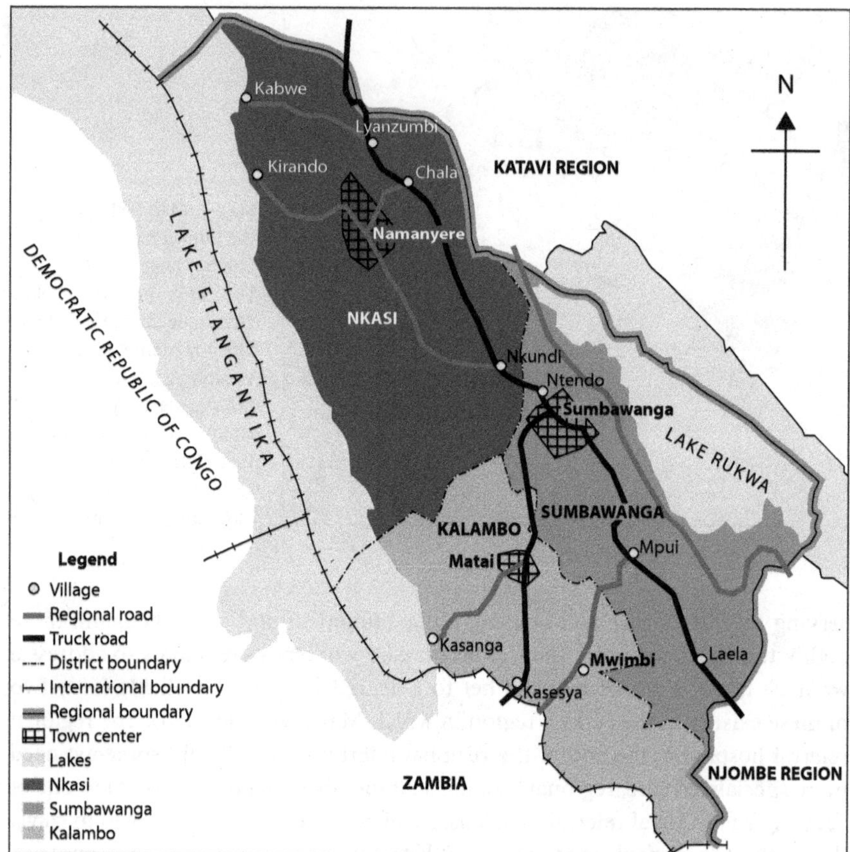

MAP 2. Map of the Rukwa region showing the three main districts, Sumbawanga Rural, Kalambo, and Nkasi. The Sumbawanga Urban District is the hatched area around the smaller word Sumbawanga, representing the town center.

tropical, fishing and rice cultivation are major sources of income, and mosquito-borne diseases are vastly more common.

Generally, the Wafipa people for whom the Rukwa region is home are subsistence farmers, growing maize, millet, rice, beans, and cassava; newer cash crops include sesame seed and sunflowers.[48] The varied terrain provides numerous opportunities for agriculture and other economic activities but also presents substantial administrative and infrastructure challenges. Since the colonial period, there is a record of how cold temperatures and the long rainy season in this area have thwarted building projects. The tarmac road was completed only in November 2014, finally connecting the region's main town of Sumbawanga to neighboring regions. Some communities on the lake shores still lack access to cellular networks.

The region has historically been geographically and socially isolated, with a reputation as a home to powerful witches and traditional healers.[49] I was repeatedly told that powerful witches in the region were known for being able to send lightning to kill someone. When I got in a taxi in Tanzania and told the driver where I was working, I invariably got a response along the lines of "Oh! But there are so many witches there!" The name Sumbawanga roughly translates to "to throw (away) witchcraft."

While people often told me the powerful witches in the region had long since fled to the bush out of fear of government persecution, many of the traditional healers, or *waganga wa jadi,* for which people also know Rukwa, have continued to run thriving businesses in the region. People from all over Tanzania, and even neighboring countries, seek the expertise of these healers for nonbiomedical ailments. According to early anthropological accounts, a Fipa healer sees his treatment "as an attempt to restore order to the two dynamic systems, one localized in the body, the other an invisible network of social relations, which together constitute the person for Fipa. . . . A large part of the average doctor's practice is concerned with meeting people's requests for treatment that will make them more socially effective."[50] The Fipa idea that well-being encompasses one's social relations and interconnectedness with others is similar to concepts related to health and healing from across the sub-Saharan African world. The self and one's social network are intimately connected and together make the whole person in this worldview. In the Kifipa language, there is only one word for what English speakers would differentiate as medicine and magic, thereby demonstrating the conceptual relatedness of these categories in Fipa thought.[51]

Despite the power biomedicine now has globally, interconnectedness and relationships continue to shape the worldview of many sub-Saharan Africans; Afro-communitarian thought heavily influences social relations and interactions.[52] For the Fipa, these moral or ethical social commitments surface via beliefs that broken or misaligned social relations result in physical ailments, including pregnancy difficulties, especially obstructed labor. If people cannot resolve these pregnancy complications through social routes, women must seek biomedical assistance at one of the region's health facilities. There too, within the walls of biomedicine's primary institution, ethical social commitments and interconnectedness often direct interactions at the hospital.

Within Rukwa's Mawingu Regional Referral Hospital, a medical officer in charge and a nurse in charge oversaw each department. The patron and the assistant matron oversaw the nursing staff and reported to the hospital's overall medical officer in charge, who subsequently reported to the Hospital Advisory Board and the Hospital Management Team (HMT). The clinical (non-nursing) staff included medical officers (MOs), assistant medical officers (AMOs), and clinical officers,[53] who, together with auxiliary staff, reported to the medical officer in charge. The auxiliary staff included laboratory staff members, medical attendants (semiskilled paramedical workers), pharmacy personnel, and other nonclinical support staff such as the hospital kitchen workers, security guards, and cleaners/groundskeepers.

The Obstetrics and Gynecology Department was more complex than any other department at the hospital. At Mawingu, the maternity ward is integrally connected to and dependent upon several of the other hospital departments, including Surgery, the laboratory, the Outpatient Department (OPD), Medical Records, and the gynecology ward.

The hospital administration coordinated activities with the regional medical officer (RMO), who oversaw all the health facilities and services throughout the region. The RMO, at the time of my fieldwork, was visibly involved in the daily functioning of the hospital and almost always attended the hospital's morning clinical meetings. He was an ally in creating and implementing the hospital's yearly goals and was responsible for ensuring that all facilities in the region implemented policies from the Ministry of Health.[54]

HOW TO STUDY MATERNAL DEATH

Research on the causes of maternal mortality in sub-Saharan Africa, the site of half of all such deaths globally, points to the combined and interrelated effects of poverty, lack of education, gaps in infrastructure, poor communication, and inadequate health care staff training.[55] Undeniably, the biomedical health care system as a bureaucracy combines with these other complex dynamics to contribute to poor maternal health in Tanzania's Rukwa region. This case study of Mawingu Regional Referral Hospital reveals how the social world of biomedical facilities deeply and irrevocably shapes whether and which women survive obstetric complications, even when women are able to overcome structural barriers to these services. But beyond just providing us with insight into women's chances of survival, this setting of a regional hospital demonstrates the profound importance of understanding the experiences and strategies of health care workers. In trying to provide technical, clinical care services to women, health care providers, especially nurses, engage in subtle but significant ethical calculations and negotiations. To understand how these ethical negotiations affect pregnant women and their health, I have found theories of care and everyday ethics to be particularly useful tools with which to think. After discussing these theories, I finish this section with an explanation of my fieldwork methods.

Ethics of Care and Care Practices

Care and the nature of *good* care in Tanzanian maternal health care is the most fundamental thread throughout this book. Women like Paulina who arrived at Mawingu Regional Hospital at the ends of their pregnancies expected clinical care that would save their lives and protect their babies should an emergency arise. But more than that basic type of technical caring, many women expected or hoped for certain affective care relationships with their health care providers. Additionally, much of Tanzania's socialist past conditioned citizens to think of the state as a provider of social services, as a caring agent. Advocacy and awareness campaigns promoted this expectation, urging women and their partners to take advantage of biomedicine, provided by government facilities, for their pregnancy and delivery care. Beyond these elements, however, care came to play important roles across many other registers on the maternity ward at Mawingu. Providing affective care was one way nurses and doctors sought to be accountable to patients, and through their technical caring skills their own superiors, the government, and outside organizations judged providers' efficacy and professionalism.

To bring together all the forms of care, especially nontechnical, that the maternity ward and hospital setting generated, I draw on Erdmute Alber and Heike Drotbohm's definition, which states that care can be "understood as a social practice that connects not only kinsmen and friends, neighbors and communities, but also other collectivities such as states and nations. . . . Care is a social and emotional practice that . . . entails the capacity to make, shape, and be made by social bonds."[56] This definition extends care beyond an intersubjective dyad of individuals to broader possibilities. In a hospital setting, the typical observer might expect to be most attuned to how nurses and patients or doctors and patients enter into these intersubjective caring relations and practices. Clearly, the expected relationships of care are present, but alongside these exist care relationships between doctors and nurses, nurses and nurses, the hospital and its workers, documents and nurses or doctors, supplies or technology and health care workers,[57] as well as the state and citizen patients, and the state and its health care employees. All of these forms contribute to the generation of care as a multiplicity of practices in the biomedical setting.[58] Ideals about good and bad (nontechnical) care carry implicit messages about ethical care, or the ethics *of* care, and how health care providers negotiate possible and impossible care practices to enact ethical care in their settings.

The term "*ethics*" often evokes notions of a rationally derived, codified set of dos and don'ts of practice. However, Paul Brodwin's "everyday ethics" is more suited to the analysis at hand because it forces us to take very seriously how environment and context shape ethics and necessitate modifications and negotiation.[59] These everyday ethics also consider actors'—in this case, generally doctors and nurses—structural position in their work environment, which helps to determine how they identify ethical problems, as well as their visions of good care.[60] Real-time, intersubjective care practices provide fertile grounds for examining these types of ethics, which become visible as nurses and doctors determine their responsibility to care for others and the ways in which they can in their work environment. These ethics become apparent when health care workers "must revisit their deeply held priorities concerning the good, the honorable, the obligatory" in the course of working with pregnant women.[61]

María Puig de la Bellacasa argues that "an ethics of care cannot be about a realm of normative moral obligations but rather about thick, impure, involvement in a world where the question of how to care needs to be posed. That is, it makes of ethics a hands-on, ongoing process of recreation of 'as well as possible' relations."[62] Such relations become increasingly clear for the Tanzanian biomedical setting when examined through the lens of maternal mortality. This is a conversation not so much about the "oughts" of moral or ethical existence as about the "is": that is, how health care workers engage in their everyday care practices in a way they imagine to be ethical or not, moral or not, and how their health care system, poverty, and structural violence constrain the repertoire of ethical choices available to them in the context of providing maternal health services to women in the Rukwa region of Tanzania.

Examining (everyday) ethics of care on the maternity ward of Mawingu Regional Hospital reveals a nexus at which forms of ethical care that are local, specifically Tanzanian, rooted in African moral philosophies of interconnectedness, meet with forms of ethical care rooted in biomedicine and the Western philosophies that accompanied its spread in the colonial past and the contemporary era.[63]

In this local setting, the borders and boundaries of care versus abuse are not always clear-cut, and the recipient of care not always perceptible. Though women and nurses, as well as the doctors and administrators, were on the same side, striving for the same goal—the healthy birth of a baby and the continued health of the parturient mother—the institutional setting of the hospital, as shaped by state and global policies, not infrequently placed (especially) nurses and women in diametrically opposed positions, with the good of the one dependent upon the sacrifice of the other. Here the story of the Mawingu Regional Hospital's maternity ward should serve to demonstrate that the nurses and doctors worked in many ways unseen by women to buffer pregnant women and their babies from systemic deficiencies with no compensation and often at great personal cost, achieving some quiet forms of good care at the expense of other more visible goods.

These multiple versions of "good" that reflect not only particular, situated or subjective values but also different ways of ordering reality are an inherent attribute of care; care "implies a negotiation about how different goods might coexist in a given, specific, local practice."[64] In the context of maternal health care, "different goods" enter the picture as each different actor seeks to give, receive, or demand care. The complexities and ambiguities of care practices arise throughout the book and form a central component of health care workers' struggles to create and enact ethical care in their daily work and encounters that demanded the intersubjective (re)creation of moral or ethical care practices. It is this ethics of care that I pursue here and begin to elucidate in the context of this specifically Tanzanian setting with specifically Tanzanian care practices, as well as the role this ethic of care plays in reducing, or sustaining, current rates of maternal death.

Fieldwork

Maternal mortality is an especially sensitive topic because of the deeply human desire to hold someone or something accountable for these never-anticipated deaths. As the nurses and doctors with whom I worked repeatedly told me, pregnant women are not supposed to die; pregnancy is not an illness, though they and lay people recognize the great danger that can threaten pregnant women during the pregnancy but most of all during their labor and in the immediate aftermath of giving birth. I arrived in Sumbawanga for the first time in 2012. Dr. Charles, Dr. Joseph, the medical officer in charge, and his wife, Dr. Akilah, had started working in Rukwa in late 2011, primarily through a program administered by the Benjamin Mkapa Foundation, named for its founder, the third president of Tanzania. The program recruited new medical doctors to work in underserved areas of the country through incentives for housing support and salary supplements. This cohort of doctors spoke differently of the region. Compared to those whom the government had assigned to work in Rukwa, they were filled with a certain zeal and commitment to improving maternal health care that had more ideological roots. They had willingly come to Rukwa as reformers. Likewise, the Rukwa regional medical officer told me the government had moved him to Rukwa in early 2012, just one month before my own first visit. His reputation as a successful reformer in another remote area had most likely made him particularly suitable, in the eyes of the government, to work in this new location. There was a sense of movement and change following on the heels of their arrivals, and the 2010 Demographic and Health Survey, which had clearly shown that the Rukwa region was behind the rest of the country on nearly all indicators related to maternal and reproductive health. Therefore, when I arrived and started discussing plans to investigate maternal health in the region, I met with an exceptionally receptive audience; they were eager for allies. Because many of the providers and administrators were new, they were less threatened by my proposal to investigate the roots of these deaths, knowing, as they did, that the roots significantly predated their own arrival and thus their responsibility. They all felt a certain mandate to reform and improve care and joined a stronghold of a few others long engaged in the crusade to help pregnant women.

At Mawingu Regional Hospital I participated in nearly all aspects of the life of the hospital. I worked at the hospital at least five days per week and started each morning attending the clinical meeting at 7:30 a.m. On the ward, I observed surgeries (primarily C-sections and the occasional fistula repair or evacuation postabortion/miscarriage), assisted nurses with the intake and discharge of patients, took vital signs, and filled out paperwork related to birth records, labor progress, doctors' rounds, death certificates, and patient consent forms as dictated to me. I also tested urine for protein (a sign of eclampsia), took blood samples to the hospital lab, collected lab results, restocked supplies, provided laboring mothers with comfort measures, delivered babies, and resuscitated newborns, as well as mopped floors, took equipment to the autoclave, helped fetch supplies, and performed other basic tasks that arose as part of daily life on the maternity ward. To contextualize events in the hospital, I also visited more than twenty communities and worked in the Tanzania National Archives.

I did not start my fieldwork with the intention of being involved in clinical tasks on the ward because I am not a clinician and am neither trained nor certified in any sort of nursing, midwifery, medicine, or paramedical field in the United States. However, despite my intentions, while I was at the hospital in 2013, one of the senior nurse-midwives who was also a nationally certified trainer of trainers in basic emergency obstetric and neonatal care (BEmONC), told me I should be more helpful on the ward and decided to train me in how to conduct uncomplicated deliveries. Simply scribbling away in my little black notebook had become untenable. Initially, I protested, telling her that I did not know *how* and that therefore I felt it would be unethical for me to perform these tasks. In her no-nonsense manner she quipped, "Well, I am going to teach you and then you will know! Besides, there will always be someone else here even if you are doing the delivery." With that, my education commenced. These interactions with Nurse Gire exemplify the complex negotiations that Gitte Wind describes as negotiated interactive observation in hospital ethnography; the ethnographer also becomes "an object for the Others' interpretation and social engagement. . . . At least some if not all of an ethnographer's informants will watchfully scrutinize all her actions, attitudes, comments and questions."[65] Gire's scrutiny of my dedicated scribbling led her to determine that this type of work did not satisfy her and, in her view, was incompatible with the setting in which I could be taught to be a useful additional set of hands.

Ultimately, I engaged in "observant participation,"[66] through which I learned, though initially unwillingly, several aspects of being a nurse-midwife and, under supervision and only when human resource shortages necessitated, worked in a version of that capacity. None of this experience made me a midwife, a specialized profession of which I am not a part. However, under the watchful and exacting eyes of Nurse Gire, I learned to properly, safely, and respectfully assist women during uncomplicated births. As she had said, there were always nurses on the ward, but after much supervised practice I did sometimes deliver babies on my own. This happened only when all of the nurses were occupied with other women. Always, the nurses and doctors knew what I was doing and came to assist as soon as they were available in order to ensure that women received appropriate, safe, and effective care. A deep respect for women's rights and dignity, as well as their bodily autonomy, underpinned all that I did.

In preparation for this fieldwork in 2014 and 2015, I pursued training in the United States as a doula, or birth support person, in the hopes of being useful on the ward in this capacity. Doulas provide comfort measures and pain management strategies for women in labor but, perhaps most importantly, serve as a witness to the woman's labor and birth, whether picture-perfect or prolonged and traumatic. This witnessing is often the most valuable tool a doula has to offer and is not terribly different from the similar gift an adept ethnographer can provide through interviews and presence. Because I was not a nurse, I was at liberty to spend more sustained amounts of time with individual women while they were in labor on the ward. I often would stay close to the beds of women who were young or expressed fear or concern amid their contractions. I would rub their backs, apply counter-pressure, hold their hands, or simply sit nearby. The greatest offering I had was time; the nurses often made fun of me for spending hours with one woman, so indulgent did this seem in their setting of personnel scarcity. In one instance, I spent hours standing beside a woman as she silently and excruciatingly worked to deliver the body of her baby who had long since died in utero. All I had to give her was my presence, my witness to her silent, determined, and grim work toward a known and distressing outcome. Most of the time, these were the ways in which I participated in births.

I want to emphasize, too, that my whiteness and foreignness surely influenced how people read my presence, opening additional avenues for participation that would have been closed in other settings. Often the only other white people in these settings in Tanzania are foreign medical professionals, and, as such, it was easy for the hospital staff members to slot me into that preexisting category with which they were familiar. Therefore, it would be reasonable to think that people, especially those with whom I interacted less frequently, would not question my actions or level of participation. In fact, as often happened, they might question why I was not doing more if they assumed I was a doctor or nurse. I stopped far short of what the nurses would have liked me to do and often requested of me: I always refused to do vaginal exams, start IVs, or perform other invasive procedures.

While academics and others in the global North may consider my level of participation controversial, it was necessitated by the environment of the hospital and was supported, facilitated, and supervised by local experts and authorities. The providers on the ward drew me into a locally appropriate and necessitated form of relationality. Local norms and forms of acceptable sociality required this level of participation during moments when the choice was either me or a woman giving birth with no help, possibly resulting in danger to the baby or the woman herself. My involvement does raise ethical questions. To not engage in the ways in which I was invited to would have been a form of ethical violation when I was there and capable of doing so. What would a denial to help, to "get dirty" alongside the nurses, and instead an insistence on sitting only in my privileged, tidy world of orderly black notebooks, have meant for relationships with others in this setting? What would have been the ethical implications of withholding my *ability* to help in some of the situations unfolding in front of me on the ward, particularly when the hospital staff members were invoking my assistance? In this way, my presence and participation are irrevocably entwined with the broader discussions in this book about the everyday, hands-on, "thick, impure, involvement" in, and production of, the ethics of care in this setting.[67]

In engaging in these activities on the maternity ward, I deferred to and respected local authority and sovereignty. I was also taught by locally recognized experts. No, I would not be qualified to deliver babies in the United States because I lack paperwork and official qualifications or certificates. Instead, an African woman in Tanzania taught me, transferring her expert knowledge via apprenticeship, which, in the global system, does not count as much as that of institutionalized classroom training in a high-income country. So too, the nurses and doctors with whom I worked would be barred from immediately practicing nursing or medicine in the United States because of complex mechanisms of power and inequity, with roots in racism and colonialism, that continue to systematically devalue and discredit knowledge and expertise from places like Tanzania.

Over the course of a total of twenty months, I spent more than 1,600 hours on the Mawingu maternity ward. I did not even attempt to conduct any formal interviews with the hospital staff members and administrators until I had been at the hospital for over a year. During that time, and through the activities in which I participated, the nurses in particular came to trust that I knew the difficulties of their work environment and would not report or blame them or violate that trust. It was this combination of deep involvement and sustained presence that led to the rich interviews that resulted and the intimate portrait of the ward and hospital that follows here . Throughout the text, I use pseudonyms for the hospital and its health care providers, as well as their clients. I have made sure no health details would reveal the identity of a woman or her family or jeopardize the jobs of the health care workers. For those people whose official title would identify them, I received their explicit permission to use their quotes with their titles. Since the time of the fieldwork, many of the nurses, doctors, and administrators have changed positions or are no longer working at Mawingu Regional Hospital.

The prevailing message women receive from public health campaigns, their government, and health care providers tells them that the hospital (or other biomedical institution) can save them from any and all complications related to childbirth if only they know how to use that institution. Knowing how to use the biomedical system encompasses embodying institutionally appropriate patient compliance, deferring to health care workers, arriving early in labor, coming prepared with supplies such as gloves and umbilical cord clamps or oxytocin injections, and knowing how to navigate the institutional bureaucracy in order to arrive in the right place within the hospital at the right time. Any deviations or delays can result, so the discourse goes, in a complication or death that is not the fault of the hospital's personnel but merely the result of the woman's own inability to effectively tap into the power of biomedicine through early and appropriate access to care. In contrast, in the pages to follow, I argue the fundamental point that the very institutions that politicians, clinicians, public health and policy practitioners, and the public have imbued with the power to save lives and have invoked as a panacea to solve *the* maternal mortality problem are, instead, at the root of systemic failures to improve maternal health outcomes and care. The role these institutions are supposed to play is repeated and elevated in a sort of collective fantasy or imaginary about how to reduce maternal deaths, without adequate acknowledgment of how these institutions have failed to progress, not clinically, but socially or organizationally, in order to reduce these deaths. This imaginary of the all-encompassing power of biomedical institutions also does much to deny the global and local inequity and systemic scarcity that forces deviation, justification, and improvisation that does not meet international best-practice guidelines. Certain forms of care (technology-based biomedicine that originally accompanied colonial conquest) have achieved ascendancy through metrics, data collection, and the reduction of bodies to numbers and checkboxes. Other forms of care, more affective and relational, have been effectively quashed within the biomedical system because of institutional scarcity, often the result of biomedical and biobureaucratic expansion that sought to accomplish too much, too quickly.

The second goal of this book, the first full-length ethnographic examination of what transpires in a government maternity ward in a low-resource setting, is to present a thorough and nuanced portrait of how health care providers and administrators work to deliver maternal health care services and uphold the ethical ideals of their professions within a bureaucratically and structurally constrained system. What emerges is a complex, discomfiting picture of shifting forms of accountability, patched together and resewn under duress, both professional and personal, as nurses and doctors sought to provide health care and save women's lives, doing the best they could under conditions of scarcity. African biomedical health care providers and administrators have long been "functionally invisible" in scholarship.[68] Understanding the complex inner processes of health care institutions and their staff members, and care as one form of an ethical "institution," has become even more important with the continued emphasis on biomedical birth to reduce maternal deaths. In every policy created and implemented, the health care workers are the ones meant to carry them out. However, they remain unnamed or unacknowledged in so many of these documents, even as policy makers and experts expect them to do ever more, often with the same, or fewer, resources.

1

The Mawingu Regional Hospital Maternity Ward

The deep-blue walls of the Mawingu Regional Hospital compound usher people arriving on the main road into Sumbawanga Town, a town of some 150,000 residents, located on the Ufipa Plateau, approximately 1,200 kilometers from Tanzania's economic center of Dar es Salaam. The hospital's large plot of land is the same one on which the hospital has sat since at least the 1920s, when the facility numbered a few dilapidated buildings. According to the current staff's collective memory, the oldest buildings still standing on the Mawingu Regional Hospital grounds date to the 1970s. Other wards have risen around this original core, fanning out on the hospital plot. The newest structures include the main operating theaters, the psychiatry unit, and, most importantly for the issues in this book, the maternity ward.

For an understanding of how a hospital can contribute to maintaining high rates of maternal mortality, some background information is necessary. Therefore, I begin by introducing the hospital and the institutional actors who will reappear throughout. These actors make up the characters in this story and include the nurses and doctors, yes, but also documents and paperwork and the physical spaces of care themselves. Situating these actors within the larger context of the Rukwa region and its medical infrastructure helps to draw attention to the importance of each. Additionally, scarcity's influence on the current state and functioning of the health care system in Rukwa becomes clear. This scarcity foregrounds many of the ethical and care negotiations and exchanges that develop throughout the rest of the book.

The first glimpse of scarcity, if you knew how to look, would be visible as you rounded the blue wall's corner and approached the hospital gates. Here you would pass the visitor's waiting area. Relatives always occupied the waiting area: a cluster of concrete benches with an aluminum roof that provided shade during the dry season and shelter from the wet in the rainy season. Here relatives from outlying villages waited for their family members to heal or perish, waited to bring family members food or take away soiled clothes for washing, waited to be told to run to a private pharmacy for a critical medication unavailable inside. Clutching brightly colored plastic or woven baskets full of food the hospital did not provide, they waited for the hospital's visiting hours, which happened three times per day for approximately one hour each. Some people, having come from a village and lacking a place to stay in town or any relatives with whom to pass the time when they were not allowed inside the hospital wards, spent the entire day in this waiting area. They waited, whiling away the long hours on the concrete benches worn smooth by many others who had passed the time similarly. This waiting area sometimes acted as a litmus test for the state of the hospital. If I passed relatives crying or if there was commotion in this area, I could expect to hear reports of a death or some other extraordinary event when I sat down in the morning clinical meeting.

Next to the visitors' waiting area, security guards manned the hospital gate and occupied a guardhouse, its spare rooms consisting of a couple of broken chairs and a telephone. The guards were responsible for ensuring that relatives did not roam about the hospital at unsanctioned times. They also inspected all cars for stowaways, ensuring that no patients left the hospital without the proper receipts confirming payment and their discharge cards signed by a doctor. Though most of them knew me, they also subjected my car to search, particularly when I would leave in the middle of the night shift. The guards would ask me to turn on the interior light or open the door so they might look in the back seat and the trunk to ensure that I was not smuggling any patients out of the hospital.

Once I was past the guards, the hospital compound opened up in front (figure 1). A dusty turnaround-cum-parking area in the dry season, it turned into a muddy and cratered expanse during the region's long rainy season. A sign listing the hospital departments greeted visitors to Mawingu's compound. To the far-right side of the compound was a meeting hall, used for the morning clinical meetings, similar to the grand rounds that take place at many hospitals worldwide. In the course of these morning meetings, the hospital staff members gathered to hear reports on the state of the hospital from the previous twenty-four hours, including the number of patients, deaths, admissions, and discharges, as well as a report on the money collected and spent. They also discussed particularly difficult cases in order to decide on subsequent treatment and presented cases in which a patient had died. The medical officer in charge presided over the meeting. These meetings started every weekday morning and included nurses and clinicians from all the hospital departments. The meeting hall was a vital venue, often the only one, for sharing information about the state of the hospital.

This part of the compound, before one entered the hospital proper, also housed offices for both hospital administrators and regional health administrators. In this

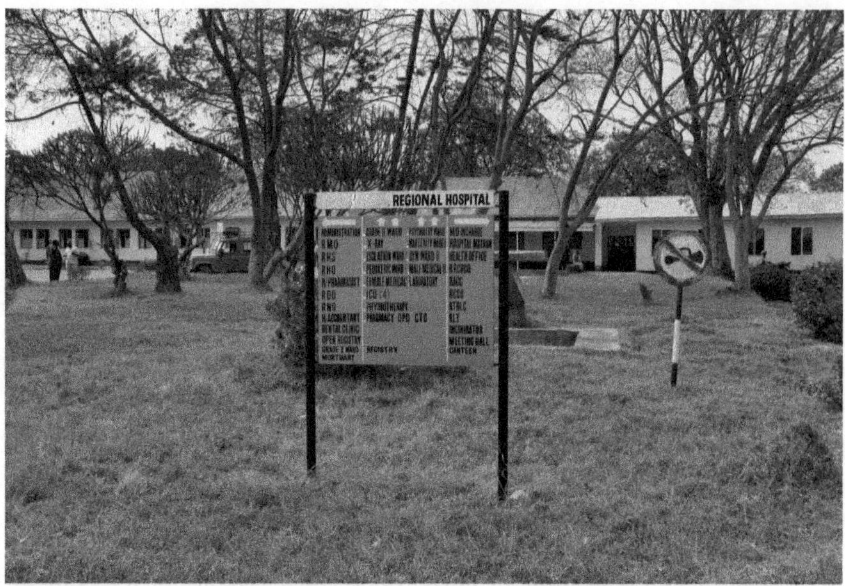

FIGURE 1. View of Mawingu Hospital. Photo by author, 2014.

area, doctors also had offices for consultations and their weekly specialty clinics, such as diabetes and gynecology. Opposite this, the regional administrative block housed the open registry, home to all hospital personnel files; the regional medical officer, the highest-ranking medical official in the region; the regional health secretary; the regional nursing officer; the hospital accountant; and the regional environmental health officer. Next to this building was the Dental Department. Finally, back near the guardhouse, was the Medical Records Department, in a small two-room building with an office and with shelf upon crooked shelf of medical charts and files numbering in the thousands.

The point of entry for nearly all patients, except those going straight to the laboratory or the maternity ward, was the Outpatient Department (OPD). Passing through the main door into the OPD, I had to pass the cash office where often a line of patients or relatives waited to pay the fees required at various steps of the hospital visit or stay. Chipping paint in the uniform colors of government health facilities in Tanzania—pale yellow on top and bright blue from waist level to the cement floors—spotted the walls of the OPD. The OPD itself was a narrow waiting room with several wooden slat benches on which patients and those who accompanied them waited. This area of the hospital could be particularly crowded and hectic but was also supposed to be the first stop for any emergency cases because the hospital lacked an emergency department. I sometimes saw semiconscious people lying on dilapidated gurneys or slumped over in a wheelchair parked near the doctor's door.

Throughout my time at the hospital, the administration changed their ideas about the ideal method of arrival for pregnant women, convinced at one time that they should all pass through the OPD to be triaged and receive a file, and at another that the best course of action was sending them straight to the maternity ward without any paperwork or notion of their condition. The maternity ward provided the single biggest administrative challenge to hospital management because the number of women coming to give birth routinely eclipsed the number of all other patients two, three, or even four times over.

At the end of the OPD was the pharmacy. A painted iron lattice separated the pharmacy worker from the waiting patients, relatives, or hospital staff members. Papers and medications were passed between these parties through the lattice or via a small opening at the level of a wooden ledge that served as a counter, worn shiny by elbows and hands. A doorway near the pharmacy led out into the hospital compound. From this vantage point, I could look out over the yard, the district medical administrative offices, and then, past a large and flamboyant poinsettia, to the hospital kitchens and, behind that, the laundry and the mortuary.

At the opposite end of the OPD was the doorway to the rest of wards. Mawingu Hospital, like many other hospitals in tropical countries, was built in a style derived from colonial hospital plans, meant to facilitate the flow of air and patients, preventing dangerous miasmas.[1] The different wards were offshoots of the main walkway.

THE MATERNITY WARD

The maternity ward was toward the back of the hospital, the furthest point from the entrance. Pregnant women arriving in labor usually proceeded directly to the maternity ward, navigating their uncertainty about both hospital procedures and its layout as they followed the smooth concrete walkway around various corners and the open mouths of the other wards. Upon arriving at the doors to the maternity ward, the pregnant woman generally entered with a female relative or friend who had accompanied her to the facility. Often the relative balanced on her head a plastic basin full of clothes and birth supplies (gloves, a plastic tarp, sometimes an umbilical cord clamp) wrapped up in a colorful *kitenge* cloth to keep everything contained. They passed through the first set of doors to the ward, then through an anteroom, to enter the ward proper (figure 2).

Several rooms with unique purposes formed the ward. These included the Kangaroo Care Room for premature babies; the antenatal room for women admitted on the ward, perhaps because of health problems or a history of C-sections, but not in active labor; the labor room; the delivery room; the operating theater; the post–Cesarean section room; the postnatal room; and the small room for women readmitted with their babies after birth because of the baby's health condition. In the center of this square was a freestanding, smaller building that contained the

FIGURE 2. Inside the maternity ward. Photo by author, 2014.

offices of the managers of the ward: the ward nurse in charge and the ward medical officer in charge (figure 3).

Interspersed throughout these rooms to which women had access was a parallel but prohibited set of rooms that were solely for medical personnel. These spaces included the nurses' changing and break room, staff toilets, a main storeroom for the ward medical supplies, and a storeroom for cleaning supplies, which the male nurses also used as their changing room. The changing room was the most important social location on the ward for the nurses. They used this small room for tea breaks during the workday and as a place to exchange gossip, money, and wedding invitation cards, to conduct side business (such as selling water, snacks, or secondhand clothes), or to discuss private issues (figure 4).

PATIENT FLOWS IN TIME AND SPACE

Pregnant women, their relatives, and health care workers flowed through these spaces in different ways but along specific tracks. Upon arrival, the patient and her companion reported first to the admission room. This large room was divided into two sections by a chest-height tiled wall. To the left were a number of beds occupied by women in active labor but not ready to give birth, as well as the more critically ill patients or those who needed close monitoring. Women who came to the ward with malaria in pregnancy, severe anemia, infections, preeclampsia, or eclampsia slept in these beds, where the nurses could easily monitor their condition without

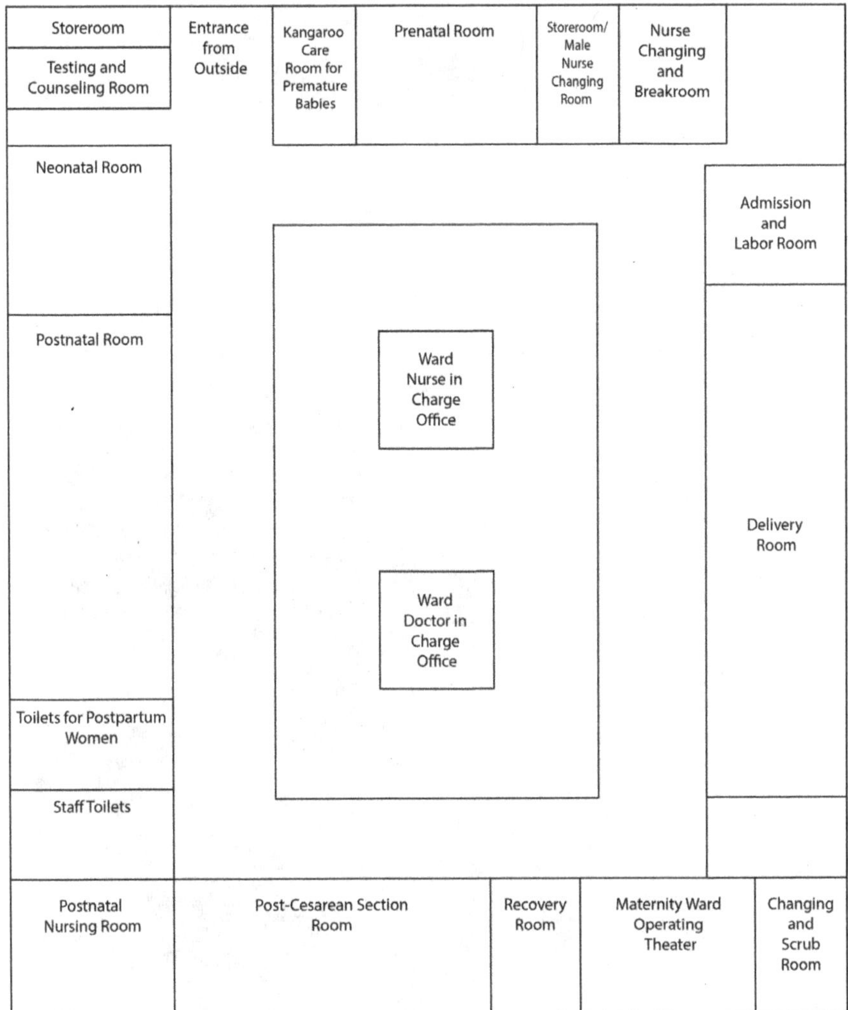

FIGURE 3. Ward floor plan, 2019.

being far from the labor room, which was adjoining. To the right of the wall in the same room was the admission area. This area housed a large desk for filling out paperwork, a wooden bench for arriving women, a waist-high examination bed, a trolley with necessary supplies (gloves, cotton swabs, antiseptic, urine dipsticks), and a handwashing station made out of a plastic bucket with a spigot and a plastic basin on the floor. All women started at this point, in the admission room of the ward. Nurses then funneled them into the appropriate other rooms, sorted and marked out depending on which stage of labor they were in or what other health problems they did or did not have.

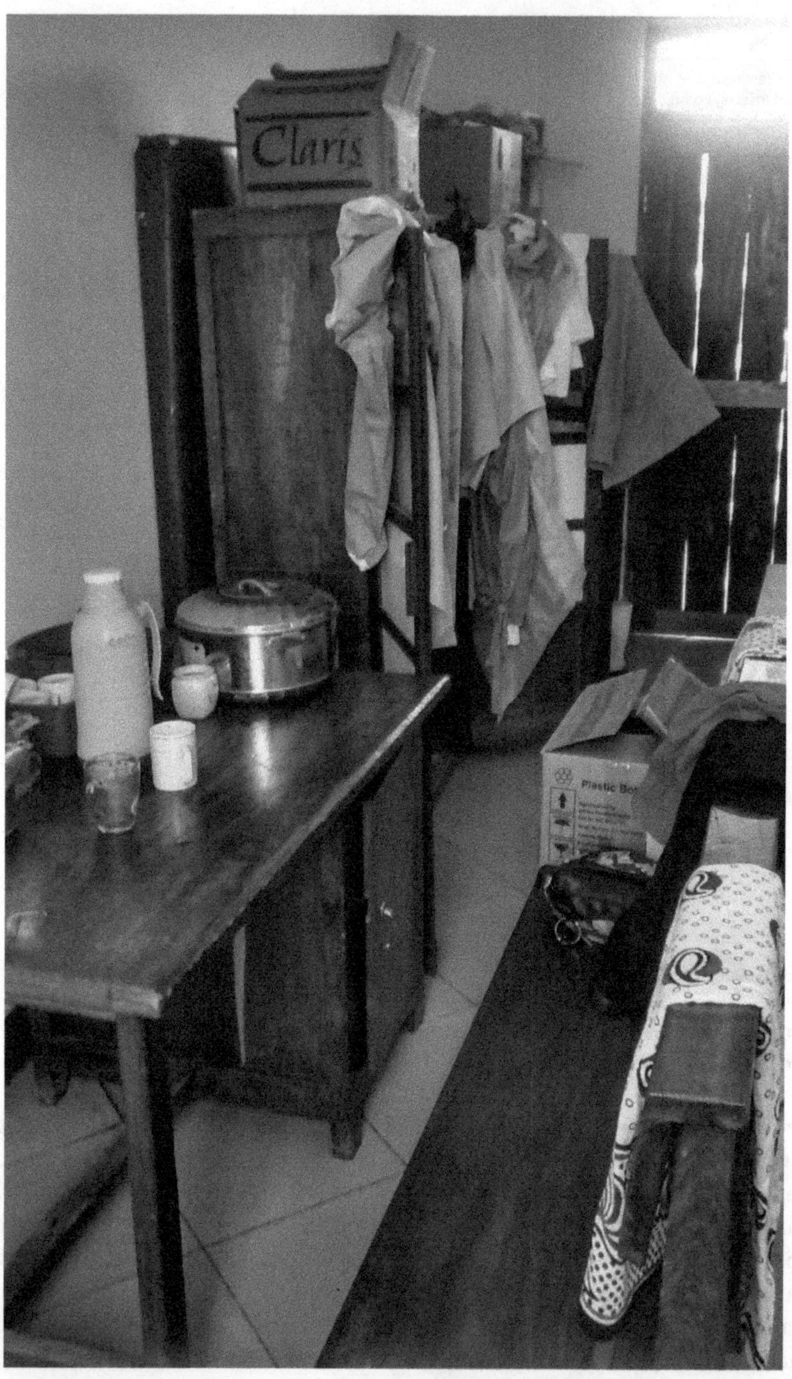

FIGURE 4. View of the break room with boxes of nurses' personal belongings, teacups on the table, disposable protective gowns draped over the cupboard. Photo by author, 2015.

While those women who lived in the areas surrounding the hospital were familiar with the procedures on the maternity ward and in the hospital more generally because of previous interactions with the system either as patients or as visitors, women who came from outside the district were often confused about how they were supposed to move through these spaces. Nowhere was it written that women in labor could go directly to the maternity ward, and waiting in line in the OPD could cost valuable time. Additionally, when women or their accompanying relatives asked for instructions, they often received gruff responses from harried hospital personnel. Sometimes it was the security guards at the front gate who were most useful in navigating the flows of the hospital. More than once, I witnessed maternity ward nurses harshly telling women they had skipped some portion of the designated procedures and instructing them to return again after they had done it properly—getting the appropriate paperwork, for example, once the hospital had implemented a new accounting and file system.

Ultimately, this confusion about procedures and these difficulties navigating the hospital spaces resulted in much consternation as women in the midst of contractions or a painful pregnancy complication were forced to traverse the hospital, sometimes more than once, in search of the prescribed piece of paper, stamp, or receipt. Delays and bureaucratic procedures that, to women and relatives unfamiliar with the hospital, seemed opaque and unintuitive could produce dissatisfaction with care but also reinforce a woman's sense that she was not in control and would do best to simply be quiet and listen to the instructions of the nurses. This instantiation of a woman's lack of power within the epistemological structure and hierarchy of the hospital served to silence her voice, figuratively and literally, as when she did not tell a nurse she was experiencing a problem she thought was abnormal. In this way, the hospital hierarchy and bureaucratic processes produced in women a sense of uncertainty about when, and how, they could ask for attention from the nurses or doctors. These experiences paved the way for women who remained silent as they began to hemorrhage or felt a change inside their bodies, which later the nurses and doctors might identify as the cause of the woman's death: infection, embolism, shock, life-threatening high blood pressure, cardiomyopathy, or uterine rupture. Women lacked the authoritative knowledge about their own bodies in labor;[2] this authority was conferred only upon hospital staff members by their affiliation with biomedicine and their training in this system. Women often told me they did not know how to assert their needs, questions, or desires in this hierarchical, power-laden setting in which they were interlopers. The result, in some cases, was stillbirth or the woman's death.

THE NURSES

The nurses, all of whom had trained in midwifery, did the bulk of the work on the maternity ward. While other groups of hospital staff members had more defined boundaries around their responsibilities, very little was outside the realm of nursing work. However, nurses were dependent upon the doctors for the ultimate decisions related to diagnoses and care plans. Within the nursing field in Tanzania were three main categories of nurses, distinguished by their levels of education and training. Enrolled nurses (ENs), in accordance with recent training changes enacted around 2011, went to school for two years to receive a certificate and primarily learned how to conduct uncomplicated deliveries. The older ENs had had around four years of training. Registered nurses (RNs) had either diplomas or degrees. RNs could subsequently continue schooling to become nursing officers (NOs) with university degrees in nursing. Many of the ENs were Fipa and had grown up in Rukwa, often doing their training at one of the nursing schools in the region. The higher levels of nurses often came from other parts of the country and were assigned to the Rukwa region via the government posting mechanisms. Occasionally, some of the Fipa nurses would complain that the hospital administration was favoring nurses from other ethnic groups, particularly those from the neighboring Mbeya region who were Nyakyusa, the same as the hospital's top nursing manager, the patron.

When I first visited Mawingu Regional Hospital in 2012, all of the nurses on the maternity ward were female. In the middle of 2014, the ward received a handful of new nurses, two of whom were male, both ENs. Later, in early 2015, we received another set of new nurses, primarily ENs, three of whom were male. In the end, approximately three-quarters of all the nurses were female. In other parts of Tanzania where I have worked, men have made up a higher proportion of the nursing staff. On other wards of Mawingu, there were more men, including several of the older, more experienced nurses. Indeed, the highest-ranking nurse at the hospital was a man and, as such, had the title of patron, in place of a female matron. His second in charge was a woman and therefore called the assistant matron. During nurse training, the students had to choose to specialize in either midwifery or psychiatry. Historically, I was told, many men had pursued the training in psychiatry; it was only more recently that more men were studying midwifery.

The archival records indicate that during the colonial period nearly all candidates recruited for nurse training programs were female; this was exclusively the case for candidates the colonial administration recruited into training programs as "domiciliary" midwives, nurses, or nurse helpers. One archival file includes many years of documents discussing the suitability of "ayahs for training in domiciliary midwifery," and it is clear these candidates were all women.[3] This trend is still visible in the profession in Tanzania. At present, the number of male nurses overall, and in midwifery services in particular, is growing, but data from 2008 show that 91 percent of nurse-midwives were women and 86 percent of nurses overall were female.[4] Clinicians, including medical doctors (MDs) and clinical officers (COs), are overwhelmingly male, with women making up only 21 percent and 28 percent respectively of these groups.[5]

Though women made up the majority of the nursing staff, hospital administrators, often the men, not infrequently made highly gendered comments, disparaging female nurses' hair when they thought it was too ostentatious, or insinuating that female nurses were looking for love interests among their patients when they wore makeup or nice shoes. These comments were insidious and worked to further undermine the nurses' access to formal power within the hospital hierarchy, linking them, instead, to more sexualized or less professionally serious stereotypes and tropes of nurses.[6]

In March 2014, near the start of my fieldwork, twenty-two nurses were assigned to the ward, thirteen RNs and nine ENs. By May 2015, the ward overall included about thirty nurses—enrolled nurses, registered nurses, and nursing officers—as well as three medical attendants and three to four physicians at any given time. The nursing patron said that, according to the ideal stated staffing-level recommendations, the hospital should have seventy-two more assistant nursing officers and twenty-nine more nursing officers, of which there were only four at the time, two of whom worked on the maternity ward. Explaining the ongoing shortage of nurses at the hospital, the patron continued: "Even yesterday you heard at the Nursing Day celebration that if you have a deficiency of nurses you cannot maintain standards. Yesterday we were told that by the guidelines of the WHO, one nurse should be serving six patients per day, but according to the research they have done, one nurse here is helping thirty or even forty patients per day. Therefore, you can see how it is difficult to reach those standards."

Nursing shortages arose because the government, that is, the Ministry of Health, did not open up enough positions in any given year or did not allocate 100 percent of the positions that district or regional administrators requested. Sometimes nurses waited a year or more before the government officially hired them. During this time, they often worked for free in a local hospital to gain experience. To try to produce more nurses more quickly, the government shortened the training time for ENs. This policy change succeeded in turning out more nurses to fill vacancies, but these new school graduates often arrived at work with little practical knowledge, unable to properly perform many procedures. This meant the older, more experienced nurses had to spend time with these new nurses to ensure that their skills were adequate before they could trust them alone during a complicated birth or an emergency situation. The hospital patron once explained to me that he made a concerted effort to assign the more highly trained and experienced nurses to the maternity ward because he recognized how demanding and complicated that work could be. He went on to say, "I have taken more than twenty assistant nursing officers [RNs] to the maternity ward because I know there is a big need. But if we had enough of the assistant nursing officers, I would expect to reduce the number of ENs on maternity [even further], they should be few there." During my time at Mawingu, there were brand-new graduates, along with nurses who were close to retirement and nurses with all manner of experience in between.

As nurses continue working in the government system, they are supposed to be promoted on a regular basis, every three years, so long as their performance is adequate. Many nurses spoke of these promotions as a right and, at Mawingu, as something that had long been denied to them because of budget constraints and poor administration. These promotions, perhaps most importantly, came with much-needed pay raises. Nurses generally belong to the Tanzania National Nursing Association (TANNA), the Tanzania Midwives Association (TAMA), and the national association for government medical workers. While the hospital employees never told me about a nursing strike in Tanzania, the doctors in the country have gone on strike to demand higher wages and better working conditions. Universally, the nurses I interviewed emphatically told me that their salaries were never enough for their daily family needs. Many of them pursued other forms of income generation, ranging from small-scale trading and selling of homemade snacks, to farming, to acting as middle-people for agricultural goods, to engaging in animal husbandry, to running clothing or home goods shops or, popularly, pharmacies.

The nurses on the maternity ward expressed their continuing feelings of being overburdened even though the hospital administrators told me they had been making a concerted effort for more than a year to increase the staffing levels on the ward. Despite these efforts, the nurses' workloads continued to increase in response to additional documentation demands produced by the hospital itself, as well as outside agencies and the Ministry of Health. This work all occurred in the context of growing demand for the hospital's maternity services.

The number of births per month on the maternity ward, 450 to 600, amounted to the busiest months' seeing around twenty births per twenty-four-hour period, on average. However, maternity care is not an area ruled by averages; some days an entire morning shift of eight hours could pass with only two births. Other days, the same eight-hour period could be nonstop deliveries, including multiple Cesarean sections, entirely overwhelming the staff members on duty and quickly exhausting supplies and equipment. Work on the maternity ward, like nursing care throughout the hospital, was arranged into three shifts—morning, afternoon/evening, and night. The morning shift was eight hours long, the afternoon/evening shift approximately four, and the night shift approximately eleven to twelve hours long.

By the time I left Mawingu in the beginning of June 2015, the morning shift generally had about six assigned nurses, including the ward nurse in charge; the afternoon shift usually had about three nurses, as did the night shift—two on labor and delivery and one assigned to the postnatal portion of the ward. The ward could quickly become understaffed if even one nurse left to run an errand, attend a meeting, or return home to tend a sick child or a funeral unexpectedly. There were around forty beds on the ward, at least half of which almost always were occupied by at least two women. Therefore, a conservative estimate might be that between forty and sixty women, plus the babies of all those who had already given birth, were on the ward each day, overseen and cared for by just six nurses, at a maximum, easily exceeding the six-patients-to-one-nurse ratio the patron cited.

On the morning shift there were also usually two medical attendants and two to three cleaners who helped fetch supplies, prepare delivery packs, maintain cleanliness, and generally run errands for the ward, including opening patient files in the Medical Records Department and taking samples to the lab. If these people were not present, the nurses did all of these tasks in addition to the nursing care. Despite efforts to task-shift (i.e., to shift certain duties from higher- to lower-level workers) and enable medical attendants, for example, to complete key tasks such as preparing equipment for delivery kits, Nurse Peninah told me,

> Another thing, so much work has to do with the nurse. Therefore, those responsibilities of sharing work, to say that the doctor does these things, the lab person these, these someone from wherever, there isn't any! I mean, any of that work, the nurse does it! . . . *Everything.* So you find that people in a lot of sectors, like the lab, a person is just sitting there, he is waiting for the nurse to do it. A person that is in the pharmacy is just sitting there, she thinks the nurse should do it. . . . You see? That is where the difficulty of the work comes in; there is none of that sharing of work responsibilities.

Later in the same conversation, Peninah told me that even though she was one of the most highly qualified nurses on the ward, as determined by formal education, she did not feel that any task was beneath her because, ultimately, it all had to be done, and if she could do it, then she would. This resulted in the endless nature of a nurse's work.

THE CLINICIANS

I trotted along behind Dr. Charles, trying to keep up, as he rushed into the ward, coming from the obstetrics and gynecology clinic that he ran twice per week in the mornings. As he explained to me, he was delayed in reaching the ward for morning rounds because "you know, everyone comes to the gynecology clinic and they don't want to wait. And because none of the other doctors are around I'm stuck doing it all myself. You see? I'm so late coming here." He grumbled as a side note, "You see? I haven't even gone to the canteen yet for my chai," referring to the small hospital-run cafeteria that offered standard Tanzanian morning "bites" of chapati, doughnut-like *maandazi,* and the requisite black and milk teas. He continued, "I haven't eaten yet since last night, how am I supposed to continue on? Hopefully there won't be a surgery."

Dr. Charles exchanged joking pleasantries with the nurses on duty as he called out for the trolley for rounds and started reaching for the nearest woman's file, tucked on top of her light-blue mosquito net, which was draped over the rusting, fly-poop-encrusted metal frame suspended from the ceiling. The women, who were in good spirits, or had been on the ward for several days, called out to

Dr. Charles. Mama Angel teased, "Oh doctor! You are late this morning. What food have you saved for me? Ugali?" Despite having not yet eaten anything, Dr. Charles responded to the standard joke with "This morning, chapati, Mama Angel! I'll bring you some later!" Other women lay on their sides or sat quietly in their beds, withdrawn into themselves out of pain, shyness, or unfamiliarity. With that joke, we were off and running for the rounds, which would cover all the women admitted to the ward. Our little party gained and lost members as we circulated with Dr. Charles; nurses entered his orbit to ask for a signature or clarify orders, and students in the clinical officer training program from the nearby school clustered around to hear Dr. Charles explain a unique case and then peeled away to find someone whose blood pressure they could take or whose file they could study. Through all this, Dr. Charles moved steadily from patient to patient, double-checking with the rounding nurse which medications were in stock or asking to verify that the woman had received the prescribed treatment when the file lacked documentation.

The clinicians, including medical doctors (or medical officers), assistant medical officers (AMOs), and clinical officers, were responsible for conducting patient rounds each day, ideally before noon, to assess each woman's condition, monitor any changes, and prescribe next steps for her care. AMOs have a four-year advanced diploma, and clinical officers have a two-year diploma. The AMOs and clinical officers tended to have more circuitous training routes, often working their way up from lower positions such as medical attendants, nurses, or laboratory staff. Medical officers, on the other hand, frequently described relatively linear educational ascents: they often came from elite private or boarding schools in the country and worked their way through the five years of medical school at the bachelor's level. The clinicians assigned to the maternity ward were nearly all medical officers (MOs/MDs) and all men during my time. The hospital and regional medical administrators, like their nursing administration counterparts, recognized the complex nature of maternity care, and just as nursing administrators wanted to place their most skilled nurses on this ward, so medical administrators sought to direct their most skilled physicians there. Though he was less present, there was one AMO, Dr. Benard, who had long worked on the maternity ward and continued to take on-call shifts. He frequently performed C-sections, like many AMOs throughout the country who had been trained to do so as part of task-shifting initiatives to alleviate the burden on MOs. AMOs and clinical officers were more common in other areas of the hospital, particularly the OPD, where they were primarily responsible for triage and treating common ailments. However, it was also these clinicians with less training who were responsible for receiving many pregnant women in crisis, especially at night.

On the maternity ward, I concentrate primarily on medical officers because they were the most common and most present. Henceforth, I simply refer to them as the doctors. Starting near the end of 2014, physicians rotated through the maternity ward much more frequently than had been common in the past, when the same three doctors had worked on the ward for about three years. There were still times throughout my stay when the ward might only have one doctor present, the others being away on annual leave, out sick, or traveling for other job responsibilities. On the day of Paulina's death, I wrote in my notes,

> Dr. Deo spent most of the last week entirely alone on the maternity ward. There are usually supposed to be at least four doctors on the ward, but two were traveling, and one, well, I don't know where Dr. Benard was, but I haven't seen him for almost two weeks. So, Deo alone all this past week. Having only one doctor seems to be common so far. Dr. Charles recently was on call essentially 24/7, alone for almost three weeks, and last month he once told me, "If you're the only one here, you're fucked. Either you die or they die," meaning the patients on the ward. In these cases, the doctors basically never had time off.

I came to find Dr. Charles's crassly ironic remark all too true as I watched the doctors and nurses struggle to provide care for their patients while doing so often meant sacrificing their own needs or well-being, including sleep or time to attend to household tasks.

The doctor would conduct rounds with a nurse who recorded a summary of the prescribed care, equipped him with gauze, gloves, plaster (medical tape), and antiseptic as needed, and drew his attention to the most urgent cases. The doctors also personally changed the bandages of women who had had C-sections or other operations, which the medical officer in charge credited as the reason for significant improvements in the hospital's rates of postoperative sepsis and infection. Further, the doctors were responsible for writing all the clinical notes for the women's files, and they saw patients in the weekly obstetrics and gynecology clinic. They were also responsible for the gynecology ward, conducting all gynecological surgeries, as well as C-sections. They rotated on-call duties for any emergencies that occurred after the 3:30 p.m. end of the working day, though they often stayed past that time to finish surgeries, paperwork, or other duties. When multiple doctors were present, they divided the duties on the maternity and gynecology wards to ensure that they could see patients in a timely manner and complete all their duties before the end of the day. Additionally, the doctors participated in meetings, trainings, and provided advice or saw patients whom they knew, perhaps through family or other personal connections.

None of the doctors were originally from Rukwa; most had been posted there by the Ministry of Health or had been recruited through the Benjamin Mkapa Foundation. Dr. Deo had finished school in 2012 and, after completing his internship in Tanga, on the eastern coast of Tanzania, had been working in Rukwa since late 2013. I once asked him how he had felt when he found out he had been assigned to start work in Rukwa and whether he had ever been there before learning of his posting. He told me, "No! I was just told, 'Tomorrow, come see your—you know, where you have been taken to. So, the next day I went, I was told that I have been planned at RAS Rukwa. I was shocked, (*in English*) Where is Rukwa? I came to know that this here is Rukwa, I felt so bad." He went on to tell me that he had been encouraged to come because Dr. Fakhiri, whom he knew from their internship time in Tanga, had also been posted to Mawingu, in another department. Dr. Fakhiri went without hesitation and subsequently encouraged Dr. Deo to also go.

"Why were you worried about your assignment?" I prompted.

"Ah, there were these stories that there are witches here, but when I came, I saw it was different. But the thing that was making me afraid was that about witches." I nodded in encouragement, and he continued, "I mean, that's to say, when we had arrived at Tunduma [the largest town closest to Sumbawanga where the paved road used to end] I wasn't seeing any electrical wires. It was necessary for me to ask people, 'Friends, there, there isn't any electricity?' They told me it was there, so I came, life started, until today. Although, when I was coming here, I had planned the fare to return entirely, but I came to delay that." Other physicians, particularly specialists, who had been assigned to the region never even made that first trip to see it for themselves.

When I started working in Rukwa in 2012, the Sumbawanga Urban District Council reported that only 51 percent of health care positions were filled and that the problem was worse in the rural areas outside of town.[7] Nurses and doctors related many stories in which health care workers assigned to the region reported for work and then disappeared again. Many others, including several of the nurses with whom I worked on the maternity ward, were actively pursuing transfer requests to move outside Rukwa. This trend is not new. This region presented persistent problems for colonial administrators, who routinely struggled to meet the needs of the people living in the area while also supporting health care personnel. This struggle was exacerbated by limited connections to other regions of the country and lack of access to reliable postal and telecommunications infrastructure due to the isolation caused by natural geographic barriers and by a lack of significant earlier, German colonial efforts to infiltrate the region. The region has only recently started to change, and colonial challenges related to retaining health care workers and geographic isolation would sound familiar to anyone who has lived in Rukwa in the last twenty years.

THE DOCUMENTS

As much as the doctors, nurses, and pregnant women patients appear to be the key players in this story, there is one character still to introduce, the documents. The corpus of text produced each day, week, and month on the maternity ward was overwhelming, and the nurses were responsible for the vast majority of it. Though the doctors, like Dr. Charles, wrote notes in patients' files and documented their clinical progress, it was the nurses who were primarily responsible for maintaining the documentation for each woman, baby, procedure, supply, shift handover report, death, or birth registration. They also documented all HIV testing, the patients on the ward who were receiving hospital meals, and the number of patients—adult and infant—on the ward at the end of every shift. Some of the record books were in Swahili, but the staff members wrote all official hospital reports, including the daily morning, afternoon, and night shift reports, in English, the country's second official language.

As time passed at Mawingu, the stack of notebooks on the nursing desk in the labor room steadily grew. This stack was paired with a smaller one in the postnatal section of the ward, and all of these eventually met up with the books and files in the nurse in charge's office in the form of monthly reports that the ward submitted to the hospital and then to the regional and national levels. Starting in September 2014, the nurses also began documenting every piece of equipment and every supply they used while caring for each woman, scrupulously listing each item and its number count in the woman's paperwork and repeating this again in a notebook newly acquired for the purpose. The hospital administration had added this documentary requirement in an effort to ensure efficiency and responsible use of supplies. Newly available numbers from a computerized accounting system had led some administrators to express concern that the maternity ward was misusing supplies because of what appeared to be vast consumption, far different from that of other wards. In fact, the ward simply had many more patients.

In the course of daily life on the ward it was impossible not to continually encounter these various documents, the paper residue of lives and treatment, rumor and clinical decisions, state and global policy. Sometimes, as with the notebooks, the paperwork remained well-behaved and stationary, while at other times the forms were unruly and tended toward wandering.

"I can't find it!" Nurse Neema threw her hands up in exasperation as she walked into the delivery room where I was sitting at the well-worn desk, fiddling with my phone. It was a slow morning, and one woman labored quietly nearby, slowly pacing with a green plastic cup of tea balanced in the palm of her hand. I pulled my eyes away from the phone. "What are you looking for? Can I help?"

"This patient says she was here last week and that we admitted her for three days and sent her home because she wasn't in true labor. Now she has returned and I can't find her records anywhere!"

"Let me see if I can find them," I told her.

"Yes, you are always pulling out those papers, saying, '*Takataka, takataka!*' Go look for this file in those *takataka*." I laughed as the tension in her shoulders eased just a touch and Neema turned to go back through the swinging doors to the admission room, on to another task.

The nurses knew that I would routinely help with ward cleaning by going through the stacks of papers in the delivery and admission rooms, good-naturedly muttering about the trash, *takataka*, that everyone stuffed into the cupboards built into the desks. I gingerly pulled open the crooked door by its worn handle. The cupboard threatened to vomit its contents into my lap as I crouched before it and reached in up to my shoulder, sweeping out rumpled papers of various sorts. Feeling like a fisherwoman bringing in my haul, I swept up partographs and half-filled lab request forms into the basket shaped by my arms as small pages from the physician's prescription pad fluttered to the floor, along with colorful pink and yellow chits from the cash collection system no longer in use. With their greater density, the shiny cardstock trifold antenatal cards plunked to the floor near my feet. I gathered the fallen bits and pieces into a pile that sprawled higgledy-piggledy across my outstretched forearms, and I moved it all to the top of the desk for closer examination. Women's forgotten tetanus vaccine record cards sat together with referral letters laced with entreaties for help from the regional hospital for this or that difficult case—a ruptured uterus here, a case of eclampsia there—that a nurse had hastily thrown into the drawer sometime between receiving the woman and intervening in her obstetric emergency. I peeled apart lab request forms, several of which had never made it to the lab, others with results written in the lab's distinctive red pen at the bottom of the page. Partographs, used to record a woman's progress in labor, had folded up on themselves, concealing the women's names and obstetric histories on the front page. After sorting the papers in the first desk's cupboard, I moved onto the next and repeated the process. After some time, I found the papers Neema wanted; stapled to the partograph of another woman with a similar name, the pages had sunk to the bottom of a pile and drifted into the back of the cabinet.

Documents and documentation requirements structured interactions and decision-making in ways both obvious and subtle. Their presence permeated the ward. Some of these documents were for ward or hospital purposes only, while others had afterlives at the regional and national levels. Here, they either went on to reinforce the region's reputation as a peripheral backwater or served to demonstrate and uphold the region's performance of improvement and compliance with the proliferating guidelines and protocols handed down from the Ministry of Health. At higher levels within the hospital, the nurses' documentation demonstrated their (in)appropriate handling of situations both normal and exceptional. Care that counted was counted care. That is, the documented care constituted the official version of reality. What was on the piece of paper might not reflect the actual sequence of events as they occurred, but the nurses and doctors could manipulate these forms so they included the accepted form of reality that protected them from repercussions or allegations of bad care—either intended, accidental, or otherwise—and, conversely, demonstrated how they were improving outcomes on the ward.

FIGURE 5. A tower of notebooks on the nursing desk in the labor room. Photo by author, 2018.

Every new protocol, guideline, or hospital system generated another notebook or record book (figure 5); these books continued to multiply to accomplish the objectives of outside biobureaucratic institutions and the proliferation of their efforts to track, monitor, supervise, train, and constrain the health care providers working both in urban centers and at the periphery, as well as the bureaucratic efforts of the hospital itself. In addition to accounting and supplies books, the ward regularly received new HIV testing logs and logs for documenting the provision of family planning services, for example. Handbooks and workshop participant activity books seemed to reproduce in desk drawers as the nurses attended various trainings related to basic emergency obstetric and neonatal care (BEmONC), Helping Babies Breathe (HBB), the nonpneumatic antishock garment (NASG), HIV testing, cervical cancer screening, or TB prevention.

Paperwork generally, makes up the stuff of all forms of administration in Tanzania. The open registry and the Medical Records Department in the hospital played important roles in this documentary landscape too. The open registry housed all the official details of a person's employment at the hospital, including evaluations, assignments, reprimands, and mistakes. The Medical Records Department held the only evidence of care given and received—the only official record of a patient's presence and, sometimes, death within the walls of the hospital. On the maternity ward, the paperwork, as an outgrowth of (bio)bureaucratic expansion, became a player in the social and professional life of the ward.

THE ORIGINS OF MATERIAL SCARCITY

Actors at the Mawingu Regional Hospital worked to provide care to patients across wards and departments, all the while against a background of historically rooted scarcity and administrative neglect in this peripheral region of the country. Though colonial correspondence refers to the facility that existed on the site of Mawingu in the 1920s as a hospital, the descriptions of the few squat, thatched-roof buildings and available services exemplify the racially stratified health disparities operating throughout the British Empire. In areas with more direct economic benefit to the colonial regime, or with a larger colonial settler population, health care services were much more robust. Because of the remoteness of Sumbawanga from centers of political administration, then as now, there were few options for medical services for both the colonial and local population.

An archaeology of what has always been the hospital's site might reveal unseen vestiges of the first facility's mud walls; of the kitchen table on which subassistant surgeon Dr. Ghanekar conducted operations in 1936 because of the shortage of other facilities and equipment;[8] or of the layered complaints of generations of health care workers—European medical officers, Indian subassistant surgeons, and African assistant medical officers—posted to this remote town. Since that time, the hospital has struggled with retaining skilled staff members because of its isolated location and the lack of private practice and social opportunities for educated workers.[9]

Prior to state reforms in the 1990s, the people of Tanzania had access to free health care services, and for-profit, private sector activities in health care were limited.[10] In 1993 the government introduced user fees and then, shortly after, created exempted groups—pregnant women, children under five, elderly patients, HIV/AIDS patients, and severely impoverished patients seeking care—who, to the present day, do not have to pay for services.[11] In 1996, the government undertook a process of health sector reform, which included decentralizing many aspects of health care planning and delivery to the district level.[12] Decentralization allowed districts and facilities, such as the regional hospital, to determine their own supply needs but also required them to pay for them out of their budgets, the income for which came from the central government, as well as user fees, insurance reimbursements, and the rural Community Health Funds (CHFs) into which families could pay. Decentralization placed the locus of control in the regions and districts but also put the fiscal burden of the health care system on economically disadvantaged populations in distant areas of the country, such as Rukwa.

Policy makers instituted fee exemptions to encourage vulnerable populations to utilize health care services to lower mortality rates. However, at many levels, these exemptions were essentially an unfunded mandate, lacking specific budget lines or any sustainable financial plans for continuing to pay for the care these populations needed, especially in the context of decentralization. While the central government budget does now include a budget line for maternal health care, the funds for these services are often supposed to come from outside donor contributions.

Regardless of the funding mechanism, all government health facilities throughout the country order their supplies from the Medical Stores Department (MSD). An act of Parliament in 1993 established MSD as a public, nonprofit organization, and it began functioning in 1994.[13] During my time in Tanzania, MSD was facing an incredible unpaid balance for supplies already disbursed. For example, in October 2014, Muhimbili National Hospital in Dar es Salaam alone had an unpaid balance of close to US$4 million.[14] A newspaper reported the collective debt of all health care facilities in the country was around US$50 million or TZS 108.6 billion as of June 2015.[15] In 2010, the WHO estimated the Tanzanian government spent $223 million on rehabilitative and curative services.[16] Using this number solely for the purposes of putting the debt owed to MSD in perspective, the debt would (in 2010) represent 22.4 percent of the government's total health expenditure. It was this enormous amount of accumulating debt that caused MSD to issue a statement limiting (or, in some cases entirely stopping) distribution until the government reached a plan to settle the balance. Yet facilities like Mawingu relied on funds from the central government to pay their debts at MSD, as well as purchase new supplies. If the government was slow to disburse these monies, because of either lack of funds in the budget from low revenue generation or delayed contributions from donors, facilities could be left without the means to pay MSD and, as in 2014, without any supplies. In September 2014, a sign appeared on the maternity ward that read, "Announcement: For now, there are no oxytocin injections. Therefore, the few there are, are only for emergencies." Oxytocin is the first-line drug of choice for preventing postpartum hemorrhage, and every woman is supposed to receive it immediately after giving birth. A shortage of this basic supply was a result of these countrywide problems.

As 2014 wound on, a perfect storm began brewing, one that would further challenge Mawingu's abilities to operate and provide services. Poor-quality services at lower levels of the referral chain resulted in ever-increasing numbers of patients at Mawingu Regional Hospital, overburdening this facility as it took on patients that could have been served closer to their homes. Poor services or lack of competent providers in village dispensaries and fewer resources for complicated problems all drive patients to higher levels of care. The hospital has seen a dramatic increase in the number of patients served each year just since 2010, but this increase in clients has not been met by a concomitant increase in physical capacity.[17] The result is a bed occupancy rate of 172 percent, such a significant degree of overcrowding that patients are often forced to share beds.

In addition to improved standards of care at the regional hospital, a lack of money in the community in late 2014 was driving more and more pregnant women to bypass lower-level facilities to give birth in the hospital. This decision was driven by rumors of good care, yes, but also by the belief that the hospital would have more supplies available, so that patients would not need to pay for supplies out of pocket as they would have had to in the village. Because of MSD's refusal to disburse supplies on credit any longer, health care facilities at lower levels became increasingly bare.

In Rukwa, people get much of their annual income from selling agricultural products, which they usually harvest after the last rains, sometimes as early as June and as late as September. They then use these funds for household expenses, including health care. In 2014, the government, one of the largest buyers of individual farmers' crops, acquired maize on loan with the promise of future payment. In November 2014, I read in a newspaper that members of Parliament were questioning the delay in payments for the more than three million tons of maize the government had already purchased on loan. In some villages, as late as April 2015, community members told me they were still waiting for the cash from the government for maize bought more than six months prior. In addition to delayed payments for purchased crops, the timing of the crisis at MSD coincided with particularly low market prices for maize in 2014. There was a bumper crop, with some farmers producing more than ever before, but the government had already amassed a surplus that could feed Tanzania for a projected three years. Therefore, the government was not buying maize from farmers at prices even remotely close to those of the harvest of 2013. For many months following the harvest, as I traveled around the Rukwa region, I could see maize in gunny sacks piled high under blue tarps, waiting for buyers who never came. This means many families had nothing to sell and had not yet received any money. Preserving what little cash they could access was vital for community members during this period because they were quickly running out of resources as the prospect of payments from the harvest months earlier became increasingly less certain. Bypassing local facilities to avoid buying supplies or medications was one strategy some families used to try to save some money.

Delayed or no payments for the maize harvest led to cash-poor families who could barely pay for the essentials, let alone unexpected costs at health care facilities. Without cash, community members also could not contribute to the community health insurance schemes known as CHFs. Without the money from these funds, most dispensaries and health care centers were unable to stock essential medications and supplies.[18] The lack of equipment in these lower-level facilities shifted the burden of care from primary level dispensaries to the district health center and designated district hospitals but primarily to the regional hospital, which struggled to stay afloat throughout this time. Patients and their families lacked information about the health care system and the CHFs because of poor communication throughout all levels of the health care sector and local governments. They did not understand why supplies were not available. This poor communication and lack of transparency created an environment characterized by high levels of suspicion and mistrust between communities and the professionals meant to work with, and for, them in order to improve their health and well-being.

The health care situation in communities throughout the Rukwa region directly affected Mawingu, most obviously by increasing the number of patients seeking care at the hospital when services were lacking at the village dispensary level. The regional hospital absorbed more and more of these clients, who often used what cash they had to *get* to the hospital. Families arrived at Mawingu with high expectations for free care and supplies aplenty but too often encountered nurses' demands that they rush out to buy medication or gloves or intravenous fluids. While the hospital accepted these patients from the districts, the district health administration did not provide any funds from their budgets to help support the regional hospital, even as they off-loaded patients from their populations. Because care for pregnant women was, by policy, free, this increased patient load in the maternity ward was particularly worrying and an enormous drain on hospital resources.

The regional hospital operated for months at a time with almost no support from the government for the care the hospital provided for the exempt groups, most significantly pregnant women. The regional medical officer repeatedly railed in morning meetings, "We should not be conducting normal deliveries! We are a referral hospital. Why are they not doing their work at the dispensaries? I would turn them away at the gates, but you cannot risk a woman giving birth there after you have turned her away. But, really, this is not sustainable!" The increase in patient load without increased resources meant that nurses and doctors, struggling to prevent deaths on the maternity ward, had to work even harder to ensure that women and their babies did not fall through the ever-widening cracks of the hospital's system. The nurses and doctors continued to strive to do their best without first-line medications of choice, or any at all: they improvised catheters from nasogastric tubes and gloves, and they cut umbilical cords by hacking at them with the tiny sharp point of a needle from a syringe instead of using scissors or razor blades.

The nurses and doctors worked together with patients to address women's needs while they were pregnant and in labor, even as the central Tanzanian government did not disburse funds in a timely manner. Supplies from MSD were slow to arrive at the hospital, and their absence worked to undermine biomedicine's reputation in the community. Beyond just the technical aspects of care that Tanzanians expected to find at health facilities, the socialist period's expectations of state care for citizens continued to permeate the ethos of Tanzania, resulting in disappointment when care failed or was unavailable. And yet, many of the country's more recent policies had resulted in a health care system that was unable to keep pace with increased demand; hospitals like Mawingu were receiving more and more patients without the necessary support from the central government. One way in which this mismatch in supply and demand manifested was through the ongoing high maternal mortality ratio in the country and at the hospital.

2

Working in Scarcity

At Mawingu, the nurses, doctors, and administrators all dealt with systemic material scarcity and sought to mitigate its effects on their care practices through the implementation of new systems and via small moments of creativity, improvisation, and ingenuity within the broader system. This environment of scarcity pervasively affected providers' motivation levels and morale. Though most of the health care providers working on the wards may not have known the details and extent of the health care system's lack of funds, they certainly saw, felt, and lived the shortage on a daily basis. Scarcity in this and similar settings is always a product of particular historical events and trajectories, as well as state reactions to them.[1] In this instance, particularities of the Tanzanian health system rooted in socialism and the country's subsequent structural adjustment program and its aftereffects have produced material scarcity. Expanding biobureaucracy heightens material scarcity further by making it more difficult to access what is present; at the same time, biobureaucratic expansion begins to limit the space available for affective care practices.

As one of the highest-volume wards at the hospital, maternity was a constant drain on resources, which led to tense interactions—among providers and between women and the hospital staff—delays in care, and the deaths of women and their babies. When scarcity and bureaucracy combined, they synergistically created a system with an insurmountable inertia, resisting comprehensive reform efforts and limiting possibilities for changes that might have improved care for women and the work environment for the nurses and doctors. In the absence of prospects for deep, sustained changes, nurses and doctors innovated and improvised in much smaller ways to keep delivering diverse forms of care every day.

THE MATERIAL NEEDS OF THE SYSTEM

"*Habari za asubuhi, jamani? Hongereni kwa kazi,*" I said as I passed two of the night-shift nurses as I entered the ward after the daily morning meeting. With

FIGURE 6. Supply trolleys after a busy shift. Photo by author, 2014.

these greetings to say good morning, I shook off my lingering drowsiness and headed into the changing room. The small room was crowded with nurses from both shifts, morning and night, as they changed into or out of their uniforms and traded stories both personal and professional. I turned my back and started to change into my scrubs. A cry went up as one of the nurses handed out wedding invitation cards, and another corner of the room erupted as Nurse Mpili demanded to borrow lotion from someone. Someone else shouted out the usual joke about how I didn't have to wear spandex shorts under my scrubs because my thighs weren't as fat as hers, and, laughing, I donned my nonslip, waterproof (amniotic fluid and blood-proof) Crocs. With that, I stepped out of the room and left the cheerful din behind me to start restocking supplies.

Nearly every morning I arrived at the hospital between 7:30 and 7:45 a.m. After the clinical meeting was finished around 8:00 or 8:30 a.m., I headed to the ward. If it was early and the night-shift nurses had not yet finished handing over to the morning shift, I would often find the ward in a state of disarray after a busy night of caring for patients. First thing in the morning there were often wrappers from gloves strewn about, empty boxes, sticky footprints on the floor where tea or IV fluids had splattered, and broken glass ampules from used oxytocin injections. Both the nurses and the cleaning staff on the morning shift embarked on tidying up the ward first thing after the shift handover occurred, so long as there were no women in need of immediate medical attention. Three trolleys in the labor and delivery rooms carried the most immediately necessary and most commonly used supplies (figure 6). I always glanced around to see what was missing or almost out, cleared away the paper wrappings from gloves, and straightened the medications before heading to the nurse in charge's office to collect the missing items we would need for the day shift. As we all worked together, the ward slowly returned to its normal daytime look, with the smell of bleach water slowly filling the ward as the cleaner, Tatu, worked her way through the space, eradicating all traces of sticky tea spills, drops of amniotic fluid, and spattered blood on walls, floors, and bedrails.

Though in February 2014 when I returned I encountered improved supply levels compared to 2012 and 2013, as the year progressed the availability of supplies did not continue to improve. Some days, the cabinet in the nurse in charge's office would be nearly empty when I went in search of bottles of IV fluids, gloves, or catheters. Under such conditions, the nurses often struggled to provide care. In order to provide adequate care, the maternity ward requires a vast number of material inputs. In fact, it was the most expensive ward to run at the hospital. In May 2012, on my first visit to Mawingu, Nurse Kinaya marched briskly around the ward with me in her wake, leading me on a tour. As the nurse in charge she was aware of the progress the ward had made recently but lamented, "We desperately need more delivery packs. You see?" She gestured to the metal supply cabinet with its door askew and contents jostling for space; two packages wrapped in sturdy green fabric sat alone on the left side of one of the shelves. "We have only those two left and it is only four o'clock," she said, using the Swahili time for 10 a.m. There were five and a half hours left in the day shift, not to mention the evening and night. "How are my nurses supposed to help every mother when we have only three full sets that comply with the requirements? Even the scissors we do have are too dull to cut the cord, we have to cut and cut until blood is spraying you!" Each delivery pack was supposed to include a metal kidney dish, into which the nurse would place the placenta, two forceps for clamping the cord, one pair of surgical scissors, two sterilized umbilical cord ligatures, and two pieces of gauze. All of the materials were placed in the kidney dish, wrapped in two pieces of green cloth (drapers), and tied with a thin piece of cloth. The sets were then sterilized in the hospital's autoclave, located in the main operating theater. The nurses used one delivery pack per mother. Depending on the autoclave schedule and staffing numbers, there could be long delays between when the delivery packs ran out on the ward and when sterile packs became available. Particularly with only a handful of packs in 2012, the nurses had operated mainly without this set of tools, which the hospital, national, and international standards all considered to be the most basic essentials for clean, safe, and skilled maternity care.

While this state of affairs had improved by 2014, maternity care was highly vulnerable to stock-outs and failures of the supply chain. In addition to the delivery packs, each woman who came to give birth needed a number of other supplies in order to receive high-quality care. From admission through the birth of the baby, nurses required an absolute minimum of three pairs of sterile surgical gloves, though they often used many more. Perhaps most critically, the maternity ward was supposed to stock oxytocic drugs, most commonly oxytocin, though ergometrine was often present as a backup. Women received an injection of oxytocin immediately after they gave birth to help prevent postpartum hemorrhage.[2] Other needed items included personal protective equipment for the nurses, such as boots, gowns or aprons, goggles or face masks, and caps to cover their heads. Also, the ward had to always have IV (intravenous) fluids on hand, as well as cannulas for insertion in a vein to start the IV and "giving sets," the tubing that connects the IV fluid container to the cannula and that regulates the speed of the fluid flow. The dizzying list continues: medical tape, antibiotics, antihypertensive medications (for women with signs of preeclampsia or eclampsia), basic pain relievers for postpartum mothers, ketamine for surgeries, nasogastric (NG) tubes in both infant and adult sizes, resuscitation equipment, vacuum for assisted deliveries, sutures of various types, antiseptic solutions, syringes, magnesium sulfate (for mothers with eclamptic seizures), blood pressure cuffs, stethoscopes, urinalysis dipsticks, cotton swabs, gauze, sterile water, catheters, and urine bags. All of these supplies and more were integral for providing care to women during their pregnancies, labor, and the immediate postpartum period.

During a C-section or laparotomy, as in the case of a woman with a ruptured uterus, in addition to IV fluids, cannulas, catheters, and surgical blades, the operating theater needed a machine to help monitor the woman's vital signs while she was under anesthesia, and either drugs or other means of resuscitation in case something should start to go wrong.[3] Without resuscitation equipment, women died on the operating table and babies did not recover from the effects of severe asphyxiation. In other cases, lack of antibiotics before and after surgery increased the woman's chances of contracting a life-threatening infection. All of these supplies came from the Medical Stores Department (MSD).

Government health facilities all had an account with MSD that they used for ordering, and they largely relied on central government funds to purchase the materials needed to keep the facility running. Mawingu Regional Hospital went for eleven months in the fiscal year 2014–15 with only a fraction of promised funds from the government, meaning they lacked the cash to purchase supplies from MSD.

Practically, because of the high, and ever-increasing, patient load on the maternity ward, each day the hospital was spending nearly three times as much on maternity services as it was able to bring in in cash from services provided in all other departments; this deficit was supposed to be closed by government funds. When I asked the regional medical officer about this situation, he explained, "What you are seeing is that more and more people are coming here because they see that the care we are providing is high quality. It used to be that not a lot of people were coming here, but now many of them come even if they should be going to the health centers or the district hospitals because they see the care here is better and it's more in demand, so we are using more medicine and equipment." Poor services at lower levels drove demand at Mawingu.

THE HOSPITAL BUDGET

Each year, the Hospital Management Team (HMT) and the Regional Health Management Team (RHMT) created an annual plan and budget for the hospital's goals and operating expenses. They forwarded this plan to the Ministry of Health and Social Welfare and the Ministry of Finance for approval. The Ministry of Health then disbursed funds into the hospital's accounts. Some of this money went into the hospital's account with MSD. When this account was empty, in the absence of supplies being issued on credit, the hospital had to use the cash collected to pay for more supplies.

The daily clinical morning meetings at the hospital always started with a reading of the accounts from the day before. This included going department by department and reading out the number of patients served, the cash collected, and the amount of money used for patients in the exempted categories. The maternity ward was far and away the largest source of exemptions, with a patient flow that surpassed that of any other ward or department. This was the main reason the amount of money spent on exemptions was always around three times the amount of cash brought in on any particular day. For example, on February 9, 2015, the report said that on the preceding day the total cost of the exemptions was TZS 1,273,127. Of that, TZS 1,073,000 came from the maternity ward, and the remaining 200,000 was from services provided to the elderly, children under age five, HIV patients, and the destitute, combined. The total cash collected for February 8 was TZS 380,000, and the total cost of services provided for that date was TZS 1,650,000. This was representative of the trend—free services were generally three times the amount being brought in through daily cash collection of user fees. Even so, this level of cash collection was an increase over the past and an improvement. This all combined to mean that the hospital was operating at a loss every single day. The shortage of money was a constant topic of conversation within the hospital's morning meeting and among the administrators, as well as a source of rumor and gossip for the nursing staff not present in the meetings.

After watching the declining supply situation on the maternity ward that had started in late 2014, I asked the regional medical officer in May 2015 about the supply problem at the hospital. His response took me on the detours and wanderings to which government funds were subject; at one moment money was released from the central government just one month before the end of the fiscal year, and shortly thereafter the central government informed the RMO they had an outstanding debt with MSD nearly equivalent to the disbursed amount. While the hospital had requested TZS 286 million for the preceding fiscal year, which was coming to a close, they had gone nearly forty-five weeks with just TZS 6 million. He explained: "There they tell us we had a debt of about 80 million shillings, so now we have 30 million shillings to buy new medications and supplies. But up until then we really only had 6 million shillings to run the hospital. . . .

You see the exemptions every day, it's hard to continue to run a hospital with only 6 million shillings for the year. We've already made an order to MSD; we should get more supplies soon." The RMO's meandering explanation demonstrated the complicated ways in which funds flowed through the bureaucratic fiscal systems of the health care sector, enhancing the feelings I had, echoed by many nurses, that the entire process was rather opaque and subject to detours, as when the RMO told me the money "went somewhere." The fiscal year ended in June, and by March 2015 the Tanzanian Treasury had released only 58.4 percent of the fiscal year's budget; it was not just a problem for Mawingu.[4] In the absence of the required ministry funds, the RMO said sometimes the amount of money the hospital received was only enough to cover the hospital's most basic bills, such as electricity and water, which had to be paid for the hospital to continue operating.

In addition, bureaucratic guidelines that the central government distributed and updated through periodic circulars put strict limits on how the hospital was allowed to spend the money collected each day from patients. The regional medical officer explained that though the hospital had succeeded in increasing the amount of money it was collecting from patients on a daily basis, Mawingu would never be able to collect as much money from user fees as regional hospitals located in more prosperous areas of the country or serving large numbers of insured patients. In his characteristic way of speaking in metaphors, to drive his point home, the RMO emphatically asked me, "How can you say these two people are competing in the same sports game when one has good shoes and equipment and the other is there barefoot? It's not a level playing field. Just the same, even to compare us [at Mawingu], to say that we are competing with another hospital and are capable of the same results, is not an easy thing!"

This concern with the availability of cash for health care services in the Rukwa region emerged repeatedly in meetings and informal discussions among the hospital staff members, particularly after the hospital increased the fees for services. Nurses repeatedly said they were afraid patients from the region would forgo follow-up care, such as bandage changing, to try to save their money, such was the level of poverty in the area. The lack of family resources to pay for health care, even when the fees were still low in comparison to other regions, was also a common theme and a very real barrier to care in the villages I visited. People unfamiliar with this region would often suggest that the hospital just try to increase its collections, or make a better budget, or lay out better plans. This, however, was far easier said than done because of the structural constraints of the region's economy, bureaucratic cost-sharing guidelines that were outdated and that severely limited how the hospital could use its funds, and national-level supply chain problems and financial shortages.

All of these constraints led the hospital to try to manage funds and reallocate them whenever possible. It often meant suspending extra pay for the staff members and delaying other crucial activities, such as car maintenance for the hospital ambulance or repairs to buildings.[5] The nurses often told me they counted on on-call and extraduty allowances as a consistent supplement to their (low) salaries. The loss or delay of these payments was always a source of much indignation and complaining. On the other hand, if these payments were released, the entire hospital seemed to be in a good mood.

The RMO told me that they tried to prioritize extraduty or on-call allowances, particularly for the physicians, when the money was available because "This way doctors can be able to do their work, not say, 'Oh, I'm not coming right now [to the hospital] even if I'm called because I haven't been paid.'" When the government issued new regulations regarding the use of funds, or increased the required amount of extraduty allowances, the hospital prioritized paying the doctors; the nurses suffered the cuts.

COLLECTING CASH AND THE EXPANSION OF BIOBUREAUCRACY

Often, the nurses told me, and I witnessed, delays in care occurred as family members tried to find the monetary resources to buy medications or essential equipment for their patient. Some mothers waited on the ward for several days before receiving the first dose of a prescribed drug. Emergency C-sections resulted from a number of clinical conditions, which commonly included preeclampsia or eclampsia and obstructed labor with suspected fetal distress. In these cases, providers, women, and their family members could not wait. Surgeries could not commence without ketamine, the anesthetic drug most commonly used, or sutures, or IV fluids, or a catheter and urine bag. Hospital protocols for the distribution of such supplies changed multiple times throughout my stay at Mawingu. For many months, the cabinet in the office of the ward nurse in charge housed all of the ward's supplies save those for anesthesia. At another point, all the supplies were no longer allowed to be housed in the wards, but the ward staff had to report to the pharmacy with prescription forms signed by the physician who had ordered the procedure or medication. This change was related to the implementation of a new accounting system at the hospital in September 2014. While in many ways this computerized system helped to significantly, and rapidly, increase the amount of money the hospital was able to collect each day, and thus was crucial for the hospital's continued operation, it also brought a host of new complications. The new system affected the maternity ward in ways that were unique and unheard of in other wards. This was primarily because prior to the new cash collection and accounting system the maternity ward staff, as providers for an exempt group, had never dealt with receipts or the collection of funds from the women who came to give birth.

Before the automated system, nurses on each ward that did not serve exempted categories of patients collected money from clients as the need arose. This meant the corner of a patient's file often sported a stack of multicolored rectangular pieces of paper that served as receipts for payments for ward admission, a bed, laboratory tests, wound dressing, medications, IV fluids, and more. This system often created confusion, particularly for patients, who were unaware of the prices of services and supplies and did not know who was legitimately allowed to collect cash. Many community members felt this collection process encouraged corruption and bribes because it was unclear who was supposed to be paying what, to whom, and when. Nurses could arbitrarily deny care, citing unpaid balances, and delay potentially lifesaving services. Nurses, on the other hand, told me they would provide care for a woman before looking for the receipts if they felt she really was in the midst of an emergency. But many nurses were unsure of the current prices to charge patients and whose responsibility it was to do the actual collecting. Poor communication during shift changes compounded the confusion. From an administrative perspective, this system more than once resulted in patients and their relatives sneaking away from the hospital at night or during the chaotic visiting hours, leaving their debts unpaid. The hospital had already incurred the cost of the physical and human resources expended and now had very little recourse for recouping the loss when a patient "absconded" without paying (hence the nighttime searches of my car).

To produce its financial benefits, the new system drastically changed how the maternity ward staff members conducted their work and requisitioned and accounted for supplies or services rendered. Though officially the women on the maternity ward never had to pay for care, the administration began to require a daily tally of the supplies used in the course of caring for each patient. The maternity ward nurses primarily saw this as yet another burden and part of a more general proliferation of required documentation and bureaucratic expansion, generated by the hospital itself and outside forces. Now, before a nurse could take a patient's samples to the laboratory for testing, she had to go to the accounting window to get a receipt, have it stamped with the word "Exempt," and have the person in this office staple it to the lab test requisition form; only then could she proceed with the sample to the lab. The process of actually getting blood test results could be significantly delayed at the accounting window, especially during the hospital's busiest hours.

I once experienced this delay at night when I wanted to take blood samples to the lab for a patient we thought might need an emergency blood transfusion. The person on duty was a medical attendant who had previously been assigned to the maternity ward. Her time on the maternity ward was short because the nurses thought she was argumentative, generally difficult, and not a good worker. She would frequently deny responsibility for tasks or refuse to do work that she thought was beneath her. This particular medical attendant then had started working at the cash collection window and had brought to that work the same argumentative and unhelpful attitude. Regardless of the patient waiting back on the ward, she would take her time, pecking out names and the ward number with one finger on the computer's keyboard. Before beginning to stamp any of the pages she would wait for all of them to emerge slowly from the printer. These types of inefficiencies seem relatively harmless on the surface but could add up to life-threatening delays for mothers and babies when combined with all the other opportunities for delay. Such delays resulting from the procedures for procuring supplies did not necessarily *produce* scarcity: after all, eventually a patient would receive the prescribed tests or medications. But the expanded bureaucratic measures now in place made it ever more difficult for the nurses to access what supplies were available, compounding their work and, often, frustration levels. In effect, the biobureaucratic expansion, best seen here via the new accounting system, produced a scarcity of time for clinical patient care. It also produced a scarcity of emotional reserves for affective caring as nurses had to engage with petulant gatekeepers and as physical time away from the ward prevented additional intersubjective care exchanges.

On the maternity ward, yet another notebook appeared with the advent of the new accounting system. As the nurses recorded in this new notebook the supplies used for each woman, they felt the effects of biobureaucratic expansion through the added tasks of documenting the number of syringes and pairs of gloves used each day in service to each patient. They felt it also in their interactions with the medical attendants who controlled the processing of receipts and "Exempt" stamps and, by extension, critical laboratory tests, medications, and vitally necessary equipment for patient care.

One might argue that all health care providers in a government system are "street-level" bureaucrats,[6] but these newly empowered medical attendants were, additionally, embodiments of the growing biobureaucracy. In a classic study of the relationship between location in an organization and access to power, David Mechanic argues that "within organizations one makes others dependent upon him by controlling access to information, persons, and instrumentalities. . . . Power is a function not only of the extent to which a person controls information, persons, and instrumentalities, but also of the importance of the various attributes he controls."[7] Despite having the least access to formal power within the hospital's organizational structure, the medical attendants became quite powerful with the expanded bureaucratic procedures involved in producing more accountability and improved cash flow. The computerized system simplified certain interactions, perhaps increasing transparency and subsequently reducing allegations of bribery or corruption on some wards. However, the system's unintended consequences included opening new spaces of inefficiency and new opportunities for delay, miscommunication, and social maneuvering by the gatekeepers.

With the increased demand for services in the hospital came this concomitant growth of the bureaucratic systems employed to track, order, and process the new patient flow through the facility. The implementation of the automated accounting system was another example of the biobureaucratic proliferation that has accompanied the expansion of health care services globally. The biobureaucracy was now operating at the level of the individual hospital via the new systems the administrators implemented, while at the same time embedding the hospital and its systems within the broader health care sector, subject to much higher-level biobureaucracy that outside powers—including the Ministry of Health but also foreign nongovernmental organizations (NGOs) and the World Health Organization—imposed on the hospital. The spaces for providing truly intersubjective care were being compressed from all sides. Accountability for supplies, money, and procedures operated facing both internally and externally.

DELAYS IN CARE AND SOCIAL TENSION

With the new accounting system implemented in 2014, the process for getting all the necessary equipment eventually became much more convoluted, especially for those women on the maternity ward who needed Cesarean sections. The nurses could not start preparing a woman for surgery, even if they were certain she would require a C-section, until the doctor had officially written up prescription forms for all of the specific, individual supplies. This resulted in multiple pieces of paper, which the nurses had to take to the cash collection window and then to the pharmacy window.

One night, when I was on the ward conducting interviews, it became clear one of the women was going to need an emergency C-section. Because only three nurses were on the ward and all were occupied, they sent me to the pharmacy with the doctor's prescription forms to collect the IV fluids, sutures, and pre-op antibiotics needed to prep her for surgery. "*Hodi, hodi dada!*" (Knock knock, sister), I called out in Swahili to alert the dozing medical attendant, Hilda, to my presence as I stood behind the metal grate at the pharmacy counter. She roused herself and slowly ambled over, shaking the sleep from her body as she did so. "Ah, so maternity needs something. How is it there tonight? Let me see the forms," she said before I could answer her inquiry about the state of the ward. "Ah, this one I don't have here, not in this size. Let me see." She peered at the form and turned to go into the back room.

"Please hurry, it's an emergency C-section. We need to prep her as soon as possible. The doctor is already here and waiting," I added to her back for good measure, though it seemed it would not make much difference in her pace.

"You need to go to the cash window and get the receipt, I can't give you these things without the receipt," Hilda called as she disappeared. I rushed over to the cash collection window, where I started again with another medical attendant, explaining that I needed an exemption receipt for the supplies for the maternity ward so that I could go back to the pharmacy and pick up everything. Once this was done, after some slow, pecking typing, I verified the exemption stamp in bright blue ink on the proffered receipt and walked the fifty feet back to the pharmacy window.

Without hurry, Hilda returned to the counter first with the antibiotics, then with the sutures, and eventually with an armful of IV fluids, adding to the pile she had started while I was at the cash window. She muttered to herself about how she would account for the difference in sizes because she was out of the half-liter bottles and could only give me the liter bottles, though this was not what the doctor had prescribed on the form. I jiggled my leg impatiently as she pulled out a pair of ill-fitting reading glasses, opened the dirty log notebook with its furled edges and began to slowly flip to today's page. I worked to suppress a sigh as she began to fill in each supply on its own line. Finally, she asked for my signature as the person who had received the dispensed supplies. With this task done, I rushed back to the ward.

At times even the most basic supplies were out of stock, particularly IV fluids or catheters, and the nurse would return to the ward empty-handed. At this point the surgery could not proceed, and nurses or the doctor would direct the woman's relatives to quickly go outside the hospital gates in search of the needed supplies. This resulted in further delays as relatives sought out money, then an open pharmacy store, and then the correct items. Sometimes the instructions the nurses had given the family were not explicit enough and the relative came back with the wrong size or strength of a medicine or catheter, which then the hospital staff could not use.

Nurse Halima, an RN, expressed to me the difficulties of the work environment at Mawingu. She was a young nurse who had been working at the hospital for less than a year at the time of our interview, and she had spent the first several months of her employment working on the private ward, Grade I. Often smiling, she was light-skinned and plump, one of the only Muslim nurses on the ward. Well educated and from a family of many other nurses and doctors in Dar es Salaam, she had an air of cosmopolitanism and quick-wittedness about her. Her short time at the hospital had already been sufficient for her to perceive the lower economic means of Rukwa's population, as compared to other regions, as well as the monetary constraints at play in the hospital:

> The supplies really are bothersome for the success of the work. [It] can be that you have studied how to do this procedure, but you can't do it, and because why? Because of the shortage of those supplies that you need to do work. And if you use more than is necessary, that is, more than has been put in the budget, it means you will do what? You ruin the entire system. . . . You find someone comes, she needs to be cared for, you fail to care for her like is necessary. And many people from here [Rukwa] they don't have any [economic] means. To say, maybe, go, buy something, bring it for your patient, maybe, for example, you say Ringers Lactate [one of the two most commonly used intravenous fluids on the maternity ward], right now there isn't any, if you tell [the relatives] to go find Ringers, they will be distraught, they don't have any money, and the baby there will continue to get tired. So this environment is difficult. But at the end of the day the [relatives] can't criticize that there are no supplies, they will blame you, like, "You, nurse, what have you done?" Or that you have caused something. But to look if the environment in which you work is difficult—they can't look.

When something was out of stock and relatives had to purchase it at a private pharmacy, it was often the nurses who took the blame. More than once, while I was present, the hospital patron held meetings with the maternity ward nurses to address patients' allegations of corruption or extortion.

There is indeed a history in Tanzania, dating especially to the late 1980s, of underpaid and overworked health care providers accepting or demanding bribes from patients and their relatives,[8] but the majority of the time I was at the hospital the supplies were, indeed, out of stock when nurses said they were; this was not simply a ploy for money. Still, more than once, patients or their relatives offered me bribes, trying to slip me a few bills in their palm as they shook my hand. As they tried to hand me this money, a woman's relatives would explain that they wanted to make sure I looked after her and helped her. Other times, as I was assisting during a delivery, I watched as a new mother tried to give one of the nurses money as thanks for her care. In most cases, the nurses refused the money, telling the mother to put it back in her handbag. Occasionally, if the mother continued to insist, the nurse would take the proffered bills. The nurse usually acquiesced after an impressive show of resisting the offer, telling the mother that it was simply her job, as the nurse, to help and that she was not allowed to take payment. After this display, the nurse would sometimes give in to the woman's continued insistence and accept the small amount of money. Surely, at times my presence might have engendered this show, but in other cases the performance might have proceeded even without me in the room. Nurses were simply not all the same in how they interpreted formalized nursing ethics and their own moral boundaries, differentially shaped as these were by years of experience, personality, religious beliefs, better or worse working conditions, and other influences.

Once I watched this happen when a woman handed money to the nurse in charge at the time, Kinaya. Citing the Nursing Code of Ethics, Kinaya explained to me that nurses were not supposed to take money of any sort but that it was allowable if they reported the money to the shift's nurse supervisor and used it for collective or ward purposes. In that instance, she sent one of the cleaners to buy a crate of sodas and some cookies for all the ward personnel to share. Despite her proclamation about not accepting bribes, Kinaya accepted the money and none of the nurses complained; even something as simple as a free soda during a long shift was a welcome bonus.

I was nearly always uncomfortable when I saw a woman reaching for money or saw money inside her bag of belongings, because I always wondered what the nurses would do. I can only know what I witnessed, and my presence most likely either removed these exchanges to other locations or reduced them, so I would not see and note that these nurses had done something unethical by their professional standards. But I did think it was not a far stretch of the imagination to picture a nurse, alone on the night shift, accepting, after a long delivery, some few bills that might pay for a ride home after her twelve-hour shift. Surely, low salaries, much-delayed promotions, and reduced extraduty pay would have led many nurses to see bribes or money of thanks not as something it would be unethical to accept but as their due and fair share for the hard work they had put in. Likewise, Kinaya, while still the ward nurse in charge, had told me that sometimes vials of oxytocin or other small supplies went missing. She told me that she thought she knew who the culprit was and that this nurse had been stealing from the ward's stock to resell the medications in her own private pharmacy to supplement her government salary.

One day on the maternity ward I was casually discussing the issue of possible misunderstandings and perceived corruption with Nurses Peninah and Rukia. As I sat in one of the rickety wooden chairs and Rukia leaned her elbows on the desk, Peninah, in her usual bold, frank manner proclaimed, arms akimbo, "You know, me, I think it's really the fault of the hospital—from the beginning there, if in the past they were training [patients] that 'you, if you go to the big hospital, it's necessary that there are these and these and these and these necessary items or you will have to pay,' they would prepare early, but right now it has come suddenly that things have run out and they got used to if you go to the hospital everything is free, and now they have been told, 'Go buy this.' She will see you, you are telling her to buy it and that you are eating [the money]!" Rukia murmured her agreement, and another bystander muttered, "Ehh" by way of confirmation. Even I was somewhat convinced by Peninah's certainty, despite knowing that the responsibility for the situation extended far beyond the hospital walls. Peninah was suggesting that broad government campaigns advertising free services for pregnant women did not convey to women that the only care that was free was that available in the hospital; if supplies were out of stock in the hospital, necessarily, the hospital could not provide them and the patient had to procure them elsewhere. However, because of the government's unnuanced messages, many people thought they would never need to pay for anything at the health facility if they were pregnant. When suddenly nurses or physicians started asking them to buy supplies outside, patients and their families easily suspected corruption.

The saying "to eat money" (*kula hela*) is a common expression connoting corruption or bribery. These misunderstandings between the nurses and the women they cared for were often a source of annoyance but also consternation because the accusations went against the formal ethical codes that most of the nurses ascribed to and sought to practice daily. But in the setting of hospital scarcity, the nurse's proverbial "hunger" leading to the need to "eat money" might be derived from low wages, limited or no promotions, and her difficult work environment that lacked the supplies she needed to care for patients. To lessen these hunger pains, she might slip a few vials of medicine into her pockets or some pairs of surgical gloves into her purse, seeing these actions not as corruption but as her due, a way to compensate herself when her employer could not sufficiently do so.

Most of the nurses were offended by the suggestion that they might be corrupt and were particularly incensed anytime they heard the long-popular rumors about health care workers withholding blood from desperate patients or their families in exchange for exorbitant payments. The blood bank often had only a limited supply and therefore encouraged family members to donate a unit of blood as a replacement unit for the one their patient was receiving. However, the lab employees did not always communicate this clearly or the relatives did not always understand and, instead, heard that they were being charged for blood or that the lab personnel were withholding the desperately needed unit until someone donated. In the Prologue, I described the care and ultimate fate of one woman who died from a lack of blood. Sometimes the urgently needed units were unavailable in the blood bank, or, if they were, family members saw no need to donate. This could mean that for a woman like Paulina, whose life was threatened by an absolutely unforeseen surgical complication during a scheduled, nonemergent C-section, death was the result.

Figure 7 shows a poster that was up in the maternity ward when I returned in 2016, reading, "Blood isn't sold, it's always free"— a direct response to these misunderstandings and previous blood-selling practices.

Additionally, blood has long been associated with various rumors of extractive and/or occult practices.[9] Blood is a powerful ritual substance but also representative of social ties via kinship, sexual relations, and reproduction.[10] This deep history may not enter immediately into the minds of a younger generation of men and women currently in their childbearing years, but it most certainly colors the overall landscape. Against this background, blood has significant meaning, and hospital personnel could quite conceivably be using it for nefarious ends, in addition to the straightforwardly corrupt act of charging money for units of blood needed for a patient's transfusion. Anxieties related to blood extend far beyond any misunderstandings of hospital procedures because of this fluid's broader meaning in this and surrounding areas of East and Central Africa.

In the same conversation about supplies and perceived corruption, I suggested to Nurse Peninah that I thought the government had started making services free for pregnant women because they had seen that a lot of women in poorer areas were not giving birth in health facilities. In response Peninah told me,

> Indeed, it was that that started this, I've seen, but instead its second effect, those people [government officials/policy makers], they didn't see it. They are coming to discover it right now. Now it [the money] has finished. How will you tell that person that doesn't have any means there in the village, "Hey, there is no equipment for service"? Will she understand you? She doesn't understand you! Again, us, we that deal with patients, we're seen to be bad [people]! Better that person who sits at administration, they don't see him, but us, we who tell her to go buy, she tells you you're delaying her because she was looking for supplies.

She went on to give an example of how these delays might affect the care of a woman who had come to give birth: "Just say that she's in her first pregnancy. Yeah, if she'd had contractions she would have already ruptured [her uterus]. But the blame will come back to the nurse who stays with the patient; you're told first you delayed treatment, second why didn't you inform someone? But you're waiting for important supplies." It is very uncommon for a woman in her first pregnancy to

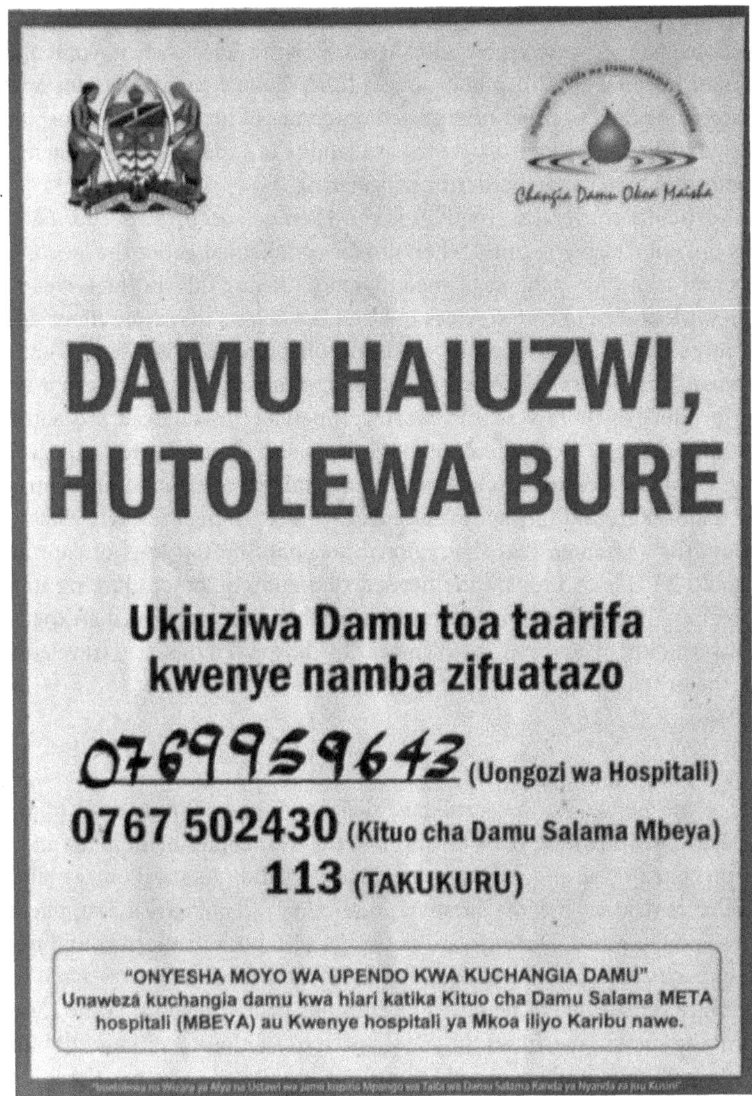

FIGURE 7. Sign reading, "Blood isn't sold, it's always free" in red and below it, "If you are sold blood, report it at the following numbers." The numbers listed include the "hospital leadership," the "Safe Blood Center" in Mbeya Town, the zonal headquarters, and the number of the Bureau for the Prevention and Combating of Corruption. Photo by author, 2016.

have a ruptured uterus, and Peninah used this as an extreme example of delay—a woman in her first pregnancy must be experiencing severely obstructed labor and a long delay in initiating a C-section if she reaches the point of uterine rupture. In her example, the woman's uterus did *not* rupture only because she was not having contractions. Nurses were visible and therefore within reach when women, their relatives, or hospital administrators sought to attribute responsibility for a woman's death, poor care, or other unexpected outcomes of her stay at the hospital. In actuality, they had little control over the availability of supplies, depending instead on lengthy and bureaucratic ordering procedures.

This particular conversation with Rukia and Peninah occurred in February 2015 but was only one of many times when nurses complained about the lack of supplies, as well as the way patients blamed them for causing this shortage. Helle Max Martin's work on health care services in Uganda suggests that accusations against nurses rooted in a lack of supplies are not a phenomenon limited to Tanzania; while nurses or doctors see referring patients to outside pharmacies as a necessary by-product of more systemic shortages, patients might read this same act as "corruption, greed or indifference."[11] Women's and their relatives' expectations that care would be free and available at the hospital was often an ideal constructed against the background of their experiences with stock-outs in their village dispensaries. They assumed that the regional hospital, the top level of care in the area, would be able to provide the needed care and equipment lacking in their communities. This expectation was often why they had incurred the expense of the transportation to, and stay in, town near the hospital if they had traveled from outside the urban district.

WORKING IN SCARCITY

Several of the nurses on the ward said that Dr. Joseph, the medical officer in charge, had been working hard to improve the availability of supplies and that they appreciated these efforts. However, the efforts did not always make supplies materialize, and nearly half the nurses reported they did not have the supplies they needed to do their jobs. During ward meetings with both the doctors and nurses, we often discussed supplies and equipment, returning over and over again to the needs that never seemed to be met. For example, nearly the entire time I was on the ward, the suction machines the nurses used to suction secretions out of newborns' airways were broken or only occasionally worked. Another time, it took nearly six months to get batteries for the electronic handheld fetal heart monitor on the ward.

After witnessing frequent stock-outs at the end of 2014, and the hospital's growing fixation on documenting supplies used, I asked all the nurses about their experience of their work environment, hoping to understand more about how they viewed the shortage of medications and supplies. Nurse Rachel lamented:

> Now you are told there are no medicines. We arrive at work, you will find me, I'm on the maternity ward there in the labor room, you find that the mother you're helping

> there, even to start a drip [IV], there's nothing. You find the labor ward has dextrose, D5%, now there you encounter a mother there who has eclampsia, PPH [postpartum hemorrhage]. How do you help her?[12] Truthfully, this environment is very difficult. . . . Many times you find we encounter the women here, they have problems. There are no supplies. It's necessary for them to buy a thing but they don't have any money. This, it becomes a problem. The mother, you just look at her. I stay there with her, all right, it is only God that helps a person to give birth or not, the baby has come out, it hasn't cried. Really, honestly, the environment is hard. I don't like it.

Almost universally the nurses and doctors felt the lack of essential supplies and equipment was the number one impediment to providing better care. They also repeatedly suggested that improving this situation would be the best intervention the hospital administration could make to motivate the providers working at the hospital. While the nurses were concerned with having the tools they needed to provide the technical aspects of care, Rachel's description also highlights her sympathy for the woman who could not afford to send a relative running to a private pharmacy to buy supplies. Aside from staying with the mother, Rachel was unable to provide other forms of care to the woman in her charge.

SUPPLIES AS THE FOUNDATION OF COMMUNITY TRUST

Faced with the nurse's demand that they purchase supplies in a private pharmacy, many community members concocted explanations that went beyond stock-outs because they did not understand how the government supply chain operated and therefore did not know that a large government facility might *actually* be out of critical supplies. The fact was that supplies were so short at Mawingu, in early 2015 as to drive the regional medical officer to comment one day during the morning clinical meeting, "*Jamani*, friends, the hospital will soon be nothing more than a guesthouse! We will be full of beds but no other services. We must improve in cash collection, otherwise we are finished!" Despite the reality, the belief that such a large facility, or any facility backed by the central government, could never *truly* be out of supplies was pervasive in communities outside Sumbawanga Urban District. Village leaders and community members repeatedly told me they did not believe that the government health facilities really did not have medicines available while private pharmacies continued to have them in stock—the private purveyor of drugs was so small, and the government was so big [powerful], how was it, then, that the small person could get supplies the government could not? A focus group participant in the village of Ngorotwa in Kalambo District told me exasperatedly, "They tell you 'Go, buy those drugs' and honestly, if you follow up in all the dispensaries, you find that these drugs don't go [there]. Now, the government, I don't know. If you go to the private pharmacies you find there the strong drugs. . . . Now why is it that the government fails to bring these for us here so we can be treated here? . . . They themselves [the government] see that we have become fruit to be harvested in the drug shops, rather than bringing us [the drugs] at the dispensary."

A second participant chimed in with "Even amoxicillin, it's just one container! Now, for this entire village, you find there's just one container. . . . The doctors, they have their own drugstore, yes, that's the business that we see, that." The insinuation that doctors or nurses were selling government-provided drugs for private gain was a pervasive concern. In this particular community, there was palpable distrust of the government's services and its local representatives—the health care providers at the health center.[13]

As the conversation in Ngorotwa continued, several of the participants agreed that their health center, and most dispensaries, were nothing more than buildings if they did not have these medications and other supplies readily available. In communities, in contrast to the regional hospital, I did not witness firsthand any examples of corruption. But this was surely related to my conspicuous presence as a foreign visitor to whom the health care workers were not accustomed. In discussions, many men and women in communities provided examples of times they had been seeking care and were charged for an item or service that should have been free. For many years, the health care sector, together with the police, was said to be one of the most corrupt sectors in the country; I heard this as part of a more general public discourse on corruption. Anticorruption efforts have been ongoing in Tanzania, but reducing corruption continues to be a challenge for the government.[14]

This exchange in Ngorotwa demonstrates how, through repeatedly failing to have supplies, health facilities worked to undermine the legitimacy of the state itself. Here, then, was a failure of the state's care for its citizens via one of its institutions with which people interacted the most, and always in times of need and states of vulnerability—sickness, pregnancy, injury. When the state failed to meet these fundamental needs, people were forced to resort to extremes and great personal expense, including selling their land, in order to make up for the state's lack of care.

Clearly, the unavailability of medicines and supplies was prevalent at all levels of health care services in Rukwa. However, patients and their family members continued to expect the regional hospital to have medications and everything else necessary for their care. The lack of drugs aggravated the relationships between patients and health care providers. Availability of supplies may be one of the most crucial elements for establishing the high quality of services available and for reinforcing the legitimacy of the hospital and of the state itself.

SUPPLIES AND DEATH

Women coming to the hospital from the community as patients trusted that once they reached Mawingu they would receive the high-quality care this tertiary facility seemed to promise. These promises became more tenuous as the supply chain and financial resources buckled under the strain of increased patient loads and bureaucratic delays. In the course of providing care for pregnant women, even how far a provider had to go in the room, the ward, or the hospital to obtain supplies could mean the difference between death and survival. Sometimes the supplies were readily accessible, but the nurses or doctors did not appropriately use them or lost valuable time while trying to make decisions on the course of care. In other instances, the hospital simply lacked the needed equipment to save a woman's life. These cases were fewer and further between because complications necessitating the specialized and unavailable equipment were much less common. As with other aspects of the health care system in Tanzania, the partial and incomplete nature of supplies and equipment was most visible when a catastrophe occurred. Easily forgotten at other times, these system weaknesses were always present in the background. The death of Kinakia exemplifies not only the importance of material supplies but also the underlying precarity of pregnancy that led some women to tell me, "When you are in labor, the grave is open."

Kinakia was just twenty-six years old and in her third pregnancy when she arrived at Mawingu on the evening of March 3, 2014. Providers at her local dispensary had referred her to the regional hospital after she had spent many hours in labor and garnered the vague diagnosis "poor progress of labor." Her records from the dispensary were incomplete, but she had no known history of problems during this pregnancy or her previous two. It took one hour after her admission for a maternity ward doctor to review her. Once Dr. Deo arrived, he agreed with the initial findings of the doctor in the outpatient department who had reviewed Kinakia upon her arrival from the village. Her cervix was about eight centimeters dilated, and both clinicians felt the baby was in a nonideal position, a face presentation. Kinakia's blood pressure was slightly elevated, leading Dr. Deo to suggest preeclampsia. When Dr. Deo took her history, Kinakia told him she had been coughing up blood and bleeding from her nose for the past day and that this had been accompanied by difficulty in breathing. The baby's vital signs appeared relatively stable at that time, but it was clear Kinakia needed an emergency C-section. Because of her history of difficulty breathing, Dr. Deo wrote in his pre-op orders that they should have suction equipment in the theater and that he suspected she was suffering from "severe aspiration pneumonia."

The surgical notes in her file give no start time for the surgery, but in the subsequent maternal death audit meeting the participants wrote that Kinakia had died approximately three hours after she had arrived at the hospital, so it is reasonable to guess Dr. Deo commenced operating at about 8:30 p.m. His notes on the surgery take up just over half a page, a stark chronicle of the last hour of Kinakia's life. Her preoperative diagnosis states, "obstructed labor secondary to face presentation" and, on the following line "?? Eclampsia." She had spinal anesthesia, as opposed to the more usual general anesthesia, so she would have been awake during the surgery. After reporting that she had given birth to a male baby weighing 3.5 kg, Dr. Deo's notes continue: "Soon after the delivery of the baby, the mother stopped breathing.

Resuscitation was done with no success. A lot of whitish mixed with blood secretions were coming out from the nose and mouth. Vitals: Nil. No cardiac activity. Pupils dilated, fixed. No sound of lungs. [Diagnosis]: Death. Possible cause of death: Pulmonary/Respiratory failure secondary to severe aspiration pneumonia."

In the morning meeting the day after her death, the physicians and nurses debated the actions taken and not taken in the theater the previous night. One asked why they had not tried to insert an endotracheal tube, to intubate. Another suggested Kinakia had not received enough IV fluids and that this lack, when combined with the spinal anesthesia, might have caused her to become hypotensive, resulting in the secretions that had suffocated her. Dr. Deo asserted that they had been unable to intubate because the one person who knew how to do it, Nurse Salome, had not been on duty on the night shift. And even if they had been able to get Salome to the hospital, they did not have any muscle relaxants available, which they said would have been necessary to help with the procedure.

Four months later, in the maternal death audit meeting to discuss cases from the preceding six months, we talked about Kinakia's death. Nurse Salome was, this time, present to discuss what had occurred and what might have been done that night to save Kinakia. Salome said, "Even up to now, we still don't have the equipment for ventilating patients there in the theater! There is a new machine, but it is still missing those other pieces to make it work!" Four months after this death, so clearly connected to an inability to intubate and resuscitate Kinakia, the hospital had not ensured the availability of some of the lifesaving tools that should have been in the operating room. The ventilation machine, too new and complicated to use without training from an outside expert, continued to sit in the corner. It also subsequently came out that the new machine was missing the needed oxygen concentrator and therefore could not function even if someone were to receive training on its use. Salome continued, "And we are talking about training people on intubating, but I can't teach anyone if there isn't any equipment to intubate in the first place!"

The ethically responsible decision on the part of the hospital and its administrators would have been to immediately find a way to acquire the missing equipment and conduct on-the-job training. But Dr. Charles and Dr. Deo could perform routine C-sections without any of these more specialized drugs, machines, or equipment. Therefore, the hospital staff members and administrators were able to continue to overlook the absence of these supplies as their everyday environment necessitated they prioritize spending money and effort in ways that would affect many more patients. This environment facilitated and demanded that the hospital prioritize spending on basic necessities instead of specialized, rarely used tools and techniques. Kinakia's death had momentarily brought these supplies back into the spotlight, but the immediacy of her death soon faded. Four months later, in the meeting hall, the administrators wrote in their action plans that the hospital needed to acquire the right parts for the oxygen concentrator and conduct on-the-job training related to the use of the machine and intubation techniques. Even in subsequent death audit meetings, we never heard a report on what the responsible parties had accomplished, so I never learned how long it took for the hospital to obtain the missing equipment. Luckily, no other pregnant women needed it, at least not in 2014.

"TELL THEM WE'RE LIKE MALNOURISHED CHILDREN"

One afternoon, I was on the maternity ward to conduct pile sorts and to try to convince the nurses to schedule formal interviews with me later in the month. I had only two months left at Mawingu and was eager to hear from as many nurses as possible. As we were chatting, the nurses told me I should do more surveys so I could show the hospital administration the results and they might be convinced to change things at the hospital to be more supportive of the nurses. Nurse Lucy interjected, "Tell them we're like malnourished children! We eat *ugali* and beans to build our bodies because we're used to it, but it's not healthy!" Lucy drew on the common staple foods of even the poorest Tanzanians to demonstrate that one could survive in a workplace lacking supplies and support but that it wasn't the sort of environment that would enable the nurses to do their best work.

Overall, the environment of health facilities in the Rukwa region and, undoubtedly, Tanzania more generally, strained health care providers in a number of ways, leading to low morale and motivation. They were often under severe financial, physical, and emotional stress as they continued striving to provide high-quality care that complied with hospital and Ministry of Health guidelines for pregnant women. Many of the nurses and some of the doctors told me they found it hard to build "good" lives for themselves, in which they were able to meet the needs of their families, such as school fees and other daily necessities, because of a lack of money and few opportunities for advancement and recognition in the workplace.

The bottom line, as the RMO and Dr. Joseph, the medical officer in charge, pointed out, was that money was always a problem. Poor cash flow and slow disbursal of funds from the central government meant the hospital was unable to further invest in infrastructure, training, or hiring of staff members. Individuals working within this system were not necessarily uninterested in or incapable of providing high-quality care—very often a confluence of structural factors delayed, deterred, or demotivated, thereby affecting how women and their babies experienced the hospital and how the nurses, doctors, and administrators understood what it meant to be a government health care provider in the Rukwa region. The ways in which the central government's bureaucratic procedures intersected with, and caused, scarcity at the regional hospital, combined with biobureaucratic expansion, took providers' attention away from caring for women in ways that complied with guidelines. When supplies were scarce and the reality of care could not meet the ideal, standard operating procedures version of care, bureaucratic documentation helped to hide the improvisation in which the hospital staff members engaged. For instance, official documentation about umbilical cord cutting elided the absence of scissors or surgical blades, as well as the danger to health care workers presented by using a needle to painstakingly cut through the cord. All that appeared on paper was that the cord had been cut.

Sometimes the delay in care or in receiving a medication or procedure resulted in the woman's death; other times she died as a direct result of a lack of a specific piece of equipment, such as an adult-sized Ambu bag for resuscitation, or the lack of a way to remove the fluids from her lungs which she aspirated once on the operating table. Providers' previous experiences of the bureaucracy, the shortages, and the system that forcefully resisted any change came to shape their work in a way that suggested that the environment itself precluded many forms of care, such as some of those required by "high-quality" care guidelines and codified standard operating procedures.

3

Protocols and Deviations

Good Enough Care

The Mawingu Regional Hospital, like the Tanzanian Ministry of Health, was influenced by and worked to adhere to national and international sets of guidelines related to providing care for pregnant mothers and newborns. These guidelines for best practice often were derived from internationally sanctioned, World Health Organization recommendations, which the Tanzanian Ministry of Health and Social Welfare (MoHSW) then took up and reviewed. Pending approval by their experts, the MoHSW would reproduce these guidelines in English or Swahili (or sometimes both), affix the seal of the Tanzanian government as official endorsement, and then disseminate these recommendations and protocols throughout the country. This was one avenue by which the state continued to act as a gatekeeper for external interventions and continued to prove its fundamental importance in health care despite a landscape of increased projectification—reliance on shifting donors and policies, and the fragmentation of what should have been health sector–wide reforms into often isolated, singular projects run by nongovernmental organizations and others—and the explosion of NGOs.[1] In one instance, a new poster appeared on the maternity ward bulletin board, illustrating the use of a new device. The poster did not bear this seal from the MoHSW, and one of the nurses immediately became suspicious of those who were sponsoring the device, a conglomeration of NGOs. She picked up her cell phone and called a friend who worked in the ministry to inquire about the legitimacy of the project and ensure that the women of Rukwa would not be guinea pigs for an untested intervention of questionable origins. In the days thereafter, it became clear it was a legitimate project, but her concerns were not unreasonable given a broad history of exploitative scientific and medical experimentation across sub-Saharan African.

NGOs were often involved in suggesting or developing new guidelines or protocols based on evidence from international trials of devices or drugs: for example, changing guidelines and protocols related to the use of misoprostol,[2] treatment of eclampsia with magnesium sulfate, and the more recent introduction of a device called the NASG (nonpneumatic antishock garment) for the management of postpartum hemorrhage. The MoHSW, together with USAID, Jhpiego, WHO, UNICEF, UNFPA, and other NGOs, developed a set of assessment guidelines related to basic emergency obstetric and neonatal care (BEmONC) entitled *Standards-Based Management and Recognition for Improving Quality in Maternal and Newborn Care* (*SBMR* Tool). This tool included standard protocols for everything from greeting a woman when she arrived at the facility, to managing an emergency situation ("First, shout for help!"), to disposing of the placenta properly. There was a version for use in hospitals and a separate version for the lower-level health centers and village dispensaries. These are most often the standards of care to which I refer. Throughout the chapter, I use the terms *standards, protocols,* and *guidelines.* Protocols and standards are more rigid and are generally a concrete set of steps defining a treatment regimen or procedure. Guidelines are less rigid and include space for assessment and subsequent modification based on patient needs and local contexts. In Swahili, the government uses the word *mwongozo,* which includes the meaning of both guideline and protocol but most often translates to guideline. If I refer to the technical, clinical care that was provided as being of a low quality, it is always as compared to these guidelines or standards that nurses and doctors were using or based on their views of the care they or their institution were able to provide, and not a result of my own personal judgments of the quality of care. I refer to these particular standards of care because the hospital staff members and other health care providers with whom I worked referred to them and aspired to provide care in full compliance with them. Providers and facilities were also measured against the *SBMR* Tool by outsiders and via internal, self-assessment activities. While the maternity ward staff members strove to meet these guidelines, their environment often constrained care, both technical/clinical, and intersubjective emotional care, to be just "good enough"—good enough to keep most women alive and to let providers work another day.

The role and influence of these standards and guidelines shaped health care workers', as well as women's and men's, expectations of clinical, technical care, and patients' roles as biomedical subjects. As part of the global health development complex, these types of protocols, guidelines, and standards for care are the yardstick by which individual providers, facilities, regions, and countries are measured. Their deservingness of aid and investment, and their individual and collective efficacy, are judged by their ability to successfully implement and adhere to these measures despite widely varying access to resources—both human and material—as well as varying infrastructure and differing effects of geographic surroundings. Global health organizations and governing bodies often present these guidelines and protocols as the solutions to improving health care outcomes and reducing morbidity and mortality, including the deaths of pregnant women.

It is clear that, on the ground in Rukwa, these guidelines were nearly impossible to meet.

Against the background of scarcity, it starts to become clear how and when and why nurses and doctors on the Mawingu maternity ward did not or could not comply with all these ideals of best practice. In this chapter, I lay out many of those ideal, standard protocols for each stage of a woman's time on the maternity ward, and I start to show how care in practice deviated from these ideals. In the midst of these deviations it is possible to begin to see the many ways nurses sought to balance their needs with those of their patients—to uphold codified professional ethics, while preserving their own abilities to continue working day after day in an unforgiving system. Sometimes the nurses engaged in emotion work to demonstrate nursing ideals of caring and pleasantness,[3] but other times they did not have the emotional reserves to act out what might have been the desired affective components of caring for their pregnant clients on the ward as they juggled expectations and demands.

THE ADMISSION

Upon finally entering the ward, passing through the doors of the admission room, which bore a sign forbidding admittance to anyone not in labor, each woman handed a nurse her antenatal clinic card. The card included basic health information, a rudimentary obstetric history (number of previous pregnancies, miscarriages, living children), HIV status, and checkboxes about chronic or preexisting health problems, including categories such as heart problems and diabetes. According to guidelines, health care providers at the prenatal clinics were supposed to test every pregnant woman for HIV/AIDS, and while most were tested, sometimes the woman's village dispensary did not have the necessary reagents, test strips, or trained providers for carrying out the rapid tests.

With the antenatal card in hand, the nurse then recorded the woman's demographic information and basic obstetric history in the ward's admission book, a ragged notebook that had pages falling out and was much repaired with medical tape, regular Sellotape, and glue. After this, the nurse instructed the woman to take her things and lie on the examination bed so the nurse could check the woman's vital signs, count her contractions, listen to the fetal heartbeat, conduct a vaginal examination to estimate cervical dilation, and do a general "head to toe" assessment of the woman's overall health. Ideally, the nurse would be conversing with the woman throughout in order to take her history. On the basis of cervical dilation, the nurse then decided where to send the woman to wait out the rest of her labor until it was time to move to the delivery room. While these examinations and measurements were all supposed to make up the initial admission exam, nurses often rushed through them or simply wrote "normal" after looking at a woman.

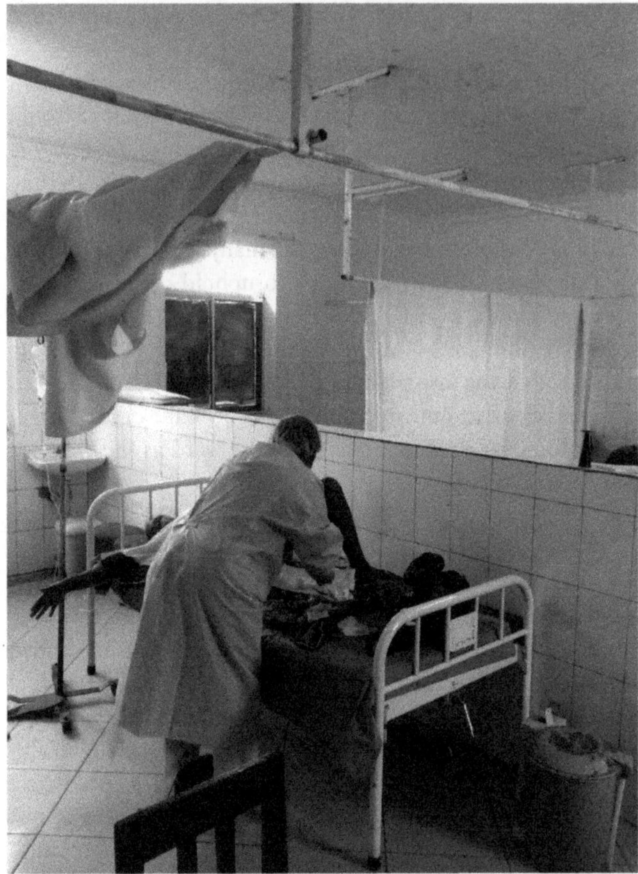

FIGURE 8. The labor and delivery room. Photo by author, 2014.

While the hospital continued to increase the number of nurses working on the maternity ward, those assigned to a shift were not necessarily present, and even when they were, the number of women arriving, in labor, waiting for a C-section, or needing other forms of care could easily stretch the nurses thin. This, not infrequently, resulted in the women having only brief, truncated interactions with the nurses in which the nurses did not ask key questions about the woman's previous medical history, problems during the pregnancy, or current health. Certainly, during the busiest times, it was not possible to obtain any kind of social history, which would have improved care by adding context to the woman's pregnancy (Wanted? Unplanned? Supported by her family? In the context of a marriage?), or to ask questions that would have eased the awkward and foreign interactions taking place. More than once, as a nurse expressed dismay and frustration, a woman resisted a vaginal exam. Nurses could certainly have tempered these violations of women's bodies, but the absence of time for these interactions was itself a product of a structurally violent situation for the nurses, in which they lacked the personnel and resources they needed. In the absence of other information or context, sometimes the nurses and doctors explained away a woman's strange behavior or noncompliance by saying she was out of her mind from the pain of contractions; other times, their inattention to a woman's faint signals for care or help resulted in that woman's death.

If the woman was in early labor, less than three or four centimeters dilated, the nurse would give her a bed in the antenatal room with instructions to come back to the admission room when her contractions got stronger. If she was between four to six or seven centimeters dilated, the woman would generally receive a bed in the admission room, closer to the delivery room. In both the antenatal and admission rooms, the women almost always shared their bed with a second woman and, at particularly busy times, maybe even with two other women. This was due to a lack of beds but, more importantly, to a lack of a place to even put other beds. If the woman had already reached six or seven centimeters, she would go directly into the labor room.

In the labor room (figure 8), women never shared a bed because of the need for enough space to conduct the delivery and the messy nature of giving birth. On busy days there was a rapid turnover in beds. Other times, women quickly progressed through the last few centimeters and gave birth in the beds in the admission room, in close proximity to other women, without privacy, and, many times, without the assistance of a nurse, who would come running just as the woman finished pushing her baby into the world.

LABORING

Once sorted in this way, the women made their way to the appropriate part of the ward to wait for their contractions to increase. Clinically, a woman's labor is divided into three stages. The first stage is further divided into the latent and active phases and, overall, is the entire time from when the cervix is closed until it reaches ten centimeters, considered full or complete dilation, and the woman is nearly ready to start pushing. At this point, from the time the cervix is fully dilated to when the baby is born, the woman is in the second stage of labor. The third and final stage of labor is from when the baby is born until the birth of the placenta.

There are few hard-and-fast rules for the amount of time a woman can or should stay in any stage of labor. However, once the woman is in active labor, in the first stage, her contractions will, ideally, remain regular and increase in strength, duration, and frequency. The general rule of thumb is that the cervix should dilate one centimeter every hour during the active phase of the first stage. Then the woman enters the second stage, which can last from a matter of minutes to a matter of hours depending on many factors including (but certainly not limited to) how many previous pregnancies the woman has had, the angle at which the baby's head entered the pelvis, the position in which the woman is laboring, the size of the baby, and the mother's own mental, emotional, and physical state. For example, a woman may have had a very long first stage of labor during which her contractions did not allow her to get much sleep. She may not have eaten much throughout her labor, and when it comes time to push she may be very tired.

Women who were feeling tired and unable to push would often say that they did not have strength (*sina nguvu*) or that they were defeated (*nimeshindwa*). The passive construction does not provide any idea of who or what may have defeated the speaker, while still conveying the sense that the speaker has tried and, not because of anything within her power, was unable to do something. Perhaps a reflection of a cultural sense of the locus of control, this phrase is a common one, not just in the hospital but in life more generally. In the case of the women, I suggest a reading of this phrase that takes it also as a sign that the speaker, the woman, was aware of her lack of control and was relinquishing it, turning it over to the nurses and biomedical intervention in all its forms. The passive voice here also acts to revoke agency and, in so doing, contradicts the neoliberal image of the patient as advocate for her own care.

FIERCE CARE AND THE SECOND STAGE

The nurses would often become very concerned about how long the mother was in the second stage of labor because, they said, this was the most precarious time for mother and baby. If a baby spent too long in the birth canal, the umbilical cord might be compressed, cutting off the baby's oxygen supply. Nurses said then that the baby would not "score well," referring to the APGAR score used to assess the baby's appearance and reflexes upon birth. Babies who did not have enough oxygen during birth could develop a number of complications, including twitches, which might be an indication of brain damage, and were at risk for birth asphyxiation, which was a relatively common cause of neonatal deaths while I was at Mawingu. In this second stage of labor, babies were also at risk for getting meconium or other secretions in their mouths, which they could then inhale deeply into their lungs when they were born and first began to cry. This created the possibility of infections, especially pneumonia.

When confronted with a woman who was defeated or was experiencing an extremely difficult second stage of labor, the nurses would frequently resort to hitting the woman's legs or using harsh language. When I asked about these behaviors, Nurse Halima explained this way, and her answer was generally representative:

> If you yell at a person, she will understand you. But if you tell her gently—me, I have tried to admit a woman gently, if I reach labor [room], gently, every area, gently. Until I came to change; it was necessary for me to be severe, why? Because that patient, she comes there, she sees you, that you have your gentleness, and [it shows] she doesn't have to be serious. Therefore, she arrives there, she is strangling the baby, she arrives there, you tell her she should lie on her back and push the baby, [but] she sits, she sits on the baby's head and the baby dies there. Therefore, if you don't use that severity—*that fierceness* helps, at the end of the day, her to get her baby, and at the end of the day that patient, she comes to thank the nurse: "Thank you, there,

> without you doing that to me like that, I wouldn't have given birth." You see? . . . Even if you go wherever, you can't hear a nurse speaking gently to a pregnant woman because the nurse is doing that fierceness to save that baby. But I don't believe that that severity, a person would do it to a person who has, I don't know, maybe I should tell you, maybe like an intestinal obstruction. If [the nurse] does that, we have to ask her, 'You, why are you doing that?' but in things with childbirth, the pregnant mother's mind, it is as though it's not there. Therefore, you have to scare or shock her. You have to yell at her, tell her, "You, you do this and this and this, and here this should be this way and this way. If you don't do these things, you will lose your baby, you will do this!" You tell her even the complete outcome. But a person, if you tell her the truth, a person sees like you are abusing her or you have asked her for bad things, therefore, this is what it's like. Except, the biggest thing is that we always speak in order to protect the baby. At the end of the day, a woman gives birth to a baby who is alive and then she complains about things like those, it's not good. While for her, you are her assistance. (emphasis added)

Halima had first worked on the private ward, and when she'd had reason to pass through maternity, she had often remarked to herself that the nurses were using mean and abusive language with the women. She could not see why and often sympathized with the women—until, she said, she was transferred to the maternity ward and quickly found her gentle demeanor did not help her in extracting the required compliance or outcomes from her new patients. Nurses yelled at or hit the women, yes, to help them find the strength to give birth but also to protect themselves as providers, demonstrating they had done everything possible to ensure a good outcome during the birth. Using a translation of a Swahili word, which Halima drew on in her explanation, I term this "fierce care" in order to draw the discussion of these behaviors into a more local frame and a more nuanced space for analysis.

Ultimately, the nurses viewed behaviors such as yelling at the women, telling them they were killing their baby, or hitting them as a form of care that they undertook to help the woman give birth. Hannah Brown cites similar behaviors in a maternity ward in Kenya, where nurses suggested that letting women relax during labor was disadvantageous and did not result in good outcomes for mothers and babies.[4] Similarly, Josien de Klerk troubles Western conceptions of care practices, demonstrating how the "toughening" of those who have lost relatives, and the concealment of dying patients' HIV status are, in fact, locally valued forms of care, though cultural outsiders might not view them as such.[5]

In my own, later work in the Kigoma region, to the north of Rukwa, I found strong community consensus around the value of strategic hitting or yelling for helping a woman to give birth. In general, community members of all ages, both male and female, agreed that a pregnant woman should never be hit. However, when my research team presented them with specific instances in which a woman might have difficulty in the second stage of labor, community members condoned hitting, usually the woman's legs, and/or yelling. These specific cases included when a woman was tensing up or closing her legs; when her fear prevented her from pushing; when she was making a lot of noise (using her strength to make noise instead of pushing); and if she was not pushing strongly enough. Community members explained their endorsement of hitting or yelling in these instances by saying things like, "It is necessary for nurses to hit the pregnant woman if she is afraid or not a brave person." A second woman explained, "A pregnant woman shouldn't be hit if she doesn't have any problem. [But if there is a problem] you hit her to ensure that other people won't say you have killed the baby. You hit her to save yourself." This particular sentiment not only describes the broader social milieu from which nurses, too, came but also combines with the hospital protocols related to the documentation and review of neonatal deaths, for which individual providers might be held accountable.

Another woman in the community, when asked if it was accurate that nurses yelled at women in order to save the baby, stated, "You can't know, even the nurse, if the baby will be alive or not. It is an outcome, not an expectation," so even the nurses had to do everything that might possibly help ensure the birth of a healthy baby. These descriptions of locally valued care practices lead to a more nuanced reading of these behaviors in which the nurses engaged, recasting them as forms of care suitable to the environment in which the nurses found themselves, not just deviations from ideal care protocols designed in other settings. Riskiness and the uncertainty inherent in reproductive outcomes in Tanzania have led to the development of expressions of fierce care, which in other circumstances—for example, Halima's mention of a patient suffering from an intestinal obstruction—would be abusive, according to community members and many nurses.

Though Halima said women often thanked the nurses for hitting them to help them give birth, the women and their relatives could just as easily report the nurse for abuse and a violation of the official, codified ethics of the Tanzania Nurse Midwives Council. Often, during the second stage of labor, the woman's fleeting pain, shame, or violated privacy were generally agreed to be elements that could be sacrificed if the baby's life was in danger; fierce care became the most suitable care. In these instances, nurses, women, and community members collectively redefined and reshaped care, entering into tacit mutual agreements about which outcome was the most important in their constrained setting. Along the way, because of persistent resource scarcity, lack of mentoring, and few alternatives, this fierce care, though not necessarily desirable, became normal both for women and for their nurse-midwives. Possibilities for other forms of care during this crucial moment in the second stage receded, fading from view and imagination.

Many of the nurses described women in labor, with no access to pain medications, as "out of their minds" or unable to listen and follow directions, as Halima also mentioned. While some women, especially young women experiencing their first pregnancy, were clearly distraught because of the pain and fear of being in labor, many others labored quietly and compliantly followed all the nurses' instructions. Occasionally, we received women who stood out as atypical examples of noncompliance, and their memory has stayed with me. One woman refused to do anything other than sit on the dirty tile floor. Every time a nurse and I helped her up onto the bed, we would turn around moments later to find her back, squatting on the floor. The doctor kept walking through the labor room that day and repeatedly berated the nurses for "letting" the woman remain on the floor because he had not seen our struggles to move her up onto the bed time and again.

Another woman's relatives told us she seemed to have experienced a significant shift in her personality with the onset of labor. She spoke of seeing spirits around her and she was extremely agitated. Because of her prolonged labor, the nurses started her on IV fluids, but the woman repeatedly pulled the cannula out of her arm and quickly made her way out into the courtyard of the ward. More than once we went to check on her and found a trail of blood from where she'd pulled out the IV, leading us to the flowerbed where she was squatting and bearing down with contractions while muttering incomprehensibly, covered in dirt.

Truly, in cases such as these, it was possible to understand how the nurses came to view hitting, slapping, or yelling as the appropriate, and needed, tools. There was nothing much else they could do with women such as these, particularly as they repeatedly defied efforts to entice them into staying put on their assigned bed, threatening to give birth in an unsanitary location with no assistance, as could have been the case in the flowerbed. These were full-grown women, with pregnant bellies, whom the nurses could not easily physically remove to their beds or elsewhere, who refused reasoning and for whom the nurses had no other technical or medical options. Understaffing and no relatives on the ward meant there was no one to continuously stay with these women. Lacking other possibilities, nurses resorted to this fierce care that contravened formal nursing ethics but made profound ethical sense in this everyday setting.

As described in the Introduction, in analyzing the nurses' actions in this context, it is critically important to remain open to care's local meanings and practices, paying particular attention to uncovering, in actions, decisions, and interactions, "what is sought, fostered, or hoped for, then and there: what is performed as good . . . [and what] is avoided, resolved, or excluded: what is performed as bad" care.[6] The ethical norms of care practices also shift depending upon the actors involved, as well as the constraints in play. Occasionally, the good and bad forms of care are obvious or straightforward, but more frequently they are complex and ambivalent: "If one looks hard enough any particular 'good' practice may hold something 'bad' inside of it (and vice versa)."[7] Sometimes, the expected care relationship produces violence, as when nurses hit, slap, or verbally abuse laboring women. When we examine these events in light of more *unexpected* or capacious care relationships, we come to understand that these actions are a different sort of care practice. Sometimes nurses used these methods not simply to vent frustration but to care for a woman's larger kinship network and her as she worked to give birth to a living baby who would solidify her place in her marital family, win her respect, demonstrate her valor as a woman, and relieve any fears of a cursed mother or baby or wronged social relations. These fierce care practices might appear ambiguous, with mixed positive and negative, kind and violent elements, because the care recipient is sometimes beyond our expected scope of perception. Western-derived approaches and perspectives miss how the individual care recipient is embedded in a broader social network, which is also receiving care in a less direct manner. While I personally do not condone hitting or yelling at women and believe women have a right to a birth free of abuse and mistreatment, viewing these actions as broadly directed care would challenge many policy makers and public health practitioners to rethink relatively straightforward, one-size-fits-all, rights-based policies for respectful maternity care in places where local forms of respectful care may look unrecognizably different depending on resources and on care priorities and practices. In the very particular instance of the second stage of labor, these explanations do not mean that hitting or verbal manipulation is acceptable but simply that we must engage with these practices on their own terms in each setting in order to understand what motivates them.

BIRTH

After the birth of the baby, the nurses would quickly cut the umbilical cord, and they had all learned active management of the third stage of labor (AMTSL or, alternatively, AMSTL), in which the nurse would first palpate the uterus for the presence of another baby and administer an injection of a uterotonic, usually oxytocin, to help the uterus to contract.[8] Then, using forceps, the provider would clamp the umbilical cord close to the mother's perineum and pull with slow, steady pressure in a downward motion until the placenta fully detached from the uterus and was delivered. The nurse then checked the placenta to make sure it was complete and thoroughly massaged the uterus to ensure that it expelled any blood clots and to verify that it was contracting, a key sign that bleeding would stop.[9] Ideally, the health care provider would explain to the mother how to check and periodically massage her uterus, as well as give her information about danger signs in the immediate postpartum period. Only rarely did I ever hear the nurses in the labor and delivery room give the woman any advice that went beyond how to check if her uterus was still contracted and telling her to void her bladder.

Most often, the nurses at the Mawingu Regional Hospital were able to let the women continue to rest in the labor room after delivery so they could monitor their conditions. This was supposed to include vital signs monitoring, though this particular aspect hardly ever happened—sometimes because other women needed assistance, others times because the blood pressure cuff was missing or broken, or no one could find a functioning stethoscope. In lieu of the more technological monitoring specified in care guidelines, the nurses who were more experienced would visually assess the mother and deem her condition "normal." Sometimes, depending on how busy the ward was, the nurses had to almost immediately move new mothers to the postnatal room because incoming women were ready to give birth and needed a bed in the labor room. These sometimes-hasty transitions were not ideal and more than once led to incoming mothers giving birth on the floor near a bed, or immediately after reaching a bed. The outgoing mothers were forced to carry all of their belongings to the other side of the ward within minutes of giving birth. When this happened, the mothers hobbled slowly along, sometimes with blood dripping on the floor from between their legs, balancing on their heads plastic basins overflowing with soiled clothes, while any free staff member carried their newborn.

Once a woman had given birth, she moved to the postnatal room across the ward, near the entrance, where she typically spent twenty-four hours, give or take, depending on her health and whether she had experienced any complications. Once she was in the postnatal room, the postnatal nurses took over her care and were responsible for ensuring she had any necessary medications or monitoring. The postnatal nurses were also responsible for providing health education related to family planning, breastfeeding, personal hygiene, and basic nutrition and baby care information. On this part of the ward, the nurses also filled out another set of documents, completing documentation started by the labor room nurses in the delivery book in which all the births were recorded, as well as filling out the birth announcement form that families took to their district administrative offices if they wanted to get a birth certificate for their child. If any of the women had not already previously been tested for HIV, the postnatal nurses counseled and tested them, providing those who tested positive with medications for the baby and further instructions for follow-up testing. The women also received a mild painkiller and an iron and/or folic acid supplement, as well as vitamin A, which they received when other nurses or auxiliary staff members arrived on the ward to vaccinate the newborns.

SURGICAL BIRTH

If a woman needed a C-section, either planned or emergency, her flow through the ward differed somewhat from the norm. If the nurses identified a possible complication or previous history that suggested the woman might need a surgical birth, they would call the doctor to alert him of a patient for review. When the doctor confirmed the need for a C-section, the nurses prepared the woman for surgery by having her sign a consent form; taking blood samples for laboratory tests (blood grouping, cross-matching, and hemoglobin levels), in case she should need a blood transfusion and to rule out anemia that might be life-threatening during the surgery; administering preoperative antibiotics and IV fluids; and inserting a catheter to drain the woman's bladder during the surgery and her recovery.

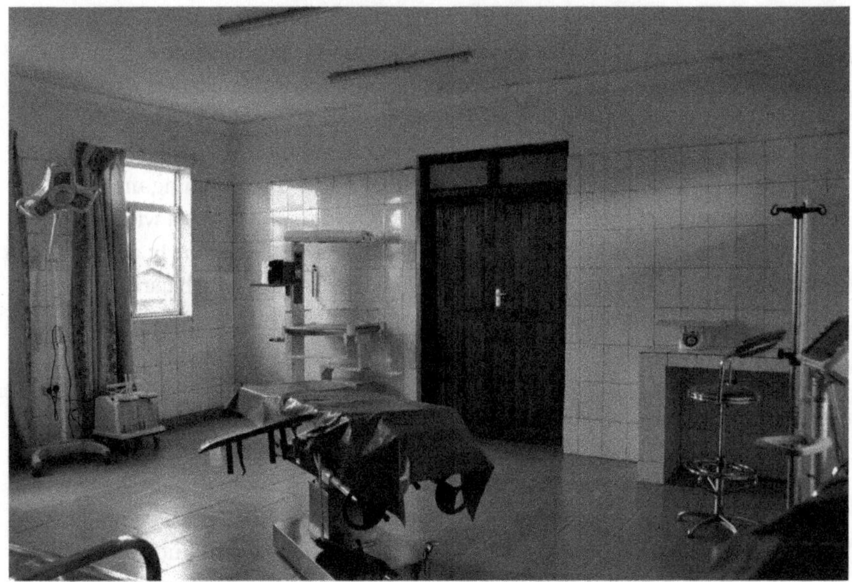

FIGURE 9. Maternity ward operating theater. Photo by author, 2014.

Once the mother was in the operating theater (figure 9), which, as of December 2014, was located within the maternity ward itself, a nurse from the labor room accompanied her to receive the baby. This nurse often had to resuscitate the baby (with greater or lesser degrees of intervention depending on a number of factors, including the type of anesthesia used) and then was responsible for weighing the baby, recording its APGAR score, sex, and time of birth, and then carrying the baby back to the labor room, where the baby would wait in a warmer until its mother awoke from the general anesthesia and was able to care for the baby.

At this point, the postnatal nurses took over the care of the mother and were responsible for collecting her from the operating theater after the surgical team was finished. The postnatal nurses transferred the unconscious and/or immobilized woman to a bed in the post-Cesarean room (figure 10), changed her perineal pad, and ensured that she was warm, clean, and secure. The postnatal nurses then were also responsible for the follow-up care of these patients, which included administering pain medication and antibiotics on a schedule and dispensing advice related to food and fluid intake, breastfeeding, urination, care of the incision site, and general information about recovery. The nurses, and often the doctor too, would try to impress upon the post-C-section mothers the necessity of using a form of birth control to prevent pregnancy for two to three years so their bodies would have enough time to heal and not predispose them to possible future complications, such as a ruptured uterus.

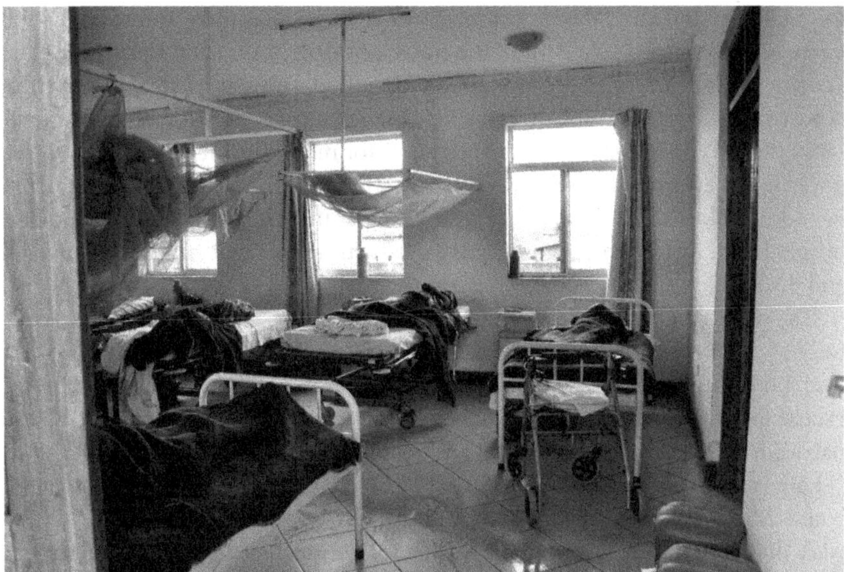

FIGURE 10. View of the post–Cesarean section room on the maternity ward. Photo by author, 2014.

UCHACHE AS EXCUSE AND IDIOM

All of the above tasks that went into women's care at each step of their time on the maternity were in addition to administrative and documentation tasks that consumed even more of the nurses' and doctors' time. The standard guidelines, like the *SBMR* Tool, did not appear to consider provider shortages, such as those the patron mentioned in chapter 1. When I interviewed the patron and the assistant matron, we talked about these tools. Patron told me, "I have looked at this tool because we have been in this program, but we are improving by only a very small percentage. . . . Once you miss resources, you will score zero; therefore this tool needs to be improved." The matron nodded her head in agreement, and I encouraged him to continue. He went on, "But the second reason for our low scores is even employees too, by which I mean the fewness (*uchache*) of employees there . . . also causes the employees to have so much work so that they lose their focus on those standards." The matron added, "It is very difficult in a setting in which there is this *uchache* of employees and so many clients, to follow those guidelines point by point while you have a queue of one hundred patients. And because they don't use these guidelines, they can't remember all of them. So the day someone comes to review them, they will find many deficiencies."

In addition to the material scarcity produced by stock-outs, hospital staffing levels were a source of frustration and great concern, preventing adherence to guidelines for care. Nurses expressed their belief that there were simply not enough of them to conduct all of the necessary patient care and documentation activities that a ward as large as maternity required, substantiated by the patron's report that the hospital was not meeting the WHO's suggested patient-to-nurse ratio. Budget constraints and unmet requests for more providers from the central government affected the hospital administration's ability to hire new staff members or promote those who had been working at the facility for many years. The hospital administration sought ways to deal with these constraints as the nurses and doctors continued to provide care to the best of their abilities.

The nurses and doctors often referred to *uchache*, or "state of fewness," specifically of providers, as a key barrier to improving maternal health outcomes at the hospital, though the medical officer in charge did not feel this was an appropriate excuse for not exerting maximum effort with every individual patient. At a maternal death audit meeting in July 2014, Dr. Joseph, the medical officer in charge, said, "I know we can't avoid death, but you get a death like this and see there were gaps." Nurse Mary suggested maybe the problem was documentation; maybe things were done but the documentation was bad. Dr. Joseph rejoined, "If you say the problem is documentation, you're doing a lot of things, then you should say the problem is that there aren't enough people, '*uchache*,' just say that, because that is the issue!" The conversation about staff levels, documentation, and care continued. Dr. Joseph told the group, "Even if you are few, I expect you to give 100 percent to the patient you are with." The RMO jumped in to ask, "Right now, where we are, it still happens that women are giving birth unassisted?" The assembled group collectively and vociferously asserted that it was still occurring. Becoming exasperated, Dr. Joseph effectively ended the discussion by saying, "It's not *uchache*, the issue is that we are not prepared when we see the patient. We are not prepared with the equipment and documentation."

In light of the fact that the maternity ward received at least eight new nurses during the duration of my fieldwork, it would appear as though the number of people was not so much a cause of poor care as continuing to invoke *uchache* was a way to locate the source of the problem of ongoing substandard care or deaths in something outside the direct control of those on the ward. Maintaining this discourse of *uchache* accomplished a status quo that served the nurses by not requiring, as Dr. Joseph asserted, higher levels of preparedness or commitment. Even as the hospital and regional health administrators sought to continue hiring greater numbers of qualified providers, the problems of miscommunication and delays in care that staff members had been attributing to their low numbers did not disappear. The nurses' continued use of *uchache* can be read as an idiom, coded from an earlier era, for a more general lack of workplace empowerment and professional efficacy, in their "under-resourced work environment that prevented them from realizing improvements in care."[10]

Uchache and the Night Shift

Despite a near tripling of the nurses assigned to the maternity ward during my time at Mawingu, there were persistent staff shortages on the night shift. On the nights in May 2015 when I spent several hours at the hospital conducting interviews with nurses on the night shift, I usually was on the ward with two nurses in the labor and delivery room and one nurse assigned to the postnatal portion of the ward. I repeatedly heard that the night shift needed more nurses. One day, I asked Nurse Mpili about it. "I keep hearing that there are not enough nurses on the night shift. But we've gotten so many new people. Why not just assign more people to each shift?" Mpili looked at me and explained, "Even just a few years ago, you would be so exhausted from working here in maternity. You know, you can't sleep on the night shift like on other wards. Because we were so few, we had the night shift maybe even three times per week. You never had time to rest or do anything for your family. Now? Now, we have so many people, you can even do only one night shift each week." Presented with the choice to either improve their own quality of life or assign more nurses to the night shift, the maternity ward had decided to maintain the low staffing levels so that everyone had fewer night shifts, thus preventing more disruptions to family life and sleep schedules. In this instance, the nurses and patients were more subtly on opposite sides of an issue. It was not that nurses actively wanted women to receive worse care at night, but nurses wanted to be able to ensure they could take care of their own families too.

The nursing profession in Tanzania still draws on the idea of Florence Nightingale as the paragon of nursing care. The image of Florence Nightingale often comes with ideas about selflessness and sacrifice in the service of providing care for patients. What is not included in this nursing imaginary is where nurses themselves are meant to find their endless reserves of compassion, patience, and energy. The nurses on the maternity ward at Mawingu strategically continued to utilize *uchache* while actively avoiding assigning more nurses to night shifts in order to preserve a modicum of quality of life for themselves and their colleagues.

MOTIVATION AND THE IMPOSSIBLE DEMANDS OF WORK

Nurses had to contend with the increasing scarcity of supplies while also handling new guidelines and procedures, as well as higher patient loads than ever before. This led to incredible stress that caused many of the nurses to tell me that they were often demoralized by their work environment. As a result, many of the nurses told me it appeared that their superiors, the hospital administrators, did not care about them. Feeling a lack of care, in the form of a work environment that did not enable them to perform to the highest levels of their knowledge and abilities, demoralized nurses. The type of care they wanted from the hospital administration, on an interpersonal level and also via the procurement of supplies and equipment, did not necessarily fall into either technical or affective care. I sometimes refer to this as institutional care to incorporate the structural, financial, resource, and affective elements necessary to realize a more caring work environment.

In my interview with Dr. Joseph in May 2015, I told him that since I had started coming to the Rukwa region in 2012 people had been telling me that the hospital staff members were not motivated. Sometimes this charge was leveled by community members; other times it was the doctors talking about the nurses. I asked Dr. Joseph what he thought he, as the medical officer in charge, or the hospital administration, could do to improve the level of motivation and morale among his employees. He said:

> I would say, number one [is] to increase the level of supplies—that will boost the morale. Because you are not being motivated if you don't have something to use, you don't have medicines for patients, the infrastructure is poor, you don't have supplies, you get demotivated. Then, from there, we may think of . . . like some competition . . . which departments works better, then we may recognize it by a letter or by certificate. . . . Probably that one would also boost the morale. But we cannot think about that sometimes because there are these problems with supplies so your head gets congested [you are overwhelmed]. I think I have to manage first these.

He also told me in the same conversation that even if the nurses and doctors said they would like recognition for their work in the form of verbal praise or certificates, what they *really* wanted was money, and the hospital simply could not incorporate higher wages or a system of monetary incentives given the already extremely difficult financial state of the institution.

I also asked the RMO about this issue of motivation and what he thought could help regional hospital staff members to be more motivated in their work. First, he asserted, "Ah, all these things we've done, honestly, if a person still isn't doing work with great effort, well this person, that is just how they are—they won't do it." This was primarily in reference to all the ways in which the hospital and regional health administration had tried in the previous three years to ensure that staff members received all the workers' benefits to which they were entitled as government employees, including payment for hospital treatment, paid vacation every other year, promotions every three years, and any back pay they were owed, as well as housing allowances for the physicians. However, the RMO went on to say,

> Also, to really ensure that the environment [at work] is better than where they are [home]. That is, infrastructure. . . . The work environment should be nicer than there at her home, where she is coming from, so she is pulled to stay at work more than staying at home. This is the secret. . . . She enters, she comes to work, she finds that she gets tea there close by, if she turns around there's lunch [nearby], yeah, she finds that everything is there. There is nice furniture. If it's a computer for doing work, it's

> there. Equipment is there. If she turns around there is a blood pressure [cuff] right here, glucose test here, stethoscope here, yeah? Nice things. She likes to stay at work. It's things like that.

One aspect of this overall environment that surfaced multiple times throughout my stay was the availability of tea, electric kettles, and sugar on the wards. The nurses on the maternity ward, and throughout the hospital, considered this to be a crucial part of making their working environment a livable place. They variably justified it to me as making it easier to have a bite to eat without wasting time leaving their workstation or being due this small comfort because of the hard work they did, or because, particularly on the night shift, no other food was readily available inside or outside the hospital grounds. In nearly every all-staff meeting the nurses requested the hospital also start providing bread on the wards, impossible because of the institution's financial state.

It may seem like a small demand, but I read these repeated requests for bread or other snacks as a bid for care. The hospital staff members viewed the provision of bread as a demonstration that the hospital administration had validated their presence and acknowledged their hard work and humanity. In many instances, issues of motivation seemed to center on the point that the nurses felt they were unseen and unheard. Very often, they were simply looking for some form of recognition from their superiors on their ward and within the hospital more generally.

While the administration was often concerned that the actual infrastructure of the hospital contributed to staff members' feeling unmotivated, this was not something that came up in the discussions of motivation and the work environment I had with nurses and physicians. Most commonly, the nurses were concerned with the availability of supplies and—another important factor—with the quality of leadership and mentorship that the hospital management displayed at both ward and hospital levels.

Nurse Anna started speaking about the hospital's infrastructure and the availability of up-to-date technology and quickly moved into a discussion of money as a motivator: "But also let's improve the environment, meaning that motivation, they should give us [to show] *they care for us*, the maternity ward, that's to say, we swim in blood and you know in the blood there is HIV and hepatitis. Therefore, even if they said 10,000 [TZS] every month for each provider on maternity, it would be motivation because of the type of environment in which we work!"

The lack of adequate personal protective equipment exacerbated the risk involved in providing care to pregnant women at Mawingu. Nurses expressed concerns about their abilities to protect themselves from the possible infectious agents present in women's blood and other bodily fluids.[11] These anxieties could color nurses' interactions with patients and even persuade some nurses to lash out against patients or avoid providing care at all, as the work environment was once again asking the nurses to provide care for patients while simultaneously jeopardizing their own well-being. In some cases, the nurses' concern for their own health and safety prevailed, but in other situations the nurses simply did what was necessary to save a woman's life or that of her baby. Nurse Gire told me that she would improvise protective equipment as best she could but that "no matter what, I don't remove [it]. I care only about saving the patient." She believed in the power of God to protect her in the absence of other, material protections.

Many of the nurses who had been working at the hospital for more than three or four years had mentioned to me, in other contexts, that the maternity ward staff members had formerly received an additional amount of money each month that was classified as a "risk allowance." They had received this money to compensate for the extra work they did in the absence of additional nurses but also to acknowledge the particular difficulties and dangers of maternity care work, especially the exposure to potentially hazardous bodily fluids. Now there were more providers and therefore no need to pay each person more for what was a more reasonable amount of work. Many of the more recently employed maternity ward nurses simply did not know that this money had ever existed and did not bring it up as something they would like to have to help them feel more motivated. Instead, they were more likely to talk about generally improving the work environment or, if discussing money as a motivator, referred to the extraduty and on-call allowances that the hospital had recently reduced.

MATERIAL AND STRUCTURAL REASONS FOR ABUSIVE CARE

Nurses did not engage in actions such as hitting and emotional manipulation only during the second stage of labor. I differentiate between the second stage and all other times in order to nuance the discussion of what different actors call disrespect and abuse (D&A), or obstetric violence. The term *D&A* appears commonly in the public health literature and in research on Africa, whereas the term *obstetric violence* has its roots in activism and legal reforms in Latin America, drawing attention to abuse of pregnant women as a form of gender-based violence.[12] The two terms share much overlap in the behaviors to which they refer; because of the slow spread of the term *obstetric violence* in my contexts in Tanzania, I often use the term *D&A* or abusive care. In a detailed review, Bohren et al. classify the most common instances of mistreatment of parturient women in the existing literature into seven broad categories: (1) physical abuse; (2) sexual abuse; (3) verbal abuse; (4) stigma and discrimination; (5) failure to meet professional standards of (technical) care; (6) poor rapport between women and providers; and (7) health system conditions and constraints.[13] Clearly, women's perceptions of their care may differ drastically from the views of their providers. Likewise, the category "poor rapport" includes a knotty combination of topics ranging from poor communication to denial of birth companions (often limited by infrastructure) and lack of "supportive care" from health workers. However, researchers and policy makers recognize, and many have adopted, this typology, so I present it here to help define abusive care. Outside the period of the second stage of labor, almost always the period for which nurses justified their fierce care, I approach most of the other occurrences of these behaviors as abusive. Abusive care was violent for women, but structurally violent working conditions for the nurses and doctors often contributed to these seemingly individually violent acts.

Nurse Martha, one of the past in charges of the ward, looked for deeper reasons for abusive behaviors and responded to my question about their causes in light of her own fraught interactions with the hospital administration, which had eventually caused her transfer to a different ward. She told me that a nurse's financial concerns could cause her to worry, causing conflict at home so that she was unable to concentrate and causing her home frustrations to bleed into her work with patients. Martha continued, "There are a lot of things that cause that state. The first thing entirely is the frustration that she has, the employee. . . . Another thing is the harassment that she has gotten coming from the administration: maybe a person has a problem, she has gone there and encountered bad language and she has transferred it to the patient." Her personal experience, as well as the insights she had gained from managing the maternity ward, allowed Martha to explain how poor living conditions, often a result of low wages, in addition to tense or abusive exchanges with the hospital administrators, could influence a nurse's interactions with the women for whom she was meant to be caring. In light of these other stresses, it could be impossible for the nurse to continue to engage in costly emotional labor with patients while her personal precarity weighed on her.

Everything Martha mentioned is an example of a failure of care from the nurses' employer, of institutional care, beginning at the level of the central government, which failed to adequately increase wages in the health sector, leading many nurses to remain preoccupied with the state of their home long after they had walked out the door. Nurses' private lives continued to permeate the boundaries of the hospital, blurring the lines between domestic and professional spaces. At the hospital, the patron was known for his harsh language. His forthrightness, in a culture that valued a certain degree of circumspection and tact, rubbed many nurses the wrong way, often offending them outright if he used language that was profane, or otherwise inappropriate for the workplace, in their interactions. Combined with their superior's attitude toward them, the difficulties of maintaining a good home life, and growing demands to meet guidelines and protocols, all as they worked without many necessary resources, it is not hard to understand why nurses might become abusive toward their patients.

In the nurses' difficult work environment, at one moment biomedicine held the ultimate authority, rendering facts about the body's unseen insides via ultrasound or lab tests and conferring status on those who knew how to interpret the images or numbers produced. In the next moment, this highly technical environment began to erode, undermined by broken equipment or a lack of supplies. In these instances, breakdown and dysfunction ate away at the social distance between patients and their health care providers. To instantiate their superiority in the midst of breakdown, nurses might flex their social status and the unrelenting authority of their system in other ways. Nurses might label a woman as being "from the village," emphasizing her lack of belonging when she didn't know how to navigate the hospital. For a woman who looked poor or uneducated, the nurses might use derogatory language as a way of reminding her of the distance in their social positions and their resultant access to authority and power. Poor women were often easy targets, as were those from minority ethnic groups who spoke Swahili less fluently and whom the nurses often simply addressed by their group name, such as "the Sukuma." On hectic days, I often heard Nurse Peninah, who was from a different ethnic group, saying to anyone within earshot, "You Fipa women, you just want to have babies until you die! Why don't you use birth control, eh?" Dehumanizing women in these ways may have been a result of stress, as well as a way for nurses to maintain the little power they had within their work environment. One result, however, was that women in these groups might have been more afraid to speak up and, subsequently, less likely to receive the help they needed during emergencies.

Lived realities such as these are extremely difficult to incorporate into, and are therefore entirely lost in the design of, many public health interventions meant to improve care, decrease disrespect and abuse, and empower women in the health care setting. When the nurses themselves felt uncared for, were struggling in their private lives, or encountered stubborn and noncompliant patients in the absence of manpower and sophisticated technology, sometimes they resorted to hitting and yelling. While violating many official guidelines, these interactions had internally consistent logics, making them more understandable, even if never ideal, in this setting.

DIFFERENT SUBJECTIVITIES, DIFFERENT MOTIVATIONS

Different parties throughout the hospital had, unsurprisingly, different ideas of what it meant to be a motivated health care provider and why their fellow providers were not more motivated. Administrators often placed the onus of responsibility on the individual. Even if the nurses received all of their rights as government employees, even if the hospital infrastructure improved, and even if the nurses' employer cared for them, the bottom line was that motivation came from the inside. The administrators felt that they could do as much as was within their power but that providers would still exist who were not invested in their work and did not *kujituma,* or put in an effort. This difference of opinion was not unique to the Mawingu Regional Hospital. Daniel Chambliss explains the conflict between nurses, in particular, and administrators as a conflict of perceived priorities and as centering on how administrators are removed from "life in the trenches";[14] this distance, physically and in terms of goals, caused administrators to fail to demonstrate the level of appreciation and recognition for which the nurses were looking.

While it was easy to see the differences in perspective between administrators and nurses, a divide that I had not anticipated appeared between the older nurses and their younger counterparts. While the younger nurses never said the older nurses were unmotivated, every older nurse pointedly said the newer graduates did not have the same level of expertise, experience, and training they had had upon graduating. Additionally, the older nurses did not mince words when asked why the hospital staff did not seem motivated and why this accusation of low motivation surfaced time and again at Mawingu. When I asked her how nursing had changed since the time she entered the profession in the 1970s, Neema told me, "Those from the past, that is us, we did work by referring to the past behind us. You provide care that you know, the basics, and a person is happy. But the nurses of today, really nursing is finished! Well, let's say that health care services are coming to an end . . . [now] that health generally is like a job, like any other job. They have removed everything that was called *wito* [a calling]. Now, if there is no calling [to nursing], when you play with a person [i.e., merely go through the motions of providing care] it is like you don't reach the goal."

The term *wito* in this context means to be called to a profession, a vocation, in a way that indicates a deep personal meaning to the work. The older health care providers all lamented that nowadays the people who entered the nursing profession did so as a result of family pressure or a lack of other options as dictated by secondary school test scores. Even community members suggested that health care providers were not invested in their profession, which was one requiring deep caring—affective, not just technical—and compassion, and instead were merely looking for money and stable employment. In her explanation, Neema went on to describe how the previous generation of nurses had started their shifts in the morning by ensuring that patients had everything they needed—medications, fresh air, a haircut, even clipped fingernails. She said that now the nurses did not work this way and had forgotten some of the very principles of nursing care. She went on to tell me about how nursing care of the past emphasized close contact with the patient, including hands-on bodily care and even washing soiled linens. Nowadays, these tasks were left to the patient's relatives, shifting certain forms of care practices that required less technical expertise but also greater emotional proximity into the domestic sphere and out of nursing.

The Rukwa regional reproductive and child health coordinator (RRCHCO) was also a very experienced nurse and had practiced for many years. She echoed Neema's observations about the current generation of nurses and added an example of how these newer nurses sought to remove themselves from direct patient care:

> Me, I see that they don't have a calling [*wito*]. . . . These days, I tell you, we that studied a long time ago, we're different from those who have studied in these recent years. . . . A [nurse] can stay on the labor ward, she is using her phone, she is chatting while a mother is in pain over there. Then this same nurse will claim, "My rights have been violated!" What rights?! Those that studied recently, so often they have gone into this profession of nursing as if they lacked another place to put themselves. . . . A lot of them, their minds are thinking, "If I go to study more, I will arrive, I should be at a high level. This patient, let me not touch her." . . . These trained personnel should be very close to the patient . . . but she who has studied a lot is far from the patient [these days], and it's not right!

The RRCHCO's comments show how she perceived the younger nurses to be selfish but also how she thought these nurses sought to escape the more emotionally laden work of intimate care in close proximity to patients by increasing their technical care abilities. The older nurses all remarked upon the growing reliance on technology as a replacement for other forms of caring, which were more about the humanity of patients and their needs as fellow humans, as in hair care, instead of simply passive subjects, receivers of care, in the form of more technically skilled expertise.

All the other experienced nurses with whom I spoke independently told the same narrative of the decline of nursing care and such practices that were in place to ensure good patient outcomes through close attention to detail: care with less distance. Gregory Mhamela's *A History of Nursing in Tanzania* refers to this type of methodical nursing as process nursing, which has its origins in the nursing methods Florence Nightingale herself started.[15] However, as time has passed, and the length of training programs has decreased and the demand for more health care personnel has continued to rise, nursing education and, in turn, practice have evolved. The younger nurses did not often speak to me about nursing more generally as a profession, though some would talk about it in terms of how their current work environments did not allow them to use all the book knowledge they had acquired in the classroom. Care in nursing education may now focus more on technical expertise, but nursing students still learned the ideals of Florence Nightingale, as well as up-to-date codes of ethics from the Tanzania Nurses and Midwives Council.[16] Their care practices began to change as soon as they stepped into the wards and sought to emulate the experienced, embodied practices of the older, more skilled nurses. Sometimes these older nurses demonstrated a true calling for nursing and a commitment to close patient care. Other times, the chaotic and underresourced environment of the hospital, combined with nurses' own personalities, home situations, and persistent feelings of lacking care from the institution employing them, led nurses to hastily breeze through interactions with patients with limited emotional engagement, producing a type of caring that appeared, from the outside, to be emotionally distant or that resulted in abuse. Yet these behaviors were the product of an environment with very little room for other options. Younger nurses began to mirror these behaviors too.

I have gone into such detail related to the workings of the maternity ward and the hospital more generally in order to paint a picture of the flow of patients through the hospital and the stages of care on the ward. The tour of the maternity ward outlines the sheer amount of work for which the nurses were responsible on a daily basis. In addition to the tasks I have enumerated, the nurses fetched supplies, attended meetings, rotated onto the HIV testing and counseling service, the family planning service, and the cervical cancer screening clinic, and were responsible for an ever-increasing amount of documentation. In the absence of medical attendants or auxiliary staff members, as on the night shift, the nurses would also mop floors, wipe down beds, wash equipment, and fold gauze for use in delivery kits.

The multiple professional demands on nurses' time occurred against the background of their home lives and domestic needs and responsibilities. More than one nurse on the maternity ward bore the primary responsibility for paying their children's school fees or those of a younger sibling, supporting aging parents, and supplementing the income of their spouse, who often was not employed in the formal sector. All of these competing demands, in addition to low wages, a lack of resources, and unsupportive interactions with hospital administrators, sometimes resulted in care for pregnant mothers that did not meet the guidelines of best practice. The global health community has deemed these guidelines *the* route to reducing inequalities, improving access, increasing the number of births attended by skilled personnel, and, ultimately, reducing deaths. Instead, the care that nurses and doctors were able to cobble together in this environment worked in most instances, keeping most women alive, sometimes with unclear reasons as to why. This care was, for most women, good enough. At times, "'good enough' care may be a wiser goal than care that is 'ever better.'"[17] Just as some ethical negotiations resulted in everyday ethics that deviated from codified professional ethics, sometimes "good enough" care that deviated from guidelines might be all that was possible.

Combined with women who entered the hospital with uncertain knowledge of the institution's procedures, which often undermined their confidence in what they knew about their own bodies, the personal burdens on nurses, and the high demand for their services, culminated in an environment that allowed some women to slip through the gaps. On the night shift, as the one nurse on the postnatal ward sought a few minutes of rest, a woman silently "changed condition and died," as the reports the nurses read the next morning often stated. During the day, the routine hustle and bustle of the ward, combined with a difficult home life or conflict with administrators, could result in nurses abusing or selectively neglecting a particularly difficult patient. That difficult patient might be the one who later died of cardiac failure after overexerting herself in the second stage, while the nurses yelled at her to push, not knowing (because they had not been able to spend more time on the initial intake and patient history) or not remembering that she had a history of chronic anemia that had contributed to heart problems while she was pregnant.[18]

There was a tension between creating good emergency care and what happened in practice. The maternity ward sought to structure the flows of women through the ward partially in an effort to deal with being overburdened with patients. This highly structured flow, as described in the beginning of this chapter and in chapter 1, was itself a form of bureaucracy within the ward. If a woman did not fit the prescribed structure because of having an unpredictable body—complications, or faster-than-normal labor—she often did not receive the care she needed. This lack of appropriate or needed care could take the form of giving birth on the examination bed or without a nurse, in the admission room, or it could take the form of delayed surgeries, lack of medicine, or neglect during a severe emergency, sometimes resulting in her death.

The biomedical institution is part and parcel of a global biobureaucratic complex while also being a fully functioning biobureaucracy in its own right. Here the boundaries of inside and out, local and global, are no longer useful. Biobureaucratic policies and protocols, as well as institutional goals, order expectations of both technical and affective care. Along with influencing expectations of care, the broader biobureaucracy of global health and safe motherhood has brought with it quality improvement guidelines aimed at improving technical care through increasing surveillance, documentation, and metrics. In actuality, some of these guidelines and technocratic approaches disallow forms of affective care or impose new tasks on nurses and doctors that then reduce workers' satisfaction with their jobs. This reduced satisfaction can result in fraught interactions between patients and providers, further decreasing the quality of care, both technical and affective.

Nurses on the maternity ward repeatedly told me that they perceived the hospital nursing administration to be uncaring, unresponsive, and out of touch with the needs of the ward staff and their very difficult working conditions. However, these same administrators were often severely constrained by the bureaucratic protocols handed down from NGOs and from national and international policies that were often out of date or impractical in their setting. This conflict, for all the providers and administrators, between guidelines or protocols and everyday lived reality contributed to deep-seated feelings of resentment and demotivation and shifted ethics toward providing "good enough" care in their setting and devising inventive ways of concealing their deviations from best practice.

4

"Bad Luck," Lost Babies, and the Structuring of Realities

In this chapter and the next, I use examples of three women's stillbirths to explore how a document-as-technology, the partograph, and health care providers' deviations from the partograph's guidelines for use, work to create different social and ethical care situations in maternal health care settings. The partograph plays several roles as a technology, a bureaucratic document, and a social tool. When interacting with the current technologies of documentation and intervention that are in use in the field of maternal health in the global South, health care providers often are forced—through circumstance, lack of resources, personnel shortages, or lack of fit with the local environment in any number of other ways—to appropriate them for off-book purposes. Much like the care procedures highlighted in the last chapter, documentation practices deviated from guidelines and standards.

For the nurses, particularly once it was clear there had been a gap in, or deviation from, good care for one of the pregnant women on the ward, there proceeded a complicated weighing of the benefits and costs of various forms of accountability and degrees of honesty in reporting, revealing, or withholding mistakes. In this chapter, it is not necessarily the deaths of mothers that bring these complicated realities to light but the much more common stillbirths that help to reveal gaps and ethical maneuvering.

Bureaucracy and its demands shape interactions and produce or reify specific forms of authority. In the setting of clinics and maternity wards, this authority is biomedical. "Bureaucratic inscription and technological intervention . . . mark the patient body and the hospital wards as sites of biomedical authority" where "care work done by nurses and doctors revolved around their mastery of hospital processes (*most prominently visible through activities involving writing*)."[1] The writing of bureaucratic documents, then, itself becomes care work but is also an integral aspect of performing biomedical authority for individuals, as well as for clinics, organizations, and, ultimately, governments.[2] Documents enter into the equation of stillbirth as the nurses manipulate them to protect themselves and their authority, question others, or respond to accusations of neglect. As these documents, here embodied by the partograph, and the broader bureaucracies that produce and collect them become objects of fixation, the documents take on more and more power in structuring interactions in clinical spaces.

STILLBIRTH AND THE PARTOGRAPH

On a sunny day in March 2015, Sarah approached me after the end of a community focus group discussion in her village. Somewhat timidly she said, "What's wrong with me? What could be wrong that is causing all my babies to die?" I asked her more questions about what had happened during her last pregnancy, and she explained, "When I went to the dispensary, I was lying on the [delivery] table and I could still feel the baby moving inside of me. Then, when the baby was born, it was already dead." Two other pregnancies had ended similarly for her. I told Sarah it sounded as if she was experiencing stillbirths as a result of some lack of provider experience or knowledge in her local health care facility and recommended she try to plan to give birth in another facility in the future, if at all possible. Sarah's likely cases of stillbirth, as well as the case of Pendo related later in this chapter, exemplify intrapartum stillbirths, which were often a result of delayed recognition, or improper treatment, of delivery complications. These types of stillbirths were prevalent throughout the Rukwa region and did not occur only in the regional hospital.

If a woman came to the maternity ward and the nurses were able to discern a stable fetal heartbeat upon arrival, that meant the baby was alive. Subsequently, a number of clinical problems could later result in fetal distress and, if not addressed with an appropriate intervention, could end in what the hospital staff members called "fresh stillbirths" or "fresh SBs." The baby's death was due sometimes to obstructed labor or rarely to a very tight nuchal cord or some other complication.[3] The social dynamics of the maternity ward and the structural processes at play intersected with these clinical symptoms and could easily turn a relatively treatable problem into a life-threatening crisis for both mother and baby. Nurses struggled to remember which women needed to be monitored at what times, because each woman was on a different schedule and the nurses continued to be shorthanded. Sometimes more urgent cases occurred that could take all available nurses away from the less immediately critical work. A woman might not have her cervix or fetal heartbeat checked because the nurses were dealing with another woman who was hemorrhaging, for example. However, at the very least, the nurses listened to and recorded every woman's fetal heartbeat during the shift handover procedures.

To explain the centrality of the partograph in the discussion of the cases that follow in this chapter, as well as in the daily life of the maternity ward at the regional hospital, I first outline the official uses of the partograph, how to fill it in, and the informal, improvisational ways in which the nurses often employed this piece of paper. In a setting in which other technologies could not be relied upon and were in short supply, photocopies of partographs made their way into nearly every health facility. The district medical officers and the district reproductive and child health coordinators were responsible for distributing these papers, sometimes even if providers did not request them.

The most basic function of the partograph is to form a graphical representation of a woman's labor. Every four hours a provider should examine the woman and plot measures on the graph, including cervical dilation, the baby's head level or descent into the woman's pelvic opening, fetal heart rate, and the strength of the woman's contractions. There are also spaces to record blood pressure, fluid intake, urine output, and the woman's pulse. The World Health Organization (WHO) recommended wide use of the partograph starting in 1993 and 1994.[4] Since the 1970s, the partograph has included an "alert" and an "action" line.[5] The action line is based on the premise that when a woman is in truly active labor, one centimeter of cervical dilatation takes one hour. If a woman's progress is appropriately plotted on the partograph and crosses the action line, it indicates that her labor has stalled and that something may be wrong. The line is so named because a provider needs to "take action" to investigate and rectify the situation so mother and baby can be safe and healthy (figure 11). Paper-based partographs are still common in many low-resource settings, though they have been replaced by electronic fetal monitoring and other technologies in many high-income countries.

Despite the partograph's ubiquity, during a total of five weeks of supervision visits during which I accompanied clinical experts from a multi-NGO project operating in the Rukwa region, it became clear that, as shown in findings from several other countries, many health care providers were not entirely certain about the proper technical uses of the partograph.[6] Many other health care workers simply could not be bothered, because they lacked mentoring and monitoring or were overburdened with other vital tasks. In other instances, women, preferring to spend as little time as possible in their local, often-dilapidated village dispensaries, arrived late in labor, and the health care worker had no time to monitor their labor via the partograph before the baby arrived. In contrast, the ideal, as nurses suggested, was for a woman to arrive while in early active labor, giving plenty of time for monitoring and ensuring that health care workers would be able to identify and address any potential complications. In all these cases, health care providers were often not employing the first-line tool for preventing stillbirths.

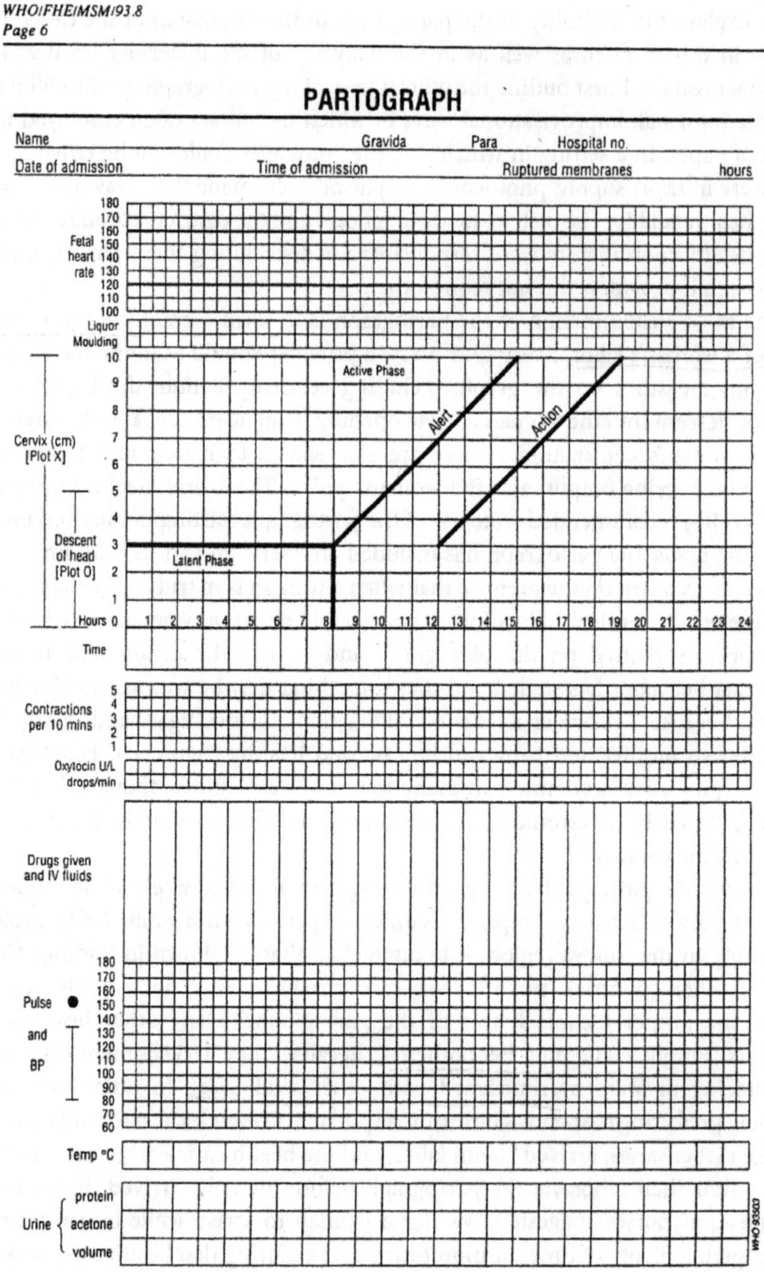

WHO/FHE/MSM/93.8
Page 6

PARTOGRAPH

Name Gravida Para Hospital no.

Date of admission Time of admission Ruptured membranes hours

Fetal heart rate 180 170 160 150 140 130 120 110 100

Liquor

Moulding

Cervix (cm) [Plot X] 10 9 8 7 6 5 4 3 2 1 0

Descent of head [Plot O]

Active Phase

Alert

Action

Latent Phase

Hours 0 1 2 3 4 5 6 7 8 9 10 11 12 13 14 15 16 17 18 19 20 21 22 23 24

Time

Contractions per 10 mins 5 4 3 2 1

Oxytocin U/L drops/min

Drugs given and IV fluids

Pulse ● and BP 180 170 160 150 140 130 120 110 100 90 80 70 60

Temp °C

Urine protein acetone volume

WHO 93503

FIGURE 11. A partograph identical to the version the health care providers in the Rukwa region were using. There are spaces to chart vital signs, the descent of the baby into the pelvis, the fetal heartbeat, and cervical dilation, among other things, all on the y-axis. The x-axis is time in hours. Reprinted with permission from *Preventing Prolonged Labour: A Practical Guide. The Partograph Part I: Principles and Strategy* WHO/FHE/MSM/93.8 p.6, Copyright 1994.

THE PARTOGRAPH'S ROLE IN SOCIAL INTERACTIONS

Though a deceptively simple piece of paper, the partograph became a key technology not only in caring for women but also in accomplishing a number of diverse social goals. As a technology, it was accessible only to certain people, and different actors employed it with greater or lesser degrees of success and expertise. When problematic bodies defied the order of the partograph, by not following the convention of one centimeter of cervical dilation in one hour, nurses and doctors had to use their judgment and experience to decide if they should let a woman continue to labor or do something to intervene. The partograph was also a central aspect of teaching nursing and clinical officer students during their time on the maternity ward. Nurses and physicians presented the partograph as the most important tool in the midwife's or obstetrician's practice, and they imbued it with an almost supernatural power to predict when a woman or her baby needed help. But there was always one caveat—the partograph had to be used properly in order to be effective.

While, on the surface, this might seem to be a purely good technology that can function to save women and babies from complications and life-threatening situations, this paper technology's shadow side is that women whose bodies do not conform to the rule of thumb of one centimeter of dilation per hour set in motion a cascade of clinical, social, and ethical quandaries for health care workers. The documentation on each woman's partograph is a record of her care and a record of the competence of her health care providers, who must accurately measure the data to be plotted on the graph. Partographs form an important record of the health facility's proficiency in providing high-quality maternity care. Indeed, as part of a woman's medical record, the partograph is a piece of organizational infrastructure,[7] but one that facilitates interactions between different worlds. These worlds include, in this case, those of patients, nurses, doctors, the hospital as institution, the Ministry of Health, and international donors, but, more broadly, the worlds of surveillance, bureaucracy, and care. The partograph makes up one part of the expanding bureaucratic system that the Tanzanian state uses to try to improve quality of care in its public health facilities.

Sometimes, moving beyond its official uses, nurses would use the partograph, and their careful documentation on it, to bid for the doctor's attention in an effort to secure care for the woman. If the nurses felt that a woman should have a C-section or that the doctor needed to examine her in order to rule out the need for an operation, they would write on the partograph "Dr. to review" and then wait for his judgment call. On the day or evening shift, the doctor would usually come to the ward within a short time of receiving a phone call from the ward nurses notifying him of a patient. On the night shift, the nurses had to call the nurse supervisor, who then called the doctor on call. The nurse supervisor sent the hospital car and driver to pick up the doctor at his house and bring him to the hospital. This could take more than an hour depending on where the car and driver were and on the (un)willingness of the doctor to return to the hospital after having worked the entire day.

More than once, nurses felt a doctor needed to review a woman but there were delays in his arrival or, once on the ward, he refused to examine the woman. In one case, the nurses reported that the doctor had passed through the ward, refusing to even touch the patient but still proclaiming that she would be able to give birth without problems, which was not, in the end, true. In most instances, the doctor's refusal to do an exam was because, upon hearing the details from the nurses, he decided the information did not suggest an emergency. He might decide the nurse's assessment of the woman's progress was sufficient, thereby expediting his return to bed. In such cases, the nurses used the partograph's back page to document the events that transpired in order to protect themselves from accusations of inaction when the inaction was, in fact, due to some delay or refusal on the doctor's part. Nurses frequently stated that doctors were never blamed when things went wrong. Nurses took to using the partograph and other documentation as a way to protect themselves and to prove the doctor's culpability. Nurse Peninah told me that she had learned such documentation practices at her previous posting at one of the zonal referral hospitals and that she continued to use them. She explained, "The doctor, you have called him at such and such time, you write it. I started to look for him at such and such time. He hasn't arrived since several hours have passed, you write it: 'Since I called for him, maybe two hours have passed, he hasn't arrived.' Therefore, you're on the safe side." In this way, Nurse Peninah sought to protect herself and strategically draw attention to the role doctors played in provision of care that was delayed or otherwise not up to standards.

Peninah's use of the document to record the roles and responsibilities of other actors in the patient's care was also a way in which she was utilizing the little formal power available to her within the hospital's hierarchy, which tended to privilege the more specialized or technical knowledge of the doctors. Additionally, the hospital desperately needed to retain as many physicians as possible, and the administration was unlikely to reprimand them unless they grievously endangered a patient's life or directly caused the patient's death. The nurses also would not necessarily have supported disciplinary action against a doctor that was based on their notes on the partograph. Rather, they were first and foremost concerned with protecting themselves and deflecting any allegations of their own wrongdoing. Peninah's strategy also sought to protect the nurses on the maternity ward from unpleasant encounters with the patron should the ward nurses' actions come under scrutiny on account of a woman's death or severe complications.

In other cases, nurses filled in the partograph ex post facto because of a push by the hospital administration for better documentation or a supervision visit from an outside agency (Ministry of Health representatives or NGO program officers, in most cases). During these visits, the outsiders entreated the ward staff to try harder to check off the boxes in the record book of births, making sure to appropriately write "yes" or "no" in the column about whether they had used a partograph. Nurses would, by rote, simply write "yes" regardless of the actual existence of a partograph for that particular woman, copying what they saw in the row above their entry. In this way, the ward collectively was able to invoke the *idea* of the partograph to accomplish bureaucratic documentation requirements and to project high-quality care that complied with hospital, national, and international recommendations and rules.

Good care came to be synonymous with good documentation regardless of the particulars of the care that women actually received. By writing that they had used the partograph in the officially sanctioned government record book, the nurses legitimated their care practices and conformed with guidelines. In these moments, a culture of accounting for compliance with guidelines took primacy over a culture of actual care practices in which the nurses could have been engaged. Systemic fixation on documentation of care drew providers away from "deep compliance" in favor of surface-level documentation of compliance meant to appease bureaucrats and fulfill reporting requirements.[8] This fixation then opened up myriad opportunities for manipulating these powerful documents.[9] Additionally, data fabrication helped nurses to accommodate reporting requirements in the context of resource and personnel scarcity.[10] Data fabrication or falsification on forms like the partograph created parallel realities or "paper maternities" based on documented care but diverging vastly from the care women received in actuality.[11] Analyzing some of these instances in which nurses manipulated the partograph or the idea of the partograph makes visible how forms of caring emerged or re-formed. It becomes clear that more surveillance and more bureaucracy may create less care of the type policy makers imagine but more care of a previously overlooked kind—that of health care workers for each other. Documentation requirements responded to and structured formal ethics of care, but these requirements undermined the more relational caring that could have engendered *actual* high-quality care instead of the paper appearance of it.

UNCERTAINTY AND THE PARTOGRAPH

While the partograph was an ideal tool on account of its simplicity and ready availability, the environment of the maternity ward forcefully limited and redefined how the nurses were able to use it. Because Mawingu is a regional hospital, there were often students on the maternity ward doing rotations or "practicals" as part of their training. Their presence complicated some of the unspoken routines and norms on the ward. It was often unclear who was responsible for filling out each woman's partograph when these visitors were on the ward. Students frequently neglected to sign their names or ask a nurse if they were unsure about how to complete the paperwork, preferring instead to try their best on the basis of their nascent book knowledge of the partograph.

In the spring of 2015, a second batch of newly graduated nurses joined the maternity ward. They often left the hospital as soon as their shift was over without properly completing the paperwork for their patients, and they did not take an active part in delivering reports to the incoming nurses at the shift handover. Poor handover procedures led the incoming shift to sometimes overlook women or assume that a patient was fine because the outgoing shift had not indicated otherwise. Like the new graduates, other nurses were unsure about when to start the partograph because of their relative lack of experience in maternity care. If the nurse started the partograph too early, when the woman was not actually in "active" labor with regular contractions, they opened the door to a host of potential problems. A woman who is in active labor should progress regularly, again, ideally following the rule of one centimeter per hour. If she was not in active labor when the nurse started her partograph, it could appear as though the woman was spending much too long in labor and needed an intervention to help her. Students and new nurses often did not have the skill level to measure cervical dilation and determine the relative strength of contractions in order to accurately ascertain if a woman was in active labor and also to subsequently take accurate cervical measurements that would appropriately reflect the woman's labor progress. In some cases, I saw the more experienced nurses reconstructing an alternative partograph that hid either mistakes in measuring cervical dilation, such as those made by nursing students, or delays in care, most often without any malicious intentions. In so doing, they were reconstructing an alternate reality, one in which the woman's care followed the expected, ideal trajectory. After rewriting the partograph, the nurses would often throw away the original and would tell me they were doing so to reduce confusion or correct mistakes from when someone had initially started the partograph.

Recreating the partograph was a way in which the nurses attempted to reshape their reality on the maternity ward, bringing it into line with desired bureaucratic or best-practice expectations and goals. The partograph contributed to the production of care on the maternity ward, as well as actively constituting social realities.[12] The document, because of its origins as a way to prevent prolonged labor and poor fetal outcomes, enlisted providers in a broader fight to reduce intrapartum stillbirths and maternal morbidity.

Collectively, measurement and handover problems constructed a great deal of uncertainty. Instead of being an objective technology that nurses and doctors employed to track women and tame their laboring bodies, the partograph became a site of improvisation and a relational strategy, open to interpretation, re-creation, and disappearance. The more experienced nurses were able to use the partograph not just to record labor progress and spot potential problems early on but also to tap into the document's social elements; they used it to invoke protection (for themselves or their colleagues), record blame (for doctors' delays), and solicit care for their patients.

Structural constraints recreated technologies and documents in ways that throw into question their veracity and efficacy as evidence of idealized forms of care: for example, they resulted in nurses either "cooking" the data or using the partograph as a "postograph" after the woman had given birth or even departed the facility.[13] All data are inherently cooked through the activities that bring them into being in the first place, and "Data reflect the capacity and expertise of all their handlers."[14] At Mawingu Regional Hospital, the nurses cooked the partograph data when they filled in partographs after a woman's birth or when they replaced a partograph showing that a woman had long passed the "action" line with one that demonstrated a more moderate, desirable labor progress. They often engaged in this cooking to achieve goals for care or surveillance well beyond the originally intended use of the partograph. Knowing that their colleagues, and they themselves, were engaged as partograph chefs, nurses and doctors had to know when to take the partograph in front of them as fact and when to see it more as a representation or performance of idealized care. Holding open this space of uncertainty, regarding the partograph as an accurate reflection of care or as a re-creation, allowed the partograph to fulfill the most capacious role as record, re-creation, and social tool. Outsiders might think increased certainty would improve the partograph and its efficacy. In fact, more certainty would close off some of the most critical aspects of the partograph's functioning. Currently, the partograph's uncertainty works for nurses, in particular, in much the same way Alice Street suggests doctors in Papua New Guinea used uncertainty in medical files: to create "a device that distributes agency and perpetuates contingency"[15]—perhaps the most important function of the document. This role of the partograph becomes quite clear in the following cases of two women, Pendo and Zuhra, whose babies were stillborn at the hospital.

THE CASE OF PENDO'S BABY

We were crowded into the nurse in charge's office, in a meeting the doctors had called to address a case that had unfolded over three days. Normally, these types of meetings did not draw many of the nurses. Most did not view the often long and meandering meetings as sufficient reason to give up their precious time on their days off or did not relish the idea of coming to the ward in the morning when they were already scheduled to report for the evening or night shift later the same day. However, in this instance, the small office was fuller than usual, with nurses squeezed onto long wooden benches and sharing chairs, each one half on and half off. The hospital medical officer in charge, who also worked on the maternity service, had called the meeting, and the mood was serious.

I had more information about the meeting and the case than others because I had been present since the beginning. I had been helping to care for Pendo since she had arrived at the hospital two days before. She was a pleasant, quiet client in her first pregnancy. She had come from Dar es Salaam, across the country, where she was living with her husband, to give birth at Mawingu in order to be closer to family during this important event in her life as a woman and in their lives as a married couple. She had arrived at the hospital in early labor, with more than enough time to spare before giving birth. I often saw nurses reprimanding women for arriving late, just as they were transitioning to, or were already in, the second stage of labor. However, Pendo was in the early stages of active labor and therefore avoided any possible accusations from the nurses that she had been late to report to the hospital.

The day Pendo arrived, the nurse on the ward responsible for admissions had written her name in the admission notebook, examined Pendo, and started a partograph for her. I had seen her later in the afternoon when she was quietly walking around the ward, waiting for a nurse to tell her to enter the labor and delivery room. I remember noting to myself near the end of the morning shift that the evening shift nurses would definitely need to conduct another vaginal exam to check her progress and cervical dilation. Hopefully, she would give birth sometime in the night. The nurses had asked one of the doctors to review Pendo because they were concerned she would need a C-section. The doctor deemed her likely to give birth vaginally without complications, so there was nothing else for anyone to do but settle in to wait for Pendo's body to decide it was ready for the baby to come out.

The next morning, I arrived around 8 a.m. and started looking around the ward for any signs of activity. I went to fetch supplies from the nurse in charge's office, carefully signed out the quantity of each item in blue pen inside the battered notebook, and carried everything back to the labor room. The ward was relatively calm, and I found a moment to look over the antenatal clinic cards and current partographs sitting on the desk in the labor room. This was the paperwork of the women who were now either under observation or in the last stages of labor before giving birth. Pendo's paperwork caught me by surprise. I looked around, and, sure enough, she was the same woman who had been present with us the day before. I thought that seemed odd, especially because the doctor had told us he thought she would give birth without any problems. Added to that fact was the absence of any further information on the partograph, as would be required by best practice. The oft-repeated phrase "not documented, not done" rattled around in my head. Internally shrugging my shoulders, I thought even documentation might not necessarily indicate the realities of care that had transpired given the ways in which written reports often elided the much messier care practices that were the ward reality.

Although what one of the nurses later called "neglect" seemed possible, my first thought was that perhaps they had just been very busy in the evening and overnight. Maybe the nurses on these shifts had examined Pendo again but had simply failed to find the time to write down the results, as sometimes happened. Nurse Gire was working the morning shift that day, and I drew her attention to the nearly blank partograph. She also remembered Pendo from the day before because we had been working together then too. Nurse Gire examined Pendo, and the following is from my field notes:

> Pendo, a patient from yesterday, is still in labor, and by 12 p.m. she still hadn't delivered. Gire did a [vaginal exam] again and decided Pendo was at 9 cm and was obstructed. . . . She has long passed the action line and should probably have had a [C-section] last night or evening. Now she no longer has a discernible fetal heartbeat. . . . It seems likely the baby was in distress and has already died. I asked Gire why the other people . . . might not have detected that it was cephalopelvic disproportion (CPD)[16] and why other nurses don't use partographs? . . . Pendo is just finishing in the theatre now at 1:45 p.m. and the baby was stillborn. [Nurse] Alvina says the baby was macerated,[17] but I'm skeptical.

CPD might have been the cause of Pendo's unusually long or obstructed labor and could have explained the poor dilation of her cervix. If the baby is unable to enter the pelvic opening, perhaps because of this mismatch, or because of the formation of the bony processes of the pelvis, the baby's head cannot exert pressure on the cervix, helping it to open. If the baby cannot fit in the opening, the uterus is contracting without being able to accomplish its goal, and instead the baby comes under great stress from the squeezing, which does not result in the baby moving into the pelvis. This stress can eventually cause the baby to be stillborn.

After her surgery, I stopped by Pendo's bed to see how she was doing. Pendo had not awoken yet from the general anesthesia, but it was visiting hours, and her mother-in-law, Mama Hassani, was there looking after her. We exchanged some words about how it was a very sad situation. Mama Hassani told me that Pendo's husband had been very upset about everything but that she, as his mother, had been trying to explain to him that these things happen, and it was just bad luck, *bahati mbaya,* and the couple would have another baby. In that moment, as we were chatting, Mama Hassani's phone rang. It was her son, Pendo's husband, across the country in Dar es Salaam. I was the only "staff person" around, the only available person affiliated with the hospital, so she passed the phone to me when he wanted to talk to someone who worked at the hospital. Immediately, he began demanding answers, wanting to know how a baby who was fine could suddenly be *not* fine and why his wife hadn't had an operation sooner and how he did not believe it was *bahati mbaya,* bad luck. He wanted to know if I had done the surgery. I explained that no, I had not. In fact, the surgeon was the medical officer in charge of the entire hospital, Dr. Joseph. Nothing had gone wrong during the surgery. I tried to tell him that I was not the one to whom he should be talking, that he should talk to the nurse in charge of the ward or Dr. Joseph and they would be better able to explain to him what had happened.

While he was still on the line, I tried to hand the phone to the nurse in charge of the maternity ward who was sitting in the labor room. She waved her arms, refusing to take the phone, as did Gire, who was sitting next to her. After I hung up, I called Dr. Joseph, who suggested Pendo's husband call back in two days, on

Friday. The next day, I told Pendo her husband could call again on Friday to talk to the medical officer in charge. She told me he didn't want to talk to anyone anymore and they had been able to explain to him that this kind of "bad luck" happens.

TO KNOW HIS FACE: STILLBIRTH AND COPING

About a month before Pendo's arrival, Zuhra had been at Mawingu. She had come after already visiting her local, village dispensary where the providers had sent her on to the hospital without any documentation or proof that a medical professional had even seen her.[18] Because of the way the regional hospital organized and documented referrals, Zuhra slipped in, looking like someone who had just come from home in the absence of official referral paperwork. Busy nurses bustled through the ward and admitted Zuhra without taking time to ask if she had come straight from home or had sought care elsewhere before arriving. They assumed she had come from home, as most women did, and therefore did not ask her the questions that might have elicited the fact that she had been in labor for more than twenty-four hours before her arrival at the hospital. This one fact might have changed the trajectory of her care because it would have been a sign that her labor was not progressing as would be expected for a woman in her fourth pregnancy.

When they examined her, she had not projected the image of a woman in active labor—she was too quiet, too calm—so she did not receive a more thorough examination of the current state of her labor. In cases in which a woman was visibly in pain or distress that would suggest active labor or the impending need to push, the nurses generally conducted a more thorough exam sooner. Nurses often told other women who did not seem to be in active labor, or close to pushing that they needed to wait while the nurses completed other miscellaneous but necessary tasks before a nurse would be available to examine them. While nurses examined every woman physically, the medical history was often left by the wayside with the explanation that it took too much time to go through all the questions for every woman—time that the nurses could not justify when other women were waiting on the slatted wooden bench, just having arrived from home, or had been admitted on the ward and were due for their next vaginal exam.

After admitting her, the nurse sent Zuhra to the antenatal waiting room and, according to Zuhra and corroborated by her medical file, no doctor came to see her for more than twenty-four hours. The nurses never again conducted a vaginal exam to see how she was progressing. In the middle of her third night at the hospital, Zuhra told me she had gone into the labor room to tell one of the nurses that her contractions were getting stronger, the only time she had been bothered by the pain. Zuhra told me that prior to that moment her contractions had not been like ones she had experienced in other pregnancies: they came and went without any strength or regularity. The nurse brusquely waved her off and told her that they would examine her in the morning. The nurse told her, "It's not you who decides when you should be examined! We will tell you when!" With this pronouncement from the nurse, Zuhra went back to her bed and silently waited for the nurses to tell her when. No one came to see her that night.

When Dr. Charles finally reviewed Zuhra on ward rounds the following morning, he was struck by how soft her belly was, different from the taut skin and hard, contracting bellies of other pregnant women. Her uterus had ruptured, and the baby was floating in her abdominal cavity. Because of delayed diagnosis, poor communication, and inadequate history taking, Zuhra's baby had died, floating there in the remnants of her womb and the quickly dispersing amniotic fluid. Dr. Charles immediately ordered an emergency laparotomy, which, in the end, included a hysterectomy, since he was unable to save her uterus. The family had whisked away the baby's body while Zuhra was half awake, still coming out of anesthesia from the operation needed to save her life.

Zuhra had a very bad obstetric history, including miscarriages, and at least two of her older children had died tragically. This baby had been her hope for one more chance to raise a healthy child to adulthood. For many weeks afterwards, Zuhra's relative, a nurse on another ward of the hospital, told me that Zuhra was in a depression, unwilling to leave the house and constantly sad. Zuhra's greatest cause of sadness? She had not seen her baby boy and therefore could never know what he looked like, would never "know his face," as she told me. Despite the hospital staff's neglect in her case, Zuhra and her family never decided to pursue any action against the hospital.[19] This was despite the fact that her relative, who was a nurse, told me she could have easily provided medical insight into the course of events. She told me she knew Zuhra's care had not gone as it should have, as evidenced by delays in getting a blood transfusion after surgery and by Zuhra's reports of not being seen by the nurses in the night. Poor documentation and shift handovers may also have contributed to the lapses in her care.

On the basis of this previous experience with Zuhra, I thought Pendo might like to hold her baby, to know his face, or at least to have the choice. I asked her, and she gratefully said yes, she would like to hold him. I went with Pendo's mother-in-law, Mama Hassani, to retrieve the small corpse that had been bundled in bright *kitenge* fabric and was lying on a counter near the door, looking like a healthy newborn except that the fabric had been pulled up over and around where the baby's face was and the bundle was not moving. I transferred the small body to Mama Hassani's arms, and she carried him back to Pendo. As I watched the twenty-two-year-old taking pictures of her stillborn son with her cell phone camera and asking her mother-in-law to see the baby's feet, I contemplated the key role the simple partograph had (or had not) played in this case. There was no electronic fetal monitoring to alert nurses to a baby in distress, there were no call buttons to push in an emergency, only the vigilance and diligence of the nurses, who were overworked and often unable or unwilling to conduct the fetal heart monitoring that guidelines mandated take place minimally once per hour but ideally every fifteen or thirty minutes. Less-than-thorough reports during shift changes and inconsistent use of partographs as a key technology to chart a woman's progress in labor seemed to be, among other factors, contributors to this baby's death.

In the aftermath, Pendo's partograph went missing. The nurse in charge of the ward was certain someone had hidden it or otherwise disposed of it, she resignedly told me: "Yes, it happens like this now and then. They are afraid the partograph shows their mistakes, so someone decides to hide it or throw it away. I don't know what they do with it."

Back in the meeting to discuss Pendo's case, the partograph became of central importance. The partograph always traveled through the ward with the woman whose labor it documented, and providers conceived of the piece of paper as a continuous record of her labor, despite shift changes. It was the one mode of communication that was supposed to be present even if, as the medical officer in charge accused the nurses in the meeting, verbal communication at shift changes was less than ideal or proved to be ineffective. In Pendo's case, the partograph could also implicate the hospital staff in the death of her previously healthy baby.

MOURNING AND STILLBIRTHS AS "BAD LUCK"

Many women never questioned the "bad luck" that resulted in the death of their babies while still *tumboni*, or "in the stomach." Unfortunately, this was partly because intrauterine and neonatal deaths have historically been so common in Tanzania and continue to be so.[20] In addition, many people throughout Tanzania did not consider it socially appropriate to mourn the loss of babies who were not fully mature or fully human.[21] Hospital procedures and health care provider actions often served to deny women and their families answers when their babies did not survive. Despite cultural norms, women often found it hard to come to terms with the loss of their child who was stillborn. Nurses did not routinely give women the option to see or hold their stillborn babies, instead taking away the body and then repeatedly instructing the mother to stop crying, to not make noise, and to wipe away her tears.

Part of this outwardly brusque standard operating procedure can perhaps be attributed to constructions of the origins of personhood and socially acceptable physical spaces of mourning.[22] In northern Tanzania, the concept of toughening by which those close to people who have lost relatives encourage the bereaved to bury feelings of loss when outside designated mourning spaces (funerals) to concentrate on remaining kin relations, also provides insight into local forms of caring.[23] It was not socially appropriate for a woman to openly mourn in front of strangers in the public space of the maternity ward. However, what often appeared, from the outside, to be nurses limiting compassion for the women and not allowing them to mourn caused many community members—men and women—to accuse nurses of not caring for or about pregnant women in the hospital. This community perception led to a deep cynicism and dissatisfaction with the only care available to most women.

In some cases, the woman or her relatives might suspect the death of the fetus in utero to be related to malevolent witchcraft or jealousy. In these instances, hiding the death from other, nonfamily members could be more socially beneficial. In such cases of suspected witchcraft, women and their families might not find it appropriate to reference their witchcraft suspicions in the biomedical setting even if they did harbor such feelings. For other women, their "bad luck" was the result of the will of God or Allah and not something within their control and therefore also not something to protest. Explanations about bad luck that draw on fatalistic views of the fetus's death are a common strategy that may serve to preserve women's social status and psychological well-being in light of high rates of reproductive loss.[24]

Instead of thinking it was witchcraft or bad luck, Pendo's husband adamantly insisted that healthy babies do not *just* die. This made him more of a threat to the hospital staff, particularly when combined with the blank partograph, which would not be able to refute any of his claims that the nurses had neglected his wife. He might act on this hunch and initiate some type of investigation or lodge a formal complaint with the medical officer in charge. Pendo's husband's suspicion was not uncommon for patients' families. However, as medical personnel told me, usually families or patients who were more educated or were from the urban district of the region were the ones who tended to harbor these suspicions of misconduct. These parties often had more experience with the hospital setting, health care providers, and expected care trajectories, which helped them spot instances of possible mismanagement.

Several strong fears and social norms acted to prevent many women or their relatives from bringing formal complaints against health care workers even if they were fairly certain something had gone awry during care. Many women told me they were afraid that if they made a complaint about a nurse that nurse would refuse to help them if they ever had to return to the hospital again in the future.[25] Nurses exerted their power over patients or their relatives in this way, often by forcing people to wait for care. Throughout my time in the Rukwa, Singida, and Kigoma regions of Tanzania, I witnessed this play out in health care facilities ranging from village dispensaries to regional hospitals. Though this practice is entirely at odds with the ideals of compassionate care embodied in Florence Nightingale or other paragons of nursing, in the daily reality of the ward, desperate, tired, frustrated nurses with little formal power sometimes exerted the power they did have in this way. On the maternity ward, social sanctions and punishments sometimes resulted in women giving birth unassisted, alone in the midst of a full ward. Nurses did not generally immediately abandon a woman in labor but did so after proclaiming her to be noncompliant or otherwise difficult, combative, or unsuited to the norms of a biomedical delivery on account of her unruly behavior. The nurse would then move on to other work with other patients. While withdrawing assistance from a woman in labor might appear to contradict professional ethics, the nurses were preserving their capacity for care for more grateful or willing recipients, determining, in the moment, where their care might have the greater impact. Because of the constraints of their work environment, the nurses' actions in these situations conflicted with their own ideals of professional self-presentation but were part of a broader negotiation surrounding effort and effect. If a woman did not engage in the intersubjective care relationship as a compliant recipient, the nurse would move on to another.

THE PARTOGRAPH AND GOOD CARE AS DOCUMENTED CARE

By making Pendo's partograph disappear, the nurses had irrefutably protected themselves from possible disciplinary or legal action, which could not advance without evidence, even if someone should overcome the social reluctance to embarrass, name, or punish. Reluctance to name transgressors was pervasive and often appeared to debilitate the hospital administration's efforts to address subordinates' bad behavior. Indeed, a number of nurse managers told me of their frustration with this practice, saying it made it difficult to improve the quality of services. For example, instead of saying, "Nurse X verbally abused a patient on Saturday, the twenty-third," the nursing patron would tell the maternity ward's nurse in charge, "People are using bad language" and then expect her to prevent her staff from committing the same sin again. In the meeting about Pendo's case, however, Dr. Joseph insisted directly that the nurses produce the partograph from wherever it had been hidden. The nurses who had been on the morning shift told him they had not seen the original partograph since Pendo had gone for surgery. More agitated and impatient, Dr. Joseph said, "Now, there, we are being destructive. Now, bring it, let us see it. Here we are not talking about it to argue. . . . But I remember [what happened], even if you all have hidden it. Me, I have to tell you, you all should know that, for this, I am not happy at all." The meeting continued and the issue of the partograph emerged again and again, deployed in order to question the nurses' practices during shift changes. During these times the nurses were supposed to give complete reports on each patient, and then the nurses on the incoming shift were responsible for the continued monitoring of the women, including vital signs (pulse, respiratory rate, blood pressure, and temperature) and progress of labor as indicated by the fetal heart rate and cervical dilation. Maintaining organized documentation to be handed over to the incoming shift was a key part of interactions between incoming and outgoing shift members.

One of the ward doctors, Dr. Deo, also reminded the nurses, "Then, another thing, the partograph can be a legal thing: that is, actually, if you fill it out it helps you. Now, if you examine the patient and then you haven't filled it out—not documented, not done. This is in the open, therefore, even if you have examined her, [if] the results aren't available, you could start the way [for legal consequences]." The lack of documentation, the missing information on the partograph, was in and of itself evidence of wrongdoing, of treatment and care that did not comply with guidelines and that failed to meet the larger biobureaucratic demands for documentation and data. In a variety of health care settings, health care providers use documentation and ledgers of data as proof for outsiders or internal administrators that women have been receiving care that meets guidelines for best practice. Less formally, these record books sometimes serve as "hedges against any future accusations of corruption and mismanagement,"[26] in much the same role as the partograph when properly filled out. However, in this case, the documentation was missing and could not protect the providers. Both doctors and some of the nurses expressed distress about Pendo's case, saying there had been a clear error in medical judgment that they named as neglect.

Matthew Hull suggests that (bureaucratic) documents are "mechanisms for protecting the integrity of the government" but "are often the means through which it is undermined."[27] In the government hospital maternity ward, in a country with a history of socialist state care, the partograph played a similar role in undermining the Tanzanian government via the hands of nurses and doctors. Various health care providers and experts idealistically conceived of the partograph as a way to protect their integrity because it helped them to make timely and accurate diagnoses of problems. When Dr. Deo referred to the partograph as a legal document that could protect them, he was referring to this component of the technology. However, alternatively, these very documents were also the perfect evidence of wrongdoing, either as left blank or as inappropriately filled in. The partograph then undermined and called into question providers' expertise, communication skills, and decision-making, and, ultimately, public confidence in their services. Documents and documentary practices, such as those surrounding the partograph, sometimes took on a life of their own, "returning in the transitional moment to incriminate their producers," despite providers' other intentions and goals for them.[28]

As policy makers and experts conceived of the partograph, it was meant to be a tool in reducing the incidence of stillbirths and complications for the mother. The partograph invoked the health care providers as allies in this struggle and in the global health goal of reducing numbers of preventable stillbirths, holding providers accountable for providing good care that would reduce these deaths. Data on intrapartum stillbirths, or a *documented* reduction in them, then worked to help states account for health care policies that conformed to global initiatives, such as the Millennium Development Goals. The partograph was a technology that monitored bodies, but it could also be problematic if a woman's body and labor did not follow the prescribed pathway of birth. Her body could be difficult to interpret and plot on the partograph if she gave birth extremely quickly or if her labor became delayed in some way, thereby complicating understandings of who was skilled enough to be in charge of these deceptively simple pieces of paper as technology—as in the case of new nurses or students.

Sometimes the doctors and nurses created and recreated new realities by plotting and replotting a woman's labor on the partograph. Because of poor communication and differing levels of provider expertise on the maternity ward, the partograph created uncertainty. Most often, if a woman was progressing slowly in labor, the providers immediately suggested that the first person who had examined the mother upon admitting her to the hospital had measured her cervical dilation inaccurately, overestimating how many centimeters she had reached. Therefore, that person had started the partograph too early. This uncertainty about the expertise of the examiner undermined some of the power of this simple tool. In other situations, the nurses used the partograph to try to make bids for the doctor's attention, to protect themselves from a physician's lack of cooperation or judgment, or to conceal wrongdoing and neglect. The partograph was a physical reminder, in black and white, of when care did not go as imagined or desired, resulting in the death of babies. As they acted on the partograph, the nurses in particular but, also the doctors, worked within messy, thick ethical spaces to produce, call down, and recreate different types of care at different times depending on whose well-being was most at stake in the moment—either that of the mother/baby or that of health care worker colleagues. Nurses engaged in the unethical and deceptive destruction of incriminating partographs in order to engage in ethical care of their colleagues and themselves, even as this form of care foreclosed other care for the woman and her family who had lost their child. It became ethically more important for the workers on the ward to protect each other, in order to maintain their social order, than to preserve a record of mismanagement that could provide a family with answers.

Pendo's case is a representative example of what thousands of women in the Rukwa region, and Tanzania more generally, underwent on a regular basis. In the next chapter, I continue Pendo's story to analyze how the providers attempted to create accountability in the absence of easy-to-use formal accountability procedures when they knew care had gone wrong. With the proliferation of bureaucracy and surveillance comes a concomitant proliferation of care. However, this prolific new care often goes unseen or unaccounted for in this surveilling bureaucracy because it is care *for* health care workers *by* health care workers and not just care for their patients; that is, it is the *wrong* kind of care for the public health practitioners and policy makers working on improving maternal health and intrapartum care. Therefore, when the partograph works to calculate or demonstrate care given, it is always and only the care given to women as patients that the auditors are interested in and to which they are attuned. What eludes their gaze is the care that has proliferated in the interstices and boundary lands, the ways in which nurses and doctors care for each other by protecting their professional reputations and by undergirding their colleagues' performances of clinical caring through records on bureaucratic documents.

5

Landscapes of Accountability in Care

As I have demonstrated through the cases of Pendo, Zuhra, and Sarah in the previous chapter, women and their families interpreted stillbirth in multiple ways. Providers and women imbued this unfortunate event with different meanings that then had different consequences for their projects of constructing morality, responsibility, and accountability across different levels. This makes stillbirth a perfect case study for accountability and responsibility, particularly because stillbirths are much more common than maternal deaths, both at Mawingu and globally. Stillbirth and the partograph from the previous chapter demonstrate how the hospital staff and administration constructed alternative avenues for assessing morality and ethics in the absence of a formal disciplinary mechanism. They were often understaffed and lacking many of the crucial supplies needed for their ideal, best practices of maternity care. These struggles, combined with the larger biobureaucratic system's imposition of standardized rules and guidelines for disciplinary proceedings, documentation, and data collection, necessitated ethical and moral negotiations that invoked and depended upon a particularly Tanzanian form of everyday ethics of caring. Faced with constraints and a lack of usable formal routes for discipline and accountability, the maternity ward at Mawingu demonstrated an ethics of care that generated robust but subtle informal accountability mechanisms. Some of the descriptions in this chapter may be disturbing. The language reflects that of the nurses and doctors in this setting.

STILLBIRTHS, BOTH FRESH AND MACERATED

Pendo and Zuhra's cases illustrate the ongoing challenges facing the health care system in Tanzania. Work environments were characterized by scarcity of people and supplies, as well as sometimes poor communication practices and few routes for holding health care providers accountable for mistakes due to bureaucratic and structural constraints. Stillbirths were a particularly grim consequence of these challenges. While Tanzania made progress on the Millennium Development Goals related to reducing child mortality, on some other indicators the country did not fare as well, including "poor progress in reducing stillbirths, with around 47, 550 stillbirths per year, of *which 47% are intrapartum, which is a sensitive indicator of poor-quality care at birth*" (emphasis added).[1] This statistic indicates that the challenges leading to stillbirth were not confined solely to hospitals such as the Mawingu Regional Hospital but were occurring throughout the country.

Different types of stillbirths brought with them different quandaries and speculation about causes and responsibility and carried different implications for providers and the hospital. Pendo's stillbirth was intrapartum, what the nurses and doctors at Mawingu called a "fresh" stillbirth, and fresh stillbirths were often related to provider skills or lack thereof. "Macerated stillbirths," another classification, were displaced onto other forces. This type of stillbirth, macerated, received its name from the appearance of the baby, who had usually died sometime prior to birth, an intrauterine fetal death, most times of unknown cause. The baby's flesh was often mottled, peeling off, or necrotic, and sometimes the small body was severely misshapen. If it was in an advanced state of decay, women were at a heightened risk for infections. These births, the delivery of a macerated stillbirth, often took much longer,[2] and they were emotionally, as well as physically, difficult for both the mother and the nurses involved in assisting the woman. Sometimes the woman had to stay lying on her back for hours while the deceased baby's body was partially protruding from, but not fully expelled by, her body. Instead of the nurse making the quick, deft movements that often freed the living baby at this stage, both mother and midwife steeled themselves for the tortuous process of emergence of a being who had long since ceased to live. However, there was never any talk of who was to blame in these cases; it was generally accepted that the fetus had died of unfortunate causes, natural or otherwise, that were unrelated to the actions of the providers at the health facility.

ACCOUNTABILITY AS VIEWED FROM THE OUTSIDE

People working in NGOs and in the government on maternal and neonatal health projects and policies told me they thought nurses fabricated the state of stillborn babies, writing down more macerated stillbirths than "fresh" as a way of protecting themselves and producing statistics that showed their facility in a more favorable light. Here, once again, providers were seeking to comply with the demands for documentation of improvement, as well as complying with national, and global, demands for data collection. However, they were subverting the original purpose of these data collection initiatives by fabricating outcomes and events, thereby throwing into question all data produced by similar facilities throughout the country.

I did not have to look even to people outside the maternity ward for this insinuation about "cooking" data. One of the nurses in charge told me quite frankly that she was convinced her subordinates were writing down babies as macerated when they had not been. Nurse Alvina had been in Pendo's surgery and commented that she thought the baby was macerated, an observation that would have shifted the responsibility for the baby's death away from the ward staff and onto other forces, before Pendo's arrival. Differing interpretations of whether a stillborn baby was fresh or macerated could have accounted for many of the misattributed stillbirths. After all, how mottled and necrotic does a baby have to be to be macerated? Sometimes it was abundantly clear, as when the small body oozed fluids and the skin easily peeled off, but other times the distinction was rather less easily made, and the nurses had to use their best judgment to decide how they should classify the baby. Rather than reading the nurses' actions as necessarily duplicitous, and suggesting nurses were purposefully trying to fabricate the numbers, we might conclude that perhaps sometimes it was simply a matter of different interpretations of the state of the stillborn baby's body. Nurses with more training or experience would have been able to more accurately differentiate between a truly macerated stillbirth and one that was more borderline fresh. Regardless of the degree of interpretation required, the bottom line was that nurses had an incentive to conceal fresh stillbirths, which would reflect poorly on the care they had been able to provide. With Pendo's baby, it was unlikely that Nurse Alvina was right about it being macerated because less than twenty-four hours before her C-section Pendo's baby still had a heartbeat. Usually it took much longer for the fetus to begin to decompose in utero.

Certainly, the nurses and doctors would have all liked to see a reduction in the number of fresh stillbirths, but it was easier for them to switch their priorities to accounting for poor care by concealing the true number of fresh stillbirths, or by hiding partographs that would indicate neglect or other wrongdoing, than to fundamentally change their operating procedures. This was, at least in part, due to the difficulty they encountered on the procedural, administrative, and bureaucratic levels every time they sought, as a ward, to initiate changes. Such resistance from individuals and the system further disincentivized efforts to improve outcomes and reduce deaths. At the hospital level, a real commitment to fundamentally improving care in order to reduce intrapartum stillbirths would have required prioritizing maternity care and investing in continuing education, mentoring, and supervision. All of these needs would have been inconvenient, as well as simply unsustainable because of budget limitations and lack of personnel.

At a higher level, the central government would have had to make the fundamental shift in perspective that these lost children, and their mothers, were a priority for investment. As of yet, this does not seem to be the case. As one Ministry of Finance employee told me, the government has the resources, and if they decided to prioritize maternal care, no more women would die from pregnancy-related causes. It is simply that the government does not yet have the will to make this problem a greater priority.

In the context of everyday life on the Mawingu Regional Hospital's maternity ward, *accountability* comes to take on at least two different meanings. First, the term can be thought of in relation to accounting for money—aid, investment, resources, supplies, equipment.[3] Second, it can mean being accountable, as in being subject to report, explain, or justify actions (or inaction). I primarily use it this way on the personal, instead of fiscal, level to talk about providers' responsibility for care or other tasks in the biomedical setting. Providers talked about being accountable to themselves, to their superiors, to patients, to their profession. In turn, the hospital is accountable, at an institutional level, to the central government. As public sector employees, all health care workers are also responsible to the government, their employer. In a public health landscape in which NGOs and foreign organizations appear to dominate and drive policy, the state still plays a vitally important role as the employer of most health care personnel in the country and as a builder of health infrastructure.[4] Because health care workers were agents of the government by way of their employment, when community members tried to hold them accountable for care they were also attempting to hold the state accountable.

A bevy of global organizations (the World Health Organization, the International Monetary Fund, the World Bank), NGOs, and foreign governments, which donate funds to the health sector, hold the central government accountable for expenditures and advancement toward achieving health indicators.[5] With the expansion of NGOs, direct budget contributions, and other forms of foreign aid and assistance to countries like Tanzania, these organizations have demanded increased accountability in a number of ways while often escaping it themselves by circumventing state structures or providing parallel systems *within* state structures.[6] In the end, especially as government employees, the providers at Mawingu were also accountable, by extension, to these other actors who imposed conditions on monies or pushed policies and protocols.

FORMAL SYSTEMS OF ACCOUNTABILITY

Despite this ascending pathway for accountability, the formal, government systems for reporting a health care worker's mistakes or negligence were circuitous and prolonged, working to put off the actual moment of discipline. Supervisors could not initiate the formal disciplinary procedures unless a patient or her relative made a formal complaint. Dr. Joseph, the medical officer in charge, told me that even if women and their relatives suspected something had gone wrong with the care at the hospital, they almost never moved beyond suspicion to make a formal complaint.

Sitting in his office one bright afternoon, as the cool dry-season breeze pushed in through the half-open window, Dr. Joseph told me with frustration, "Sometimes they know something has gone wrong here in the hospital with their relative, but they come and tell me, 'I don't want this person punished, I just want you to know what is happening in your hospital.' What can I do then with that information if they refuse even to go on record with their complaint?" He went on to explain that it was not easy for him to initiate disciplinary proceedings without these formal complaints against a provider. The fact of the matter was that the Tanzanian Ministry of Health and Social Welfare had strict guidelines and protocols for disciplining health care providers that, because of their complexity and lengthy proceedings, resulted in excellent job security for government health care workers. Dr. Joseph explained this situation further, giving these disciplinary procedures as an example of how the bureaucracy above him, over which he had no control, affected how he was able to work:

> Some of them [health care workers] completely misbehave, okay, but I cannot take action. I would comment that this person is misbehaving, but I have to start with a lot of issues; say, okay, from the department, make sure you document his mistakes, and thereafter, when you feel like now you are tired, you bring it to me. I have again to sit with him, discuss once, twice, or thrice. From there, and then I have to give some warnings—verbal, then written, then thereafter I cannot say, "Now! You're fired!" I have to recommend that "I have this employee who had so and so, please take action against him," or I just bring him before you for your attention. And then you will decide. Yeah? And then you will decide, whether to take action or not. You see?

In these formal proceedings, the people who would ultimately decide the fate of the employee in question were the regional medical officer (RMO) and, as the last step, the regional administrative secretary (RAS), who was responsible for the hiring and firing of all government employees in the region. What most often seemed to be the result of these procedures, if they were even initiated, was the transfer of an employee from one department or post to another in which Dr. Joseph or the nursing administration felt he or she would be able to do less damage. For example, while I was present, one lab technician was suddenly moved to the Medical Records Department and then to the mortuary. The prevailing rumor was that he was constantly drunk while at work and that the hospital leadership, being unable to fire him, had transferred him to departments in which less expertise and specialized competency were necessary. Speaking generally, Dr. Joseph told me that he had recently been dealing with an employee who had been unable to fulfill his duties but whom he was unable to dismiss. He was continuing to look for how the situation might be best resolved to protect patients and the other staff members who might rely on that provider.

These proceedings were easier to initiate if, as Dr. Joseph mentioned in the start of our conversation, a patient or relative came forward. If this occurred, Dr. Joseph could also launch an investigation through the offending provider's licensing body, the national nursing or medical organization. But community members' reluctance to come forward was often also partly due to strong cultural norms related to not embarrassing others, maintaining smooth social relations, and saving face. Other researchers have documented this same preference and face-saving ethos in other East African settings,[7] but it has a long history for Fipa people specifically too. In precolonial Ufipa, there was a woman specifically in charge of levying fines against people who engaged in a certain class of offenses, including verbal obscenity.[8] Sanctioning those who engaged in these forms of public obscenity was an important mechanism for the Fipa to maintain their ideals of intensive social interaction that was also courteous, thereby preserving social cohesion.[9] This female-led system no longer exists. But in the present day many patients and their relatives preferred not receiving redress—even in the form of an apology—for suffering, neglect, or malpractice when the only route to redress was through the act of naming a negligent provider or initiating a case against him or her.

In other settings, families might resort to the court system to hold health care workers to account. But the medical malpractice legal landscape in Tanzania remains largely undeveloped.[10] In 2015, a woman and her husband did successfully win a case against a doctor whose mistakes during a C-section left her struggling with permanent infertility.[11] In 2013, a medical student told me of a case of a malpractice suit brought against a hospital and health care workers in the Kilimanjaro region of the country, one of the wealthiest regions with a highly educated populace. A lawyer working for the prime minister's office was unable to provide me with any further information about this field of law in the country.[12]

There is evidence that malpractice litigation in health care skews scarce resources further toward those who can already access them, withholding important care from more marginalized segments of the population.[13] Additionally, John Harrington argues that the colonial and socialist history of Tanzania has resulted in "no widespread perception of litigation as a means of providing for the accountability of the agents and institutions of the state—including the great majority of medical professionals who worked for it."[14]

At Mawingu, in any instance of mistakes in patient care, the nursing administrators and the ward nurse in charge usually met privately with the person who had made the mistake. These values related to minimizing public embarrassment were integrated into the hospital's management style at all levels. The social value placed on minimizing conflicts and not directly accusing others of wrongdoing, combined with a lack of other providers, and a legal landscape that did not easily facilitate malpractice litigation, made it especially difficult for families to come forward with accusations of neglect or complaints about bad care. Families already lacked power and authority within the biomedical system, and this further intensified their hesitancy.

I came to know the medical officer in charge to be a man who often, if not continuously, thought about ways to elicit the complaints and grievances of clients and their families in order to improve the care his hospital offered. In other discussions, Dr. Joseph confided that he wished someone would encourage a patient who had been wronged to come forward with a formal complaint, demanding some form of restitution for, in these types of cases, the loss of their child. He suggested that even one such legal case against a provider at the hospital would awaken all the providers anew to their responsibilities, hopefully making them more careful and compassionate in the future. In the absence of formal accountability structures that would actually be able to hold health care workers immediately responsible for mistakes or lapses in judgment, the hospital's bureaucratic, institutional environment fostered the growth of robust informal systems of accountability based on the negotiations of everyday ethics of concealing or revealing mistakes. Brodwin argues that the real-world effects of everyday ethics are rarely lasting because of the constraints limiting implementation of imagined changes.[15] While this was true in many other instances, in this case, at Mawingu, everyday ethics, the moral and ethical convictions of the health care workers, but also those of the community members reluctant to accuse providers, led to the very real creation of profound and durable, though fluid and sometimes hidden, informal systems of accountability.

INFORMAL SYSTEMS OF ACCOUNTABILITY

Much like Pendo, Zuhra delivered a stillborn baby because of the rupture of her uterus, caused by similar lapses in communication and gaps in care after her arrival on the maternity ward at Mawingu. Zuhra's case serves as another example of how women, their relatives, and the hospital staff struggled with the consequences of stillbirth and issues of accountability. In Zuhra's case, the family told me they did not believe it would even be useful to complain. They were, instead, resigned to the hospital's status quo and lacked faith in the hospital administration's ability to create change within the institution. Zuhra's relative, who was a nurse, intimately knew the administrative workings of the hospital and told me, "I know exactly what went wrong. Even she did not get the units of blood she was supposed to. But what can we do?" I suggested she file a formal complaint, and she responded, "What would happen anyway? No, it is not useful." I also suspect she may have been concerned that doing so would affect how her fellow staff members and superiors at the hospital perceived her.

Reporting on the mistakes of one's fellow providers was not well received, and one nurse told me it was common to not report mistakes unless the administration somehow found out about them. Nurses instead preferred to protect each other, giving colleagues a chance to mend their ways before superiors found out about their misdeeds. Nurse Peninah explained to me,

> If the employee makes a mistake, the first thing, if she hasn't already gone to Patron, or to the [ward nurse] in charge, you find that we ourselves, if we are there on the ward, we'll sit and tell each other, "Man, here we messed up, you did this, but let's do

> this." And if you see that it's not entering [into a person's head], what they should do, you find that other people will tell the in charge that "this person is like this and this and this and we have been there with her." The in charge will call her personally. You see? The in charge, if she isn't able to handle the person at all, then she goes to the leadership now. But things like that take place rarely; really everyone stops here. Bu now, you find those things that have been called by Patron there, either a person went out from [the ward] and they have gone to tell about it there, or Patron himself has arrived here and encountered someone doing something and called them there [to his office]. But, many times, you find that the issue is finished here, here inside. Maybe only if a person is really violent or argumentative [the issue goes to Patron].

Peninah's description shows the informal ways in which the maternity ward nurses worked to regulate themselves and their colleagues in order to keep their ward issues within the family, so to speak. The maternity ward drew enough criticism and negative attention as it was; they did not also need to bring down further criticism for their mistakes. These sorts of self-regulatory mechanisms also helped to maintain smooth social relations among the nurses on the ward and reduced conflict between management levels within the hospital. If Zuhra's nurse relative had gone to the hospital management to complain, she would have been breaking ranks with the other nurses at the hospital and jeopardizing her own social position and, subsequently, the social capital she needed to accomplish her daily work. These implications of reporting suspected problems deterred Zuhra's relative from coming forward with a formal accusation.

Peninah's comment about the infrequency with which issues were called to the patron's office suggests that for a maternity nurse to report directly to the patron was a violation of an unspoken agreement the nurses had to keep their problems or mistakes to themselves, to protect themselves professionally and socially. But this standard way of handling mistakes among the nurses also was a reaction to the patron himself and the administration more generally. Past interactions with the hospital administration had demonstrated to nurses time and again their low position in the institutional hierarchy. Administrators nearly always prioritized the accounts of physicians and patients' relatives over those of the nurses until an inquiry was initiated and the nurses were brought into a meeting to account for the details of a case. In these meetings, the nurses would repeatedly assert their innocence, often in opposition to the accounts of lay people (relatives) who were not present in the meeting but whom the nurses portrayed as confused and unable to understand the complicated biomedical institution. Usually any complaints against the staff members that moved beyond simply notifying an administrator were mediated, and the hospital administrators preferred to sort out the sequences of events in meetings, the findings of which were relayed back to the people who had made the complaint. I saw this happen particularly regarding the availability of supplies, and it was most often simply due to misunderstandings or miscommunication on both sides, as opposed to what might be termed malpractice. With these interactions in mind, it is no wonder the maternity nurses had little trust in their superiors and sought first to deal with mistakes among themselves by enacting a more informal system of accountability.

ACCOUNTABILITY, LANGUAGE USE, AND THE MAKING OF MORALITY AND ETHICAL RESPONSIBILITY

Even in Pendo's case, in which the nurses and doctors admitted neglect, they skirted around the issue of blame, and there were no direct consequences for the providers' actions or lack thereof. The medical officer in charge told everyone gathered in the meeting regarding her case, "So in fact . . . there isn't a person who is going to come here to take action against you, nor will we write you a [disciplinary] letter, now we will not do anything." In the same monologue, not only did Dr. Joseph touch on communication, handover practices between shifts, disciplinary procedures, the trust patients had in the hospital's services, motivation, and staff scarcity, but also he spoke in a pained manner about the ethical and moral consequences of staff's collective (in)action in Pendo's case. Certain pervasive themes arose in all aspects of my participant observation and interviews. Here, Dr. Joseph invoked all these themes at once in an attempt to motivate his staff to work for improved care. His rhetorical techniques also aimed at awakening the nurses to the repercussions of their actions and care for the women and families directly affected.

In an earlier effort to convince the nurses to sympathize with Pendo and other, similar, patients, Dr. Joseph used two metaphors about why a health care worker might be insensitive to a pregnant woman in her care. In the first, he suggested that people without children might be jealous and resent other people having children, thereby preventing them from doing so. He compared the person without children to someone who wants the 10,000 shilling bill that another person has. One bill can't be shared, so the person who wants the bill tears it in half out of irritation and spite so that neither person can have it, the torn bill not being legal tender. In the second metaphor he said, "Second scenario, me, I have money, or isn't that right? Yes. Therefore, you don't feel the pain of a person that doesn't have money, okay? So similarly, you have a child, you don't see the pain of a person that doesn't have a child. You think, like, a baby, you can go to the market and buy a baby, and so you are being comfortable." For those health care workers on the ward who had never struggled to have a child, Dr. Joseph was insinuating that they might take for granted the ease with which they started a family, just like going to the market, and that this might cause them to overlook the pain of those who had struggled and desperately wanted the child they were carrying.

Within Swahili speech patterns, metaphor is very common. In the most practical sense, speakers often employ metaphor to criticize another party. The use of metaphor is crucial for the social act of saving face because the veiled nature of the criticism leaves room for the speaker to remove him- or herself from the criticism and creates a space for the listener to not understand the veiled implications.[16] Here, the thinly veiled criticism was that a nurse's personal problems—jealousy because she herself had no children or callousness because she now had them and had forgotten the struggles or hopes of those who did not—might cause her to neglect her duties, even if not from some actively malicious intent of which she was aware.

Dr. Joseph also drew on religion, something to which all the nurses and doctors told me they ascribed, as well as humane practice ("Humanly, it's not acceptable," using the Swahili word *kiubinadamu,* which is derived from the word for humanity), and invoked the nurses' own childbearing or reproductive pasts. Left without an official avenue through which to discipline his staff, Dr. Joseph instead entreated the maternity ward nurses, telling them,

> But me, I'm telling you, if we continue on this way, you should all really know that this heaven, it's there, just we aren't going there. We help a lot of people, but we will do just one mistake and we won't go there, there, where all those who believe in God should go, but *even if* we don't believe in God, humanly [as humans] it is not acceptable. Therefore, I saw that I should deliver this message, that let's just not continue this way or we see that there is no punishment that we can get and we just do that, but it's not a good thing. Why should you *not* do something [only because] you will be punished?

In the last sentence, he was trying to center the responsibility for the events squarely on the nurses, instead of employing other rhetorical devices to provide them with a more comfortable distance from the neglect and negligence. He went on to tell them that they should make changes in the way they thought of patients and that they should share reports, particularly during shift changes, so that they did not forget any patient again in the way they had forgotten about Pendo. He encouraged them to focus on providing good care, not simply preventing bad—two very different goals. No woman should become lost in the shuffle of the busy ward, as had happened to Pendo and her baby.

In an effort, once again, to impress upon the nurses the gravity of the situation, Dr. Joseph told them, "I had already finished writing my lie here 'poor progress of labor,' and I conclude[17] [it was due to] . . . but I'm protecting people here. You all should know I'm doing it because I don't want it to get out of our hands, out of this house, okay? But I'm sure, me, I'm taking on another sin for writing a lie, and I vowed that I shall not relay this, but, friends, if we do this, it is not good." In this last reprimand, his open transparency about his actions was a shift away from veiled, metaphorical language as he tried to make an example of himself. Again, in the repetition of "sin," Dr. Joseph used language heavily laden with religious significance, his particular frame of reference for morality. Before studying to become a doctor, he had started studying to become a priest and was still, when I met him, an observant Catholic. Those nurses who knew him, as well as those with strong personal religious beliefs, would have been duly chastened by this implication of sin that could jeopardize not just their earthly life but the one they hoped would follow after.

In these attempts to impress upon the nurses the gravity of the situation, we can see what Michael Lambek so aptly refers to as "living the gap," or "what it means to live in a world with ideals, rules, or criteria that cannot be met completely or consistently."[18] It is in this gap that we find everyday ethics, when people like Dr. Joseph "must revisit other deeply held priorities concerning the good, the honorable, and the obligatory."[19] The medical officer in charge often struggled, in a deeply personal way, with the constraints of the bureaucratic system in which he worked and the ways they prevented him from enacting his highest ethical standards of patient care and discipline. Instead, the system itself increased the probability of poor service or more extreme cases of neglect, such as Pendo's. And it is of the utmost importance to remember that these cases arose, not simply from personal faults of individual providers, but from clashes of many groups of people and facilities with far mightier institutions. Financial, medical, and sociocultural processes and institutions shaped and limited how the nurses and doctors came to be able to practice care in the Mawingu Regional Hospital; these constraints shaped what was or was not possible in the practices of care and, by extension, shaped the very meanings of ethical caring in this setting.

Dr. Joseph also told the nurses in the meeting about the stillbirth of Pendo's baby that even if they made mistakes, mistakes were not a reason to stand on the sidelines the next time they encountered a difficult case. Instead, each nurse or doctor was responsible for putting forth his or her best efforts to care for patients and additionally responsible for reminding colleagues to complete tasks such as documentation. Here again he was attempting to impress upon his listeners, the nurses, that they were responsible not only for their own actions but also for the actions of their colleagues and that everyone was collectively accountable for the care the hospital provided to patients. These ideas about collectivity and collective accountability may not be unique to this particular health care system. We might expect to see such in-group cohesion in any system in which a group must work closely together. However, in the context of Tanzanian, and more broadly African, ideas about interconnectedness and collective decision-making and living, Dr. Joseph's entreaty takes on even greater significance. This collective accountability is one of the most significant aspects of a particularly Tanzanian ethic of care, different from what might be found in health care institutions peopled by workers from a different philosophical origin, outside of a deeply embedded Afro-communitarian way of being.

In a divergent manner of speaking about the tragic stillbirth, Nurse Gire asked to make a statement before they concluded discussing Pendo's case. She said that those gathered (she was specifically referring to the maternity ward staff) should also acknowledge the good work they do, and she proposed the "compliment sandwich" in which you deliver good news, bad news, good news, always making sure to end on an encouraging note. She then proceeded to say:

> Those challenges, what do they do? They stimulate you all to build yourselves anew. This case is a challenge. I think, now, it has already balanced us, if we were already starting to slack off. . . . It's necessary for there to be challenges so you all do well. Don't depend on it, that every day you will do everything well, this philosophy doesn't exist. Therefore, take the challenges as challenges and let us not be content for them to repeat and repeat themselves. If it happens through *bad luck*, like these, we can't avoid bad luck, friends. To break a cup, aren't you holding it? You want it not to break but you find that it slips away from you. . . . Therefore, challenges like these, let us accept but let us not entertain them [happening again] apart from accepting them. (emphasis added)

Gire was involved in Pendo's care from the very beginning, but though she clearly stated, earlier in the meeting, that staff had neglected Pendo, she did not use the same impassioned rhetoric as the medical officer in charge, Dr. Joseph. Gire's comments were much more representative of how providers commonly discussed stillbirth. Instead of calling these events a tragedy or sin as Dr. Joseph had, Gire used the much more neutral term *challenge* (*changamoto*), which speakers often employed throughout my time at the hospital to present areas for improvement when they did not wish to use the more negatively construed word *problems* (*matatizo*). In her comments, Gire also used a metaphor to convey the inevitability of "bad luck" (*bahati mbaya*), which was likely to befall the ward from time to time. Her use of metaphor here may have had the same face-saving application, as well as bolstering the ward's collective identity once again, after Dr. Joseph had worked hard to individualize the nurses present by confronting them with the moral peril in which they stood. Gire's much different tactic was also a poetic way of reassuring her colleagues that they needn't feel too bad for what happened to Pendo; perhaps she was seeking to improve morale so they could all face the day's work.

Gire's use of the term *bad luck* is especially significant here. At no time in the discussion of the case did either of the doctors use bad luck as a way of explaining what had happened. They were much more clearly focused on dysfunction in the ward, particularly as related to documentation and communication practices. Dr. Joseph and Dr. Deo, in all of their comments, clearly laid responsibility for the death of Pendo's child at the feet of the nurses and, more generally, the maternity ward staff. Gire, whose comment was the last in relation to Pendo's case, displaced some of the blame from the nurses. By using the term *bad luck*, she very clearly was acting to move responsibility and blame onto other, less controllable and more indeterminate forces.

Gire's use of *bad luck* was much more similar to that of Pendo and her mother-in-law, discussed in the previous chapter. The term drew upon feelings of resignation regarding events that had long been common experiences for women and families in their childbearing years. This resignation was a usual response for women and their families, who might not have shared health care providers' exposure to or belief in the authoritative biomedical explanatory models or might not have experienced other possibilities for pregnant women. But when the nurses, who were trained in the management of difficult births and abnormal deliveries, employed the term *bad luck*, it was not in the absence of other ways of understanding the event. It seemed, therefore, to be a way to shift responsibility and blame away from themselves and onto larger, more diffuse forces during these tragic events.

Likewise, nurses often referred to stillbirths as "missing" the baby (*amemiss mtoto*). This term is a bit more difficult to decipher and, while clearly a carryover from English, could mean something very different in another context, as when the speaker might mean the woman "missed" her child (because she had not seen the child in a long time, etc.). This construction is also a particularly interesting way to disembody the actions or events that led to the stillbirth, simply suggesting the woman "missed" her baby the way one might "miss out" on an opportunity, with no apparent locus of control or responsibility.

When providers, patients, and their family members called neglect or malpractice "bad luck," whether or not they believed this to be true, they were effectively enabling providers to continue to evade accountability and responsibility for their actions, part of a broader bureaucratic and systemic challenge regarding accountability. The Tanzania Nurses and Midwives Council's *Code of Professional Conduct for Nurses and Midwives in Tanzania* clearly states in section 4: "The nurse and midwife is responsible for maintaining professional standards for quality care and [must] *be accountable* [sic] for her action. Therefore, she shall observe the following: . . . 4.3 accountability for her actions or omissions through formal lines of authority and responsibility, 4.4 respecting and complying with rules and regulations in a manner that promotes *public confidence*, the integrity of nursing and midwifery services and profession" (emphasis added).[20] However, the question the medical officer in charge wrestled with nearly every day was how nurses could be held accountable through formal lines of authority and responsibility in meaningful ways when the government and Ministry of Health had effectively constructed disciplinary procedures that were so bureaucratic and prolonged as to be non-threatening and absolutely ineffective.

In an effort to provide a framework for ethical action and caring in the absence of easily accessible formal mechanisms for enforcing sanctioned ethical standards, the medical officer in charge drew on his own moral values. In a singular manner, he tried to embody and convey the moral and ethical physician who takes responsibility for his actions, even as he lives the gap. Despite being unable to initiate a case against the nurses on account of bureaucratic constraints, he reflected on how his actions (or lack thereof) eroded his moral scaffolding. The way the hospital treated Pendo shook the foundations of goals he valued, such as the ultimate goal of reaching heaven, and his responsibilities to his patients. In the absence of formal lines of authority and responsibility to ensure ethical and moral conduct, Dr. Joseph was attempting to construct another avenue for impressing upon his staff how unacceptable their actions had been. Were his words weakened without the force of concrete disciplinary consequences behind them? Perhaps. However, through his rhetoric he was embodying the caring physician who was deeply wounded by this neglect of Pendo. My interpretation of part of the reason why so many of the hospital staff members respected and liked Dr. Joseph as the medical officer in charge was that he was not afraid to face these types of cases head on and was a genuine person as well as an authentic leader. In his discussion of Pendo's case, he did not simply yell at the nurses, reprimanding them for their inaction or incompetency, but put himself into the conversation, placing his moral being on the line together with theirs.

In the regional hospital's labor and delivery room, nearly every morning I was met by the tiny bodies of stillborn babies lying on a table near one of the doors (figure 12). These bodies were perhaps the best indicator of how well a particular shift performed, how skilled a labor ward was, or how well equipped physically the ward was. I could always tell if it had been a good or bad night by the number of bundles present on that table. While Dr. Joseph passionately discussed what had gone wrong in Pendo's case and was transparent about how he had tried to cover up wrongdoing and neglect, most stillbirths did not draw a similar level of attention and discussion. Instead, nurses and families referred to "bad luck," which allowed the nurses to avoid addressing the underlying problems in their department and on their ward.

Several health care providers, working both within and outside of the government health care system, told me they sometimes felt health care providers and administrators were reluctant to straightforwardly name and discuss problems and that this made it difficult to address these issues and improve care, their ultimate goal. Instead of simplifying the tangle of bureaucratic communication and documentation practices to ensure that women did not slip through the cracks, nurses and doctors sometimes changed diagnoses, intraoperative findings, and partographs to hide evidence of substandard care to further other goals related to their everyday ethics of care in their setting. These everyday ethics of care relied heavily upon collectivity and the ward's internal social cohesion. Sometimes, as in Pendo's case, many providers were complicit and knew of the mistakes that had occurred. However, in other cases, an individual nurse might have made a mistake and, fearing confrontation with either the patient's family or the nursing administration should her mistake become known, would hide the evidence of her error. Because of the shortage of resources, which extended beyond the sole control of

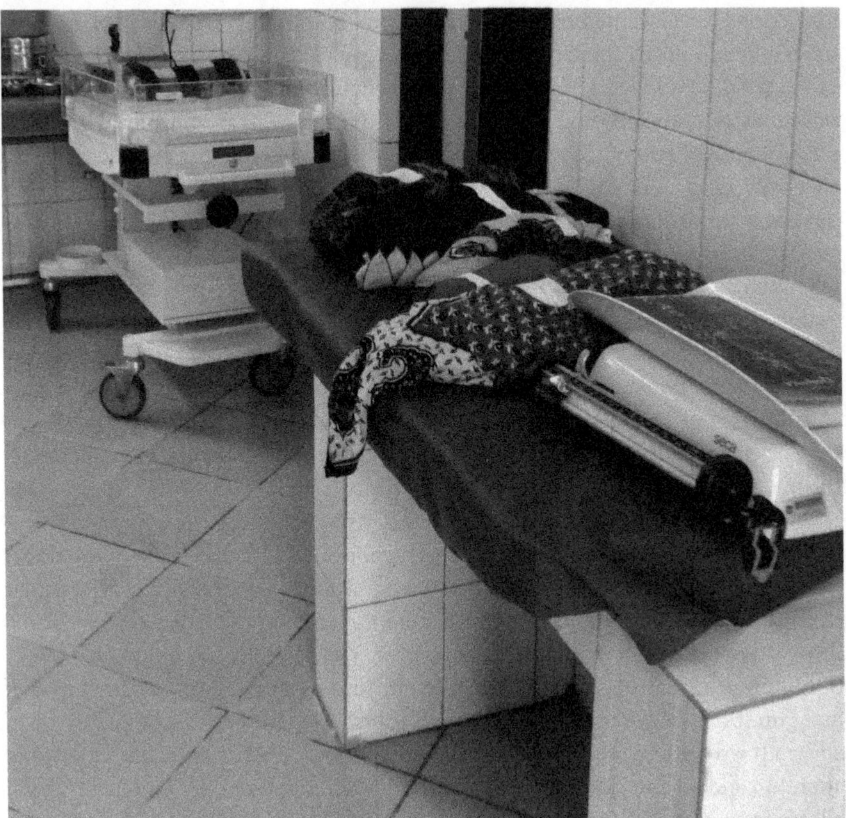

FIGURE 12. Five bodies of deceased babies lying on a table in the maternity ward of Mawingu Regional Hospital. Photo by author, 2015.

the hospital to regional and national levels, providers were often severely limited in what they were able to accomplish in terms of meeting the externally imposed guidelines for best practice.

In the absence of disciplinary threats or recourse, informal mechanisms of accountability, as well as tampering with evidence via disposing of important documents, were social acts meant to prevent criticism and embarrassment of the ward's staff members, thereby ensuring smooth social relations in this highly interdependent community of nurses and doctors. Additionally, social ideals about not losing face and not causing others to lose face (particularly through public embarrassment and criticism) may have dissuaded patients from making formal complaints and led to discipline being impossible. This impossibility was further ensured by strict and convoluted bureaucratic guidelines for dispensing warnings and disciplinary action within the government health care sector. All of these processes contributed to a system that did not easily adopt changes to routines. Instead of receiving acknowledgment of wrongdoing or medical errors, the patients and their families were left with no real choice other than to engage in the cognitive work of shifting blame once again. They shifted it from themselves onto luck and God in an attempt to come to terms with a tragedy that was still all too common in their communities. Ultimately, patients had no other avenue for coping with these events because of how health care providers, administrators, the system more broadly, and its documentary accoutrements, as epitomized by the partograph, constructed the realities of stillbirth.

In this environment that made change or reformation feel nearly impossible, the nurses and doctors had little possibility of revolutionizing their care practices. Instead, they were swept up into a global system that promulgated the idea that good care was documented care, incentivizing accounting for deviations from guidelines while simultaneously disincentivizing changes in practice that would result in different care for women and babies. Within this system, maternal and neonatal deaths, as well as intrapartum stillbirths, not only could happen but were nearly impossible to avoid.

6

The Stories We Tell about the Deaths We See

Death audit meetings were a much more infrequent but formal accountability mechanism, and one that linked individual deaths and health care workers with their institution, the region, and the rest of the country. The Ministry of Health requires audits of all maternal deaths, as well as neonatal deaths and stillbirths, though the latter two audits never occurred while I was at Mawingu. Thus I concentrate here on the maternal death audit meetings to examine not only documentation and data or accountability but also the discourse that took shape in the discussions about women's deaths that resulted from the audit and the roles these had in shaping responsibility for maternal deaths. Maternal death audit meetings became a bureaucratic technology and tool of reproductive governance that, in opposition to their planned purpose, worked to normalize poor reporting and the number of deaths that occurred in the region.

I first observed a maternal death audit meeting in 2013 while conducting a pilot study at Mawingu. At that time, I still had not decided to study maternal mortality, but the discussion and the information presented at the meeting piqued my interest and contributed to the ultimate direction of my work. In this initial audit meeting, the participants determined that four of the six deaths under review would have been avoidable if the hospital had more efficiently managed the woman's condition or had taken a more comprehensive patient history. It was clear from the discussion that bureaucratic mishaps, systemic malfunctions, and social relations contributed to these lapses in care provision and that while drugs and procedures might be vital for ensuring a woman's survival, simply reaching a hospital (by overcoming sometimes considerable barriers) did not guarantee lifesaving help.

In these meetings, the discussion of a case always ended with the same question: Was this death preventable?[1] Nine times out of ten, the answer was yes, this death was preventable. What varied vastly between deaths was how the death occurred, what transpired on the woman's slow or rapid road to death, and who was, ultimately, responsible for ensuring that such a death would not happen again in the future. Though maternal deaths in Rukwa, in Tanzania, and many parts of the world, have declined since the 1990s, globally nearly three hundred thousand women still die each year during and following pregnancy and childbirth, most in low-resource settings, and most from just a small handful of causes. In Tanzania, the Ministry of Health and Social Welfare issued standardized guidelines for facility-based maternal and perinatal death reviews in 2006, though these had been taking place in some facilities from as early as 1984.[2]

During a maternal death audit meeting, the designated health care providers and administrators went over the details of women who had died from pregnancy-related causes. The usual participants at Mawingu included the regional medical officer (RMO), the medical officer in charge, the maternity nurse and doctor in charge, all of the district medical officers, the regional and district reproductive and child health coordinators (RRCHCOs and DRCHCOs), representatives from various hospital departments including the lab, and maternity nurses. A WHO publication describes the maternal death audit in this way: "A maternal death audit is an in-depth, systematic review of maternal deaths to delineate their underlying health, social, and other contributory factors, and the lessons learned from such an audit are used in making recommendations to prevent similar future deaths. It is not a process for apportioning blame or shame but exists to identify and learn lessons from the remediable factors that might save the lives of more mothers in the future."[3] And the WHO suggests, building on its text on maternal death audits from 2004:

> [Maternal] deaths should be routinely reviewed or audited as an integral aspect of healthcare quality improvement.... This approach not only takes advantage of innovations in statistics reporting, but simultaneously improves response mechanisms to avoid future deaths. Over the past years, many low-income countries have introduced action-oriented review mechanisms, described under various names including maternal death enquiry, review, or audit. These require analysis of the circumstances of each death, identification of avoidable factors and action to improve care at all levels of the health system, from home to hospital. Much of the responsibility for follow-up actions lies with district and local health authorities.[4]

While officials and clinicians can employ this process in any setting, in any country, it is particularly useful in countries that lack reliable vital statistics and civil registry systems or where a lack of resources may make it difficult to accurately diagnose the cause of death in a more immediate way. During the audit meeting, the participants also discuss potentially contributing factors extending from the woman's family and community or the referring health facility. These discussions enable district health administrators to analyze how they can improve the referral system, infrastructure, and communication in the future in order to save more lives. At the end of the discussion of each woman's case, the group agrees on an "action plan" to be carried out in the ensuing months to address the preventable aspects of the woman's death. These meetings play an important role in collecting data, legitimating state efforts to reduce maternal deaths, and demonstrating the efficacy of individual health care institutions.

Since 2013, I have participated in or been present at a total of four such meetings. While Tanzanian Ministry of Health guidelines, as administrators and providers at Mawingu Regional Hospital described them to me, suggest that hospitals or regional health administrations hold these meetings on a quarterly basis, in practice the meetings occurred much less frequently. Sometimes the regional hospital would go seven months or more without convening such a meeting. By the time the maternity ward doctor in charge had called the meeting and notified all the appropriate district and regional-level administrators, the details of each woman's case were long forgotten, turned into an indistinct blur by the passing of time. No two women's deaths followed the same trajectory, making each case unique but with all-too-common underlying similarities. It was these commonalities that the death audit system was designed to pick up and turn into action plans and points of intervention.[5] In this way, no death is in vain; each woman leaves behind lessons that can be carried forward to prevent the death of another.

In an era of audit and accountability, of counting and an obsession with metrics as the next global health panacea, the maternal death audit meeting holds a new and loftier role as a way to track these deaths, count them, enumerate the "true" extent of the problem that is maternal death, and collect data on the ongoing causes of these deaths.[6] Policy makers, governments, and global health practitioners contend that these data, by extension, provide them with the keys to reducing or eliminating such deaths. While the numbers and the forms are meant to strip the dead women's lives down to their clinically important constituent parts, these tools of audit culture are in no way value free, no matter how much their inventors might wish this to be so.[7]

Indicators, such as a country's maternal mortality ratio, are key instruments of governance: "Indicators influence governance when they form the basis for political decision making, public awareness, and the terms in which problems are conceptualized and solutions imagined. Conversely, the kinds of information embodied in indicators, the forms in which they are produced and disseminated, and how they function as knowledge are all influenced by governance practices. The production of indicators is itself a political process, shaped by the power to categorize, count, analyze, and promote a system of knowledge that has effects beyond the producers."[8] In this context, the audit meetings and their attendant paperwork became a technology specifically of reproductive governance, which the state often enforces through the production and deployment of demographic statistics such as those tracking birthrates and maternal death.[9] Lynn Morgan and Elizabeth Roberts define reproductive governance as "the mechanisms through which different historical configurations of actors—such as state institutions, churches, donor agencies, and NGOs—use legislative controls, economic inducements, moral injunctions, direct coercion, and ethical incitements to produce, monitor and control reproductive behaviors and practices."[10] Often women are the targets of mechanisms of reproductive governance,[11] but in death audit processes this complex comes to bear forcefully on administrators and clinicians. The nurses, doctors, and health administrators are at once targets of reproductive governance and tools of these regimes as they also work to shape women into responsible reproducers through their interactions with them on the ward on a daily basis. The data they produce in these meetings include vast quantities of information not just about women but about the data's producers themselves and the health system in which they work through what is both present and absent; in producing these reports, the administrators themselves become targets of reproductive governance. In this instance, these parties are responsible for facilitating society's social and biological reproduction through preventing the deaths of pregnant women. Meeting participants must carefully negotiate how much to reveal about their own culpability while also meeting bureaucratic requirements, which if unmet would trigger other sanctions on the hospital and its leaders.

Much like the partograph, a document-cum-technology whose in vivo form is reconstructed for every new use to which nurses and doctors put it, the numbers and checkboxes of maternal death audit meetings cannot be divorced from the values, ethics, and social and institutional powers that brought them into being in the first place and continue to shape their uses. These death audit papers are meant to standardize, but in fact what they do is strip down, reducing complex lives to "yes" or "no" answers, stuffing bodies—mothers and babies—into checkboxes that cannot possibly contain the messiness and conflicting narratives of lives lived and lost, narratives that employ different lenses, take different perspectives, and arise within diverse contexts. Bureaucratic documents, and development projects generally, often seek to "render technical" complex problems that will then be amenable to technical interventions and solutions.[12] As Tania Li observes, "To render a set of processes technical and improvable an arena of intervention must be bounded, mapped, characterized, and documented; the relevant forces and relations must be identified; and a narrative must be devised connecting the proposed intervention to the problem it will solve";[13] maternal death audits and their forms seek to do just that. Yet the vast complexity of people's lives and care practices can never be fully encompassed in these documents, whose very purpose is to reduce, distill, and standardize so that the lessons from them can be presented in terms of interventions and solutions. Importantly, the forms should also comply with global notions of causes of maternal death. Lost here, too, in these forms are the true underlying causes of maternal death, including Tanzania's political economy and other drivers of stratified reproduction; the antipolitics machine is hard at work containing meaningful challenges to the status quo.[14]

When I read Form B, the second form of a two-form set sent to the Ministry of Health after each audit meeting, I could discern almost nothing about the course of the woman's illness, how she came to be at the hospital, the context in which she had lived, and, ultimately, anything about her interactions with the government hospital other than her diagnosis. In Tanzania, despite an emphasis on a qualitative, in-depth analysis of each death, the Ministry of Health forms do not provide much space for elaboration of details; "The structured reporting forms . . . are designed to collect mostly medical causes of death and as such are less suitable to guide the team through an analytical discourse on the gaps in service provision, nor stimulate action-oriented dialogue in the forum."[15] This lack of action-oriented dialogue significantly reduces the impact of the meetings, solidifying them as performative rather than functional.

Typically, the meeting started with opening remarks from the regional medical officer. Then the maternity ward doctor in charge would begin going through the case files. He read through each woman's medical record from beginning to end, pausing for questions or comments on her diagnosis or course of treatment as others present in the meeting asked for clarification. People would point out delays in the care, question the quality of history taking, or ask about the events that had preceded the woman's arrival at the hospital. The first cases received more careful consideration and discussion, with the district-level administrators interjecting comments about a facility lower down the referral chain, or about how we might determine if the woman had received adequate prenatal care. However, I found, particularly as the meetings dragged on for many hours, the attendees began to focus more and more on simply filling in blanks on the form. They began to copy action plans from one woman's form to the next by rote, without any commensurate discussion of the plan's appropriateness. This was also because the meeting's attendees identified similar problems in many of the cases. The increasingly cursory discussion ignored the fact that, in this setting, even the diagnosis is not the thing of certainty it is meant to be. Without much of the necessary diagnostic equipment, and in the absence of a pathologist, even these determinations, sometimes presented as facts, were often merely interpretations based on experience, gut, and best guesses from how a woman's illness had presented itself, what little information could be gleaned from accompanying relatives, and what the woman herself had said before her death.

The Tanzanian Ministry of Health audit guidelines include very little description of the actual review meeting, focusing much more extensively on "hierarchical reporting structure, technical committees, and administrative management of the data."[16] The metrics of global health have come to have paramount importance, clearly visible in the maternal death reporting structures, overshadowing or precluding more concerted consideration of the complexity of the lives of individuals and even institutions.[17] Likewise, the discussions about responsibility and clinical decision making, action plans, and outcome indicators in the audit meetings were never able to tell the whole story. But, then again, telling the whole story was not the purpose of these meetings; meeting participants distorted the truth for themselves and most certainly for the consumption of higher authorities.

REPORTING AND DATA COLLECTION

I had a chance to observe the national reporting structures once in January 2015 when I was in Dar es Salaam. In May 2014 I had met a woman working in the Ministry of Health's Reproductive and Child Health Section headquarters in Dar. In January, I visited her office and we discussed her work responsibilities. At that particular time, her boss was away and she was in charge of compiling the weekly reports based on data coming from the regions.

As I was sitting in her office, her computer pinged and she opened an email with the data from the entire country. There were two deaths for the Rukwa region, and under "location" it said Sumbawanga. I asked her if there was any other information about these deaths because I had just come from Sumbawanga and would have been present during the time period the report covered. She speculated the deaths had occurred at Mawingu, but I knew of no deaths that had occurred at the hospital during that same period. While the deaths under the heading of Sumbawanga could have occurred elsewhere in the municipal district, I told her those data made me uncertain about the rest of the information she had been getting. She told me she would call the Rukwa RRCHCO to clarify the details of the deaths. This was a particularly clear demonstration of the uncertainty inherent in these reporting structures. If I had not been present to ask about the data because of my experiences in the region in question, she would not have made a follow-up phone call and the deaths could have been misattributed to the regional hospital or to nowhere in particular at all.

Reporting requirements were routinely a challenge for many of the health care facilities in Rukwa. Some of the doctors at the regional hospital told me they were unsure about how to properly fill out the MTUHA (Mfumo wa Taarifa za Uendeshaji wa Huduma za Afya, Health Management Information System) books for the end-of-month reports for their wards. The hospital often submitted reports late to the regional or ministry levels, and this was a major area the hospital was targeting for improvement during my time there. Maternal death audit meetings often opened with the RMO reminding the district administrators to submit their reports of deaths in a timely fashion.

At the meeting held in May 2015, the RMO said that everyone was to report the number of maternal deaths every week to the ministry and the RMO's office.[18] He said it was very important to be following these reporting guidelines because it was an order that came directly from the president himself in 2014. Even if the districts reported zero, the ministry would be satisfied. After this proclamation, two of the DRCHCOs admitted they had not yet turned in all of their data; one said she had been late to the meeting because she was trying to find the relevant information from her office.

The RMO went on to draw attention specifically to the Sumbawanga Rural District (Sumbawanga DC) for its consistently late reporting, which had been a problem for more than a year. Highlighting the important role these data could play, he said, "In 2014, when the regional commissioner was in front of Parliament, she sent a request back to me, asking for the number of maternal deaths in the region. I told her that the maternal mortality ratio was 116 per 100,000. Later, when I finally received the late data from Sumbawanga DC, I had to tell the regional commissioner that actually the real number for the year was 142. This was even an increase over the previous year's rate of 139 or 138 per 100,000!" The RMO then pointedly asked the Sumbawanga DC representative at the meeting, "Do you think the regional commissioner would be understanding if we continued to provide her with bad data to use in front of Parliament and the president? You know, that last time, with that late data, the regional commissioner had to admit our region had not seen any reductions in maternal mortality despite even the passing of another year!" Not only did the RMO consider Sumbawanga DC's tardiness to be problematic and disrespectful, but he saw it as a threat to the region's reputation on a national stage. By providing the regional commissioner with data of dubious veracity, the RMO was also threatening the commissioner's credibility publicly and in front of her superiors.

Reporting could go wrong in any number of ways. In some instances I became confused about how the hospital was counting deaths and who was supposed to take responsibility for which deaths. In theory, any woman who had died at the hospital was supposed to be counted and documented as a hospital death. This sounded, to me, like a fairly black-and-white system. Either she was alive when she arrived, or she was not. However, in practice, there was a much less distinct line. The hospital did not want to appear to be making no progress in improving care and reducing deaths, so they were often selective about how they counted the deaths. This selective counting was an effort to shift responsibility onto other sources and away from the hospital. When a woman arrived at the hospital "already dead," it became less important to remember the details of her case, to record her passing, or to track the life of her statistics after her death. The hospital workers and administrators were happy to absolve themselves of deaths that were not theirs. In this case, the ethical negotiations of care and work were straightforward; she was clearly not their problem.

In mid-2014, I was away from the hospital for about six weeks. At the beginning of July, I tried to follow up and collect information on the maternal deaths that had occurred while I was gone. I had heard there had been two or three deaths. I asked Dr. Charles first, and he said that if the deaths hadn't occurred in the maternity ward, if the women hadn't been technically admitted to the ward already, then the deaths would be recorded in the Outpatient Department (OPD), not maternity.

He and I agreed that it was hard to follow up with deaths in OPD because of their high patient load. The doctors saw so many patients that it could be difficult to differentiate in memory or to remember the specifics of a particular case and how they had dealt with it bureaucratically after they had addressed the immediate health issue. Dr. Charles told me, "Maybe a good place to start would be to go to supervision and see if they have a record because they usually write down all the deaths that occur." I wanted to know then who was responsible for discussing the death and following up, doing the death review. He said, "It depends on where the woman came from, but the districts are supposed to do death reviews to follow up too."

I went to the nursing supervision office and found the supervisor; she told me to ask another nurse in charge of data collection. That nurse then said we should go together to the OPD to try to follow up. We went to ask Dr. Salome, one of the main OPD doctors, who told me she remembered one case from April; the woman had arrived from the village, had been treated for pregnancy-induced hypertension, and had gone home to stay with relatives in Edeni, in town. The woman had then developed further problems, relatives had brought her back to the hospital, and she had died on the way to the hospital. Dr. Salome had verified the death, dead on arrival; she said she had written it on a piece of paper and sent the body to the mortuary. Technically, then, Dr. Salome explained to me, the death didn't occur at the hospital and the death report was sent to the district from which the woman came, to be counted in the records there.

Dr. Salome continued, "I don't remember any death like that from June or the end of May. But maybe it was another doctor here who received her? You know, it can be hard sometimes here. We don't have the MTUHA book for deaths here in OPD." The data nurse, Lulu, nodded and interjected, "These OPD deaths are really difficult to trace. If you knew the dates, we could look at the roster to see who was working there and find them to ask more." But I did not know the dates and was working only on hearsay. I asked, "So then what am I supposed to do?" She told me I should go back to the maternity ward to check. "But," I said, "they didn't reach maternity to be admitted, so where are these deaths counted? Deaths *za wapi?* [Deaths of where?]" All the doctors in the OPD office at that moment murmured in agreement that it was an OPD death but that it would be difficult to find even the woman's name. Turning back to Nurse Lulu, who had accompanied me from the supervisor's office, I asked, "What about a report from supervision?" She told me that often those reports were given orally if the person had not been admitted to the hospital, so there probably would not be any further documentation on the part of supervision. And with that, she told me, "Why don't you go back to maternity and make sure there is no documentation there? I think you will find something there. Here, in my office, we haven't yet gotten the data from June because the month just finished." I returned to the maternity ward, to the start of my search, with no further information about these two deaths.

Back in the ward, I was ranting to Nurse Gire out of frustration about the problem of tracing the deaths. She told me, "I was here for the one who arrived here and almost immediately died. It was eclampsia, I think." I told Gire that Dr. Charles had said, "That woman who came here, she came and was already gasp, gasping, and then she died after only a very short time." Gire responded, "You know, the way we do this, if the woman isn't included in our admission book here, then perhaps it wasn't recorded as a death here. If she was in the book, then it's required that her death be recorded here. If she dies in OPD, then the information, her files, and everything, go back to the district she came from. They are supposed to follow up there. You see?"

After this explanation, Gire went on to tell me about when she had been a reproductive and child health coordinator some years ago: "At that time I started a form to collect better data at the village level about maternal and neonatal deaths. Really, I got better information, and I told them to bring the forms to me every first of the month for the previous month." With pride, she continued, "I got much higher numbers than others were getting, and I told the RMO at the time that this was a severe problem that needed to be addressed. But now, I don't think those forms are still being used. The data that are being reported nowadays are certainly not accurate!" Getting worked up, she said, "I don't believe that deaths have been reduced. and even the number for Tanzania seems unbelievable! We see here in this hospital! I do this work related to maternal mortality from my heart [*kutoka moyoni*], but it is hard, and it makes your heart heavy."

Gire then asked me if we had done the maternal death audit meeting yet this year. I said, "No! We have still not yet done it, since last year in October or November! We probably have twenty cases to discuss—we can't finish them in one day anymore! Now we have the ones from the end of 2013 in addition to those from this year." Shaking her head, she said, "We need to see if the RMO is around. He should push for the meeting from the top so it happens within the next week, to bring some pressure so it finally happens. The longer we wait, the more details of the cases have been forgotten!" I agreed and said, "It seems to me then it's not very useful for us in order to improve care if no one remembers the details of the case." Gire nodded her assent as another woman walked through the labor room door carrying her basin filled with her belongings. I moved away, leaving Gire to work as I went in search of the ward nurse in charge, Kinaya.

"*Samahani* Nurse Kinaya! Excuse me! Do you know about those deaths that occurred here in May and June? Where can I find information on what happened or who these women were?" In her brusque, matter-of-fact manner she said, "The medical officer in charge knows about them. He's the one who said not to document them because *tunaongeza vifo siyo vya kwetu* [we are increasing deaths that are not ours], it looks like we've killed them, but they came already in a bad condition!" Making a mental note to ask Dr. Joseph, I thanked her and moved on.

That day I did not receive information about the women's names, their home villages, or any other details that would have made it possible for me to follow up. When I asked Dr. Joseph, he simply explained that they kept no records of such deaths at the hospital because the women had not been alive long enough after arriving to actually be officially admitted. He, and others at the hospital with whom I spoke did not feel that the hospital had any responsibility to count these types of deaths of women who arrived "already dead," either literally or figuratively—almost dead—in the case of those who expired shortly after arriving. I asked him if there was even any record of the names of the women, and he told me no. As the system currently functioned, it was feasible that their names would be impossible to find again, and their deaths might go unrecorded at any level. This experience was another instance that caused me, and others such as Nurse Gire, to be suspicious of any reported declines in maternal death at the hospital, in the region, or in Tanzania more generally. This narrative that the women had arrived "already dead" surfaced over and over again in maternal death audit meetings, but even more in the narratives the nurses and doctors constructed when they gave me a more individual explanation of the phenomenon of maternal death in the regional hospital.

These accounting moves and the discourse of women arriving "already dead" served to shift responsibility and accountability outside the hospital. In this way, the providers and administrators were, in an ethical and state-sanctioned manner, able to shrug off these deaths and leave others to worry about their implications. There was no need to increase the work, the numbers, or the emotional burden at the hospital by reporting deaths that had come from elsewhere. In not entering into a relationship with these women as patients or as statistics, the hospital was also refusing them as seekers and recipients of care. The hospital was severing, arguably before the tenuous claim was ever formalized in admission books and logs, the care connection that would have obliged the nurses, doctors, and administrators to take on a dying woman and, as a result, the statistic of her death. Here, they could hide behind seemingly formalized bureaucratic rules about who constituted an admitted patient of the hospital and, bolstered by the bureaucracy, ethically turn down care for the woman. Denying this care relationship was a way of enacting other care relationships, including care for the maternity ward, care for the hospital, and care for the region's reputation on the national level.

AUDIT MEETING ACTORS AND PROCEEDINGS

In the Rukwa region, maternal death audit meetings were the responsibility of the regional hospital. I asked more than once if the districts, three rural and one urban, also were supposed to hold such meetings to discuss the deaths in their settings, those that had occurred in district-level health facilities or in the community, but

I never received a clear answer. The only aspect of the protocol that was readily apparent was the role of the regional hospital. The maternity ward doctor in charge was responsible for calling the meeting. With the support of the regional medical officer's office, he sent letters to all of the district medical officers (DMOs), DRCHCOs, the RRCHCO, and the relevant regional hospital staff members. The regional hospital was generally represented by the medical officer in charge, the maternity ward doctor and nurse in charge, a rotating selection of approximately three maternity ward staff nurses, the other physicians assigned to maternity, and, occasionally, a representative from the pharmacy or the laboratory.

This mixture of administrators at various levels, together with regional hospital staff, led to complicated dynamics and subtle power plays. Directly or indirectly, the regional officials blamed the district health administrators for failing to control or properly supervise the health care workers in the many lower-level facilities within their purview. The district officials had little direct control over these subordinates spread throughout many dispensaries and health centers covering huge land areas. This was in contrast to the much more immediate, direct effects the regional officials could have on the regional hospital. The result was that the district officials often became defensive as they had to listen to action plan after action plan in which they were the chief responsible party and the lowest providers in the region, working in the most peripheral dispensaries, the ones meant to be radically changing their practice to prevent these deaths. The district officials barely had the resources to visit their facilities, lacking funds for gasoline or working vehicles that could traverse the region's rugged terrain. Even if they were able to reach facilities, if they regularly visited all of them, the administrators would rarely have time for any other tasks, so great would the time requirements be.

In one audit late in my stay we were discussing action plans and ways to determine if women were getting enough education during antenatal clinic visits. I, drawing on my expertise as a researcher, which the RMO and medical officer in charge had encouraged, pointed out that simply observing dispensary providers during health counseling talks was not a valid way to measure what women were learning at the antenatal clinic. Naturally, I argued, the provider being observed would change his or her behavior on the day of the visit to appear as favorably as possible. One of the DRCHCOs became incensed and accused me of not understanding what it was like in villages and their dispensaries. She told me, "Women lie. They tell you that they didn't receive any counseling to go to the hospital, especially if they are primigravida, but they did! If you ask those providers there, they will tell you they are counseling women, but those women are still starting at home with the TBAs [traditional birth attendants]!" I politely returned that I had, in fact, spent a great deal of time in villages and, specifically, in dispensaries in two different regions of Tanzania. I suggested it might be more appropriate to interview some women at their homes or near the dispensary to see what they were retaining from clinic visits. I also suggested that if providers said they were counseling women about their birth plans, but women were still preferring to start out with the TBAs, we should probably take that as an indication that the counseling was inadequate, inappropriate, or unsuited for the women in question. The DRCHCO continued to bluster that I did not know what I was talking about.

After the meeting, Dr. Deo told me that the DRCHCO had gotten so upset because she knew I was right and that she did not want to make more work for herself. I said I should perhaps just not say anything again in the meetings. Dr. Deo looked at me and said, "No, you must keep telling them these things! One day they will have to listen!" My more critical reflections and suggestions, though perhaps empirically sound, were unwelcome because I had upset a balance in which meeting participants complied with documentation requirements and an official technologization of maternal mortality while escaping additional work and new routines, which this resource-poor region would have been unable to adequately support. My foreignness made it easy for the participants to suggest I was unaware of the implications of what I was suggesting, as indeed at the time I was, but not in the ways I had perceived them to be accusing me of being unaware. I was, naively, fixated on suggesting methods or action plan steps that might *actually* have produced valid outcome indicators, but that was not, in fact, the intent of these meetings. I was operating on an entirely different plane, one likely characterized by a privileged positionality derived from growing up in a world in which I could control many outcomes and in which validity, accuracy, and efficiency were paramount goals. In short, I had developed my subjectivity in a landscape very similar to that which had produced the idea of maternal death audits as technical interventions. I was not from the landscape that actually produced most of the world's maternal deaths, so the important performative aspects of these meetings were somewhat lost on me at the time; unknowingly, I had broken the fourth wall when I had tried to offer what I thought were useful improvements to action plans. I had also undermined the DRCHCO, already in a less privileged position in this meeting of district and regional authorities, her bosses. Bregje De Kok et al. write that for maternal death audits to be most successful (i.e., to change practices), they ought to take place in an environment supporting self-reflection, constructive criticism, and egalitarianism, but local institutions and cultures often do not, or cannot, fully operate in this ideal fashion.[19] This assessment, however, is predicated on a particular idea of what makes an audit successful. At Mawingu, changed practices were not necessarily the ultimate goal of these meetings, more because of systemic constraints than because of any real lack of will, but they could be successful in other ways.

Despite the inclusion of hospital outsiders in the meeting, representatives from the OPD and the hospital lab were notably absent in most of these meetings. For those deaths that occurred at night, if the maternity ward nurses faced an emergency, the OPD clinician was the first to see the woman. The OPD also was responsible for triaging incoming patients and determining whether they should be admitted to the maternity ward, the gynecology ward, or elsewhere. At this time, as part of triage, the OPD personnel would write a preliminary diagnosis and differentials and would order lab tests and any medications or procedures they thought necessary. Therefore, to understand delays and their part in the process, I always felt the OPD doctor in charge would have added a great deal to the conversations during the audit meetings. Likewise, laboratory personnel were important because they were responsible for ensuring that blood was available for emergency transfusions. The lab was also responsible for confirming any of the diagnoses put forth, most notably malaria in pregnancy or infections. Without inclusion of representatives from all of the departments with which maternity worked, it was difficult to adequately address any delays or gaps in care that had occurred at the hospital. Without including the OPD, it would be impossible to improve continuity of care that would ensure that a woman in critical condition did not become lost in the shuffle of busy wards. The essential role of the OPD is also clear in the description of my quest to locate information related to the two women who had died at the hospital but for whom there were no records. The OPD doctors never had representation and never formally heard the outcomes from these meetings, whether because no one believed them to have a place in the conversations or simply because their inclusion was not part of the meeting routine.

The infrequency of meetings meant that, in addition to more thorough consideration of cases we discussed in the beginning, for the sake of time we did not discuss the oldest cases at all. Those present also tried to make a case for one or more of the deaths not "really" being a maternal death so we that we would not have to spend time going over the details. They might try to suggest this if it appeared that the woman had had preexisting or underlying health problems. Physiologically, nearly any preexisting health problem can be exacerbated by the increased demands that pregnancy places on all of a woman's bodily systems.[20] For example, to accommodate the fetus, a woman has expanded blood volume throughout the pregnancy, which can put extra strain on her heart or lungs. Deciding to exclude a pregnant woman's death from the data on maternal deaths from the hospital was as much strategic as it was born of a genuine belief that her death had not been caused by her pregnancy. In other cases, the determination to exclude a woman from the count of maternal deaths could be a result of inadequate knowledge of pathology and the complex physiological effects of pregnancy. During these meetings, until the last one I attended in May 2015, we did not have a doctor who was specialized in obstetrics and gynecology, and the hospital never had, to my knowledge, a pathologist. The doctors were already too shorthanded to even consider taking on the additional work of postmortem examinations of women who had died from pregnancy-related causes. Once again, the system itself prohibited some of the very processes that could have helped the hospital gain access to the additional information necessary for improving care.

CASE FILES

While the physician in charge of maternity was responsible for calling the meeting, it was his nursing counterpart who was responsible for maintaining the paperwork and preserving the medical records of the women who had died. In theory, the maternity ward nurse in charge was to keep the files of the dead women together in one place, maintaining them until such a meeting happened. However, before almost every meeting there was a panic as the nurse in charge came to realize that one or more case files had gone missing. In these instances, differently than in the case of missing partographs, there were rarely any accusations about foul play involved in these disappearances. Instead, the disappearances were due to poor organization combined with poor communication and a lack of standard procedures for the storage of the files. Inevitably, one or more files would have made their way back to the Medical Records Department or would have been lost in a handover that was never completed.

In practice, the files were never allowed to leave the hospital grounds, but it was not at all uncommon to be unable to find a patient's records. Sometimes doctors borrowed the files to do a more thorough case review or to try to puzzle out why a particularly difficult case had "defeated" them. Once, in 2014, during a period of handover between the incoming and outgoing nurses in charge, we discovered that the files meant for the maternal death audit meeting were locked in the ward storeroom. Only the outgoing nurse in charge possessed the keys, and she had traveled out of the district. Other times, the medical attendant was responsible for opening a patient file after the woman had already died, carrying the papers, which might have been stapled together (or not), to Medical Records. She was then supposed to return to the maternity ward with the new file, its loose papers now tidily constrained, held within the cardstock covers with staples or piece of string onto which hole-punched pages were strung. It was more than possible that some files never made it back to the maternity ward after this detour to Medical Records. Alternatively, they may have made it back to the ward but then been subsequently misplaced when no one knew why a file had been left lying around. Nurses frequently "filed" miscellaneous paperwork of uncertain origin or uncertain trajectory in various cupboards, cabinets, drawers, and boxes.

This "filing system" on the maternity ward was infamous, and during a meeting early in my field stay, Patron called out the maternity ward for putting discharged patients' files in boxes in the corner of the room, in what had yet to become the maternity ward operating theater. He said, "The files have been there for more than a month and have not been taken to Records! The patients have been discharged, but the files are still there! What is this system there on your ward?" But though the system did not follow the hospital protocols, it was a system; the afterlives of these "misfiled" files had important effects on subsequent events, such as the maternal death audit meetings. Kinaya, the nurse in charge at the time of

Patron's reprimand, went straight back to the ward and instructed the nurses on duty to take files to the Medical Records Department as soon as the patient left. Kinaya muttered under her breath, "I'm talking, talking, but nothing changes," after Nurse Happy listlessly acknowledged this new duty, leaving little certainty that files would actually begin making their way to the records building.

These files were, themselves, characterized by missing information—the wrong times (or none at all) or dates, written hastily while doctors buzzed from one patient to the next on ward rounds. Incomplete medical histories neglected to include details of previous pregnancies and their outcomes. Scrawled doctors' notes in at least three different handwritings wove a carpet of barely legible English instructions, differential diagnoses, and observations on the patient's condition. In every audit meeting we had a discussion about the quality of medical histories, and either the ward doctor in charge or the medical officer in charge implored everyone present to improve intake interviews and timekeeping, which they often portrayed as systemic problems preventing the hospital from further improving care. Here, between the cardboard covers, upon which the woman's name was often misspelled at the whim of the Medical Records personnel, was brought into being a woman in critical condition—a life, or death, hanging together or falling apart on the pages. Missing information made it nearly impossible to reconstruct her pathway to and through the maternity ward.

EXTRAPOLATING WOMEN'S LIVES

Against this backdrop of uncertainty and barely contained file chaos the actual meetings took place. Because of the length of time that had often passed between a woman's death and the review of her case, the files were all that the meeting attendees had when assessing the progress of the woman's clinical condition, overall health, decision-making skills, family dynamics, and reception and treatment at the hospital. The meeting attendees extrapolated missing information on the basis of where the woman was from, how many previous pregnancies she had had, or the state in which she had arrived at the hospital. For example, the antenatal clinic cards and several of the hospital forms, such as the doctor's notes page, included a line at the top for the patient's religion. The woman's religion was also one of the blanks that needed to be filled on the Ministry of Health forms. Often, the woman's antenatal card did not indicate her religion, and the meeting attendees would infer it on the basis of her name or that of her husband: for example, Asha, married to Mohamed, was almost certainly a Muslim, whereas Anna was more likely to be a Christian. Though these interpretations were based primarily on stereotypes and generalizations about Christians, Muslims, and particular ethnic groups, the meeting participants accepted them in order to fill in the required blanks on the form.

In addition to the uncertainties about such missing individual attributes or demographic information, there was often some uncertainty about how the woman's obstetric emergency had unfolded. If the details of her treatment within the hospital were certain, those events that had preceded her arrival often were not clear, based only on what had been gleaned from relatives or the woman herself before her condition had taken a turn for the worse. Occasionally, the woman had arrived at the regional hospital accompanied by a referral letter and maybe even a representative from the referring health facility. In these cases, more information about what had occurred before arrival at the hospital was available. But many times the person accompanying the woman knew little about what had transpired or, even if a health provider, did not have many details about the woman's condition. This was sometimes because of the brief period of the woman's stay at the referring facility or, in other cases, because of a lack of skills and knowledge on the part of a referring provider. If providers did not have training in the recognition and treatment of obstetric emergencies, they might not even have been able to identify the exact complication beyond the fact the woman was bleeding, for example, or that she had been unable to give birth after a prolonged period of time.

In other instances, the woman arrived at the hospital perfectly healthy and her death came as a sudden and unexpected shock even to the providers involved in her case. While no one ever expected a woman to die, some women arrived at the hospital in obviously poor health, and their decline and subsequent death were consequently less of a surprise to the ward staff members. In one particularly bad week in March 2014, just one month after I had arrived at the hospital, several women died within the span of a few days. The most shocking of these deaths was that of Paulina, whose story opens the book. She had reported to the hospital for a scheduled C-section before her labor started. She was in her midtwenties and had had her previous two children via C-section, which was a standard indicator for another surgical delivery. With increased scar tissue in the abdomen and multiple previous incisions in the uterus, there is a greater risk of uterine rupture if the woman experiences strong contractions during labor. In this case, Paulina had arrived early with plenty of time to prepare and schedule her surgery.

The next day, Nurse Lucy, who had been assisting in the operating theater and had gone to receive the baby when it was born, reported back to us on the ward that Paulina had died. She had needed a blood transfusion, but she was blood type O negative, a rare type compatible only with other O negative blood. There was not enough blood available at the hospital; Paulina received only one unit of blood. In later discussions, the doctors and nurses agreed that her death was likely due to hypovolemic shock from her prolonged internal bleeding. The nurses were dazed, and in the days afterwards Dr. Deo, who had seen Paulina from the time of her arrival at the hospital, was adamant about implementing changes to procedure to prevent similar deaths in the future. On rounds with Dr. Deo almost three weeks after Paulina's death, he told me, "Now, for all cases of planned, non-emergency Caesars, we clinicians must make sure we have the results of the patient's blood type, cross-matching, and hemoglobin tests. We should have two units of blood on standby for them, too, before even starting the surgery. We must learn from these other cases and not repeat that mistake!"

To my surprise, when we later discussed Paulina's case in the audit meeting, there was no mention of this proposed protocol, nor did the meeting participants, including Dr. Deo, put this in the action plan. It appeared that once a death lost its immediacy, the nurses, doctors, and administrators quickly returned to the status quo necessitated by their environment. In contrast to how the everyday ethical negotiations in the last chapter created lasting informal structures for accountability, in this instance Dr. Deo's ethical negotiations in the aftermath about what should have been done to prevent Paulina's death did not result in any lasting change. Though he reflected on the events and sought to improve outcomes in the future should a similar case occur, the effects of Dr. Deo's everyday ethics, as individually driven as they were, faded along with the immediacy of Paulina's death.

There was little visible follow-up to address the changes that might have reduced future deaths from similar causes. In some cases, the doctors explained to me, this was because they had started trying to initiate a change or had requested a missing supply but were swiftly met with barrier after barrier or the reluctance of their colleagues and had soon given up the plan. The hospital's Quality Improvement Team (QIT) should also have participated in organizing on-the-job training to improve skills, as well as following up on the requisitioning of needed supplies, such as resuscitation equipment. However, during the majority of my time on the ward the QIT was more of an idea than a functioning body. No one was 100 percent positive about who the maternity ward representatives were, and it was unclear whether they were actually meeting and/or implementing any activities. This lack of certainty about who was responsible for following up or for implementing new protocols and guidelines compounded my feeling that the paperwork resulting from maternal death audit meetings was lost in an unknowable bureaucratic quagmire.

The amount of bureaucracy constructed, at both a national and a local level, around systematically measuring maternal deaths, accounting for them, and implementing programs to reduce these deaths would lead one to believe that the outcomes of such efforts would be consistent and replicable declines in pregnancy-related deaths. After all, dependable replicability is, or was at one time, the objective of bureaucracy—systematization for replicable, predictable, and efficient outcomes,[21] part of rendering this problem technical. However, the outcomes were more often arbitrary, underanalyzed, and lacking causal certainty;[22] perhaps declines in maternal death were due to actions on the part of the health care providers and administrators, or, just as likely, any declines were simply a chance occurrence whose continuance into the future was not something that a facility, a region, or the country could depend upon.

TABLE 1 Example of an action plan

Problem	Solution	Person Responsible	Timeline	Outcome Indicator
No working radio call, so late referral	Fix radio call	District medical officer	Within six months	Will be able to call for ambulance with working radio call system

THE FUTILITY OF ACTION (PLANS)

The outcome of the maternal death audit meeting was supposed to be action plans decided upon by the meeting participants. The underlying premise, once again, was that these action plans could structure next steps within the hospital and at the district level that would prevent recurrence of maternal deaths from the same causes. For example, if a woman was delayed in arriving at the regional hospital because the staff at a referring facility needed to call an ambulance from the district but did not have a working radio call system, the action plan might look something like the one shown in table 1.

Sometimes the woman's death could have been prevented by the presence of a specific supply or something as easily remedied—for example, perhaps there had been no adult resuscitation equipment in the operating theater or anyone with the knowledge of how to prevent the woman on the table from aspirating into her lungs secretions that she started to produce during the surgery, as was the case with Kinakia in chapter 2. Kinakia had died, meeting participants speculated, from this aspiration of fluids. This was a relatively straightforward problem with an equally straightforward solution—make sure the resuscitation equipment was present and in good working order and ensure the presence of adequately trained surgical nurses or others versed in recognizing the signs that would necessitate intubation, suction, or other forms of resuscitation.

More often than not, however, the problems the meeting participants decided to include in the action plan boxes on the last page of the Ministry of Health's audit form were not so concrete and self-contained. The needs the meeting participants identified often went along the lines of "better education of pregnant women during the antenatal clinic," and the corresponding outcome indicator was left as "a decrease in maternal deaths." Not only was it impossible to measure the success of prenatal education in this way, but the plan did not actually delineate specific steps to be taken in order to reach "better education" or identify any intermediate indicators that could demonstrate that the plan was on the right track, or give any indication of where the resources to accomplish these plans were supposed to come from within already tight budgets. This method of creating action plans that the region was incapable of executing mainly served the administrators who would be in the responsible position. With little to no time dedicated to actually producing steps that would lead to accomplishing the action item, and in the absence of the extra staffing with which to execute them effectively, the administrators sitting around the table at the maternal death audit meeting worked within national reporting structures to fulfill their bureaucratic duties while also ensuring they did not generate more work for themselves. This simplification of maternal deaths that reduced them to impossible action plans was yet another example of the way technical solutions to complex problems, and the fetishization of indicators, precluded actual solutions while all the actual contributing factors did not disappear.[23]

On-the-job training was another popular action item intended to increase providers' skill levels or knowledge of particular procedures, conditions, or interventions. Most administrators believed that any sort of long meeting or training required, at the very least, food for the participants to incentivize attendance. In a region and a hospital that was financially precarious, the prospect of having to provide food for thirty or more maternity ward staff members in order to conduct a training severely limited the possibility of in-house trainings without additional support from NGOs or the Ministry of Health. In a typical example, during the first week of March in 2014, the nurse in charge, Kinaya, organized on-the-job training for the nurses on the ward, to which they had all agreed in a ward meeting a week prior. She intended for them to all walk through the basic emergency obstetric and neonatal care assessment guidelines together, from start to finish, over the course of three days that week. On the first day, nearly two-thirds of the ward nurses were present. The following day, only three people not scheduled to be working the morning shift were present for the instruction. Upon seeing the poor turnout, Kinaya clucked and shook her head disparagingly, saying, "*Yaani*, humans, for real, it is hard to change their behaviors!" And that was the last time I ever saw or heard any concerted attempt to hold organized, ward-wide, on-the-job training. Additionally, there were no consequences if a maternity staff member did not attend meetings. Again, while Kinaya knew the professionally ethical route was to train her staff members to conduct high-quality care that complied with guidelines, her work environment meant her subordinates did not see the benefit of sacrificing personal time for training on protocols that they could only partially implement because of shortages and high patient loads. Therefore, for all parties involved, it seemed more beneficial, and more ethically sound, to drop the ruse of on-the-job trainings and proceed with actual care work.

If we assume that district health administrators *did* implement the action plans, in one way or another, in their districts after the audit meetings, they would have been the only ones who knew what they had done or the outcomes of said activities. Because of the infrequency of the audit meetings, and because of time constraints when these did occur, there were so many cases to discuss that the maternity ward medical officer in charge did not dedicate any time to reviewing steps taken since the previous meeting. Never once did I hear a report on whether the gathered administrators had made progress toward accomplishing the action plans created in a prior meeting, nor did I ever hear any reports on the stated outcome indicators. The action plans primarily fulfilled reporting requirements and were treated largely as rhetorical documents, as opposed to plans with the real potential to generate change in the system and prevent deaths. If the responsible parties were making progress on the action plan tasks assigned to them, reporting back to the gathered group could have helped create a sense of momentum and possibility, demonstrating that actions did, in fact, produce tangible results.[24]

After the meeting participants completed their action plans, the data traveled only upward. The nurses on the ward, save the few present, who were responsible for everyday care and prevention of these deaths never received a complete report on the meeting's findings. The lack of feedback and communication about action plans, progress made, or interventions planned amplified the sense that any change in the number of maternal deaths was simply a random occurrence. Perhaps it was luck. Perhaps it was due to different staff members. Perhaps it was due to the weather in the region, as when bad rains caused the roads to deteriorate and delayed a woman's arrival even further.

Dr. Charles, while in charge of the maternity ward, and Dr. Joseph, as the medical officer in charge of the hospital, told me I was the only person in the entire hospital who actually used any of the data that the hospital collected to try to draw attention to trends within the institution. I repeatedly suggested that the ward try to use the data that they collected, and that they had to use for reports every month, to help them set goals for care on a quarterly or yearly basis. I has gotten this idea from the maternity nurse in charge whom I had worked with in the Singida region; he had had great success in reducing the incidence of intrapartum stillbirths on his ward through a committed tracking of data. He used the data to show his staff trends in the number of these stillbirths. At Mawingu, instead of using these data, which were being produced to meet the demands and reporting requirements of the central government, as well as NGOs and multilateral programs, for their own ends, the hospital logged these data in the officially required books and rarely looked at them again once the bureaucratic needs were fulfilled.

PERFORMING MATERNAL DEATH AUDITS

Maternal death audit meetings are another tool, much like the partograph, that people outside Tanzania have constructed and that is meant to aid providers and administrators as they work to continue reducing maternal deaths in their settings. And yet, much like the partograph, the audit meetings rarely took the ideal form they were meant to have. As the smells of the waiting rice, chicken, and chapati from the caterer wafted over to the meeting table, the participants rushed through the details of cases, attempting to rule out a death as related to or caused by pregnancy and simply advising each other to copy the details of the action plan from previously discussed cases. The administrators, nurses, and doctors sitting around the table seemed to be engaging in a performativity of the meeting as bureaucratic requirement, as opposed to a tool for changing their ways of practicing care and serving pregnant mothers. The forms and numbers they produced traveled to higher levels and there turned into other numbers, indicators. As Claire Wendland has commented, an indicator "looks like a number and works like a fact, but it is more like the moral of a story"—one that hides uncertainty, highlighting some contributing factors while strategically deemphasizing others.[25]

Overall, while the Rukwa region was, on paper, meeting the demands of the Ministry of Health, and other organizations, for surveillance and reporting of maternal deaths, the fulfilled bureaucratic requirements belie the unsuitability of the maternal death audit system. It is clear that death audits as reproductive governance are not totalizing and do not straightforwardly produce new subjects; instead, "apparently disciplining regimes," here those of maternal health indicators and global safe motherhood, "retain resilience, unpredictability and are shaped by effects of local and biological specifics."[26] To what extent have tools of governance like the maternal death audit meeting shaped new subjectivities, or in what ways have the simplifications inherent in this globally mobile exercise rooted in public health left open a space for health care workers and administrators to resist their (re)formation as self-disciplining subjects in this global complex around ensuring safe motherhood?[27] Staff do not actively want to resist the reduction of maternal deaths in their setting, but the forms and biobureaucratic processes to which they are subjected ignore the locally specific spaces in which complex practices of technical and affective care, informal accountability, and clinical improvisation grow and are utterly unable to capture them. What this process reveals are the contributors to maternal death already well known and amenable to technical solutions, proving, perhaps, that the audits work perfectly.[28] Likewise, the expectations inherent in the forms and rhetorical processes of the audit elide the region's pervasive lack of resources, which is one of the key contributors to the failure of so many potential and attempted interventions. Perhaps the administrators' resistance to the reproductive governance trained on them takes the form of engaging in a performance of the audit meeting that rarely goes deeper than that because they are aware that the expected action plans following a narrow script are unsuited to, and often impossible in, their setting. What this means is that every subsequent meeting will see the emergence of the same barriers, the same challenges, gaps, and pitfalls as have repeatedly been identified in the past. Those problems amenable to technical interventions will make their way into action plans while the deeper roots of maternal mortality, both in the hospital and in the community, will remain unacknowledged and unaddressed. Inequity and resource scarcity remain tenaciously entrenched, escaping technical rendering in the audit process.

7

Already Dead

In general, the proceedings and outcomes of the maternal death audits were never available to the maternity ward staff members, other than those who had actually been present during the meeting. From seeing how the nurses had reacted to Paulina's death, I knew they sometimes were deeply affected by the deaths on their ward. But particularly against the background of my conversations about using hospital data *in the hospital* and the low involvement of the ward nurses in the audit meetings, I was curious how many of them knew the extent of the maternal mortality problem at the hospital. Did they realize that the hospital's maternal mortality ratio (MMR) had been increasing in the past several years? I also wanted to know how the nurses coped with the deaths on the ward because Paulina's death was the only time I ever saw them openly express any shock or dismay; surely, the nurses felt the effects of other deaths too. So, near the end of my fieldwork, I specifically asked the nurses what they knew about the number and causes of maternal deaths on the ward in 2014. All responded with very vague comments, indicating a lack of access to this information. Nurse Halima reasoned:

> Me, I've seen that the deaths are few. Why? Because I don't know. Today, I'll be on duty, I see one, because it's possible that last month, maybe I know it's only one [death] that occurred last month. But if you ask me for the year, I can't know. For the whole year, I can't know because I don't have data, and those people, we aren't told, we aren't welcome to participate in their meetings. Their meetings they do themselves, those who aren't even doing work [on maternity]. Therefore, they themselves have cut themselves off in secret, they talk, they talk and it's finished. But those of us whom this issue concerns, we aren't there in those meetings. Therefore, you can't know unless maybe you go to the records or are doing a report.

Halima reflected more than some of the other nurses on the reasons why she did not have access to more information about the number of deaths that occurred on the ward, but her answer is representative. Throughout my one-on-one interviews with the nurses, they repeatedly told me that they did not have a good concept of how many deaths had occurred overall because they had not tried to follow up. Most of the nurses were unaware of the number of deaths that had occurred, but because they had been working on the ward during only a couple of the deaths that had transpired, they felt it to be a small number. When I told them the actual number of women who had died at the hospital of pregnancy-related causes in 2014, most of the nurses were surprised and felt that the number seemed high. One responded by telling me, "Hmm, that's a lot. It shows there is still some *uzembe* [laziness] that is continuing."

In the first five months of 2015, significantly fewer women were dying than during the same period in 2014. However, no one was able to say if they thought there was a particular reason for this decline in deaths on the ward. When I went to the hospital for the night shift, one day in May, to interview Nurse Neema, we started discussing the number of deaths that occurred. Curious, I asked her, "How do you see the number of deaths?" Barely pausing to think, Neema responded, "Last year we had about five deaths of mothers." I looked at her and said, in a level tone, "You think it is only five? Here, together with the gynecology ward, it was close to thirty." Neema, taken aback, said, "Eh?! Well, that's really a lot if it's for a whole year. I think I have remembered five because those were the ones discussed in the meeting in February, and that also is a challenge that when they do a maternal auditing, staff from the maternity ward never participate the way it's supposed to happen. You find maybe only the in charge and two nurses. Therefore, we are lacking accurate data. But also feedback about why the deaths took place. But for this month I remember it is two, again they died in the following way: there's one who died with her baby inside, another was PPH [postpartum hemorrhage], it was in the beginning of April. I don't know before that."

Neema was able to remember the deaths for which she had been present or that she had more recently thought she'd heard about during a meeting. However, most of the ward staff members had no concept of how many women were actually dying every year or the causes of the deaths and how they could be prevented. This gap in communication or lack of reporting back to the ward rank and file after a maternal death audit meeting not only was frustrating to the ward staff but also shut them out, as the staff who were in the closest proximity to patients, from answers about the causes of deaths so that they could try to prevent similar deaths in the future. Ironically, in the age of metrics and the global emphasis on measuring maternal deaths, some of the people most involved—and implicated in them—never saw the data. The nurses on the ward could have benefited greatly from the audit meeting discussions of what had led to the women's deaths. They could have learned more about their own practices, the challenges the clinicians faced, and the community- or family-level events that had contributed to each death. Instead, this lack of communication of data pointedly demonstrated that these data were not for the people involved, the ones in the trenches, but for higher levels, for bureaucrats and policy makers.

COPING WITH MATERNAL DEATHS THROUGH NARRATIVE

In the aftermath of a maternal death at the hospital, before the audit meeting ever took place, nurses and doctors worked to cope with a pregnant woman's death. In this context, I repeatedly heard the narrative that the majority of the women who died were coming in "already dead." This discourse included more cases than those in the last chapter, in which the details of women's arrivals and deaths were lost because the women were, literally, dead on arrival or shortly thereafter. Instead, it came to encompass many, many deaths in which the nurses felt they had been unable to save a woman because of her life experiences and decisions preceding her arrival at the hospital. What follows in this chapter is a discussion of this narrative as a coping mechanism for the nurses and a form of care for themselves. Examining these underlying narrative structures can help us see more clearly the underlying "imprint of institutionalized practices and ideologies."[1] "Narratives shape action just as actions shape the stories told about them"; stories also "suggest the course of future actions."[2] The narratives we construct about maternal deaths operate and perform on a variety of levels, including the interpersonal, the institutional, the regional, the national, and the global. Additionally, the nurses' narratives help to reveal their ethical deliberations and how they engaged with the memories of dead women to guide their ethics of care moving forward.

It was late April 2015, and Nurse Peninah and I sat in the HIV testing and counseling room in the maternity ward, the red light on the voice recorder blinking as Peninah paused for a moment. The recorder started again as she began talking and flatly stated, "Let's say, for this year maybe, since we have started in January, we have had only two deaths. And a lot of them that happen aren't *of* here. You find there are referrals, they come from far away, and they come here and they do what? They die."

Several nurses repeatedly told me they thought the women who died primarily came from far-off villages and arrived in such a poor state that their deaths were attributable, not so much to the hospital or the ward, as to the community or family from which they came. Out of curiosity, in May 2015, after hearing this narrative arise in many of my interviews with nurses, I went back to the records of all the deaths that had occurred in 2014 and 2015 to see from which districts or villages the women had come. The fact of the matter was that the vast majority of the deaths were of women who had listed their home residence as a location within the urban district, immediately surrounding the hospital. Fully half of the deaths, seventeen of thirty-four on which I had data, were of women who came from within the urban district; 23 percent were from Sumbawanga DC (aka Sumbawanga Rural) District, 24 percent from Kalambo District, and just 3 percent, or one woman, from the furthest-away district, Nkasi (map 2). This means that transportation and bad roads, long distances, and poor access to facilities were not the primary causes of many of these women's deaths. Often other delays slowed a woman's arrival at the regional hospital, but the truth was that these women were not coming from the far reaches of the region; they were from the hospital's own backyard. Likewise, data from their medical records indicate that even the women coming from the urban district did not arrive "already dead." The median length of stay was between one and two days, accounting for about a third of these seventeen women. Four of them were at the hospital for five or more days before they died, and only two were at the hospital for less than four hours before a physician pronounced them dead. Some cases were of women who had traveled long distances to arrive at the hospital, but these were rarer.

There are a number of ways to read the assertion that women came "already dead": (1) the nurses actually believed this to be true; (2) in reframing deaths as women who were unable to be saved by the time they arrived, the nurses effectively divested themselves of responsibility; and (3) the nurses used this discourse as a way to alleviate the personal emotional burden that was the result of being unable to prevent women's deaths because of systemic constraints, lack of resources, and lack of support.

Nurse Rukia went into greater depth than Peninah, insisting that these deaths came from afar, often as referral cases from outlying communities:

> The number of pregnant mothers who are dying, it's decreasing. If you compare with the past, it's decreasing. Another time we, we get deaths, patients are brought, they're not from inside here. Eh. She comes that way in critical condition, you'll do top to bottom but you can't do anything. . . . [Deaths] come from the villages, honestly. Those people in the villages, many times they always have the habit of always delivering them there, at the traditional midwives' [*wakunga wa jadi*], they deliver them there, if they deliver they see that they have been defeated. . . . I mean, they are there, it's too late. . . . A lot of times, we get cases like that.

I prompted her further: "Okay, even if we say the number is decreasing, why do you think women and babies are still dying here, inside the hospital?" Rukia said, "The reason is just that. People come in late condition. Mhm. That is, pregnant women come in very bad condition. Eh. People die. Maybe another thing, maybe another time she has come with a severe infection, you can use an antibiotic and whatnot, but it's not possible because she is in the severe [stages] of the disease. You see, yes? They die." Throughout the conversation, Rukia resolutely denied the idea that women died because of the care being offered on the maternity ward. Instead, she blamed *wakunga wa jadi,* local midwives with little to no formal training, whom she accused of essentially forcing women to give birth at home. Informally trained women working as midwives have long been scapegoats and the targets of biomedicine's efforts to establish obstetrics as a legitimate realm of practice.[3] This was historically the case even in the United States but is an ongoing conflict in many, particularly low-income, settings throughout the world, not just

Tanzania. These generalized women, portrayed as victims of the local midwives' coercion, fit nicely within WHO's messaging and images from the start of the Safe Motherhood Initiative, in which a nonspecific "everywoman," Mrs. X, was already on the "road to death" because of poverty, gender inequality, and dangerous "cultural practices."[4]

There were, without a doubt, times when women arrived in very poor condition due to long delays seeking help, finding transportation, or being referred to the regional hospital. However, many times these deaths were not even counted in the number the hospital recorded, as explained in the previous chapter. Therefore, the nearly thirty deaths I was mentioning to the nurses did not include those of these other women whose deaths had not been recorded at the hospital. Undeniably, the narrative itself of these women coming "already" dead, as well as the almost dead, continued to do cognitive, emotional, and ethical work for the nurses.

Some other nurses, like Nurse Halima, were much quicker to admit to serious delays or a lack of emergency care at the hospital. When I asked nurses in this group what the hospital would need to continue reducing the number of maternal deaths, they focused on concrete suggestions. In their accounts, the locus of control was very much within the hospital itself, though not often actually centered on the staff of the maternity ward. Their responses tended to focus on supplies and medications, or in the case of Halima's response, the need for better triage at the OPD because the hospital lacked an emergency department.

Halima described her process of acclimating to the maternity ward and how she had learned more about how deaths were occurring once she was assigned to work on maternity. Halima said that before she worked on maternity and heard reports of deaths "I was feeling really sad. Fine, after that, I was moved here to maternity. [I] came to see, to discover more. The deaths that happen, here, here at this regional hospital are few, I mean those that are caused [by things] here, and they die here. And those, those that occur, I'm always sad, but many of the deaths, really, they come from the villages. Now, there in the villages, *I don't have the ability to do anything,* to go and do what? I don't have anything I can do" (emphasis added). She remained pragmatic about the situation, framing the deaths of the women coming in poor condition from the village as those over which she had no control and, therefore, she tended to not feel quite as bad when confronted with one of those deaths. Halima's explanation suggests that, in addition to removing the locus of institutional control and responsibility from the regional hospital, the nurses might have been using this narrative of "already dead" women to help lessen the more personal burden of these deaths. The fact that no one at the hospital made data available to the ward staff or reported on the quarterly or yearly number of deaths in a venue that was open to all staff members allowed this narrative to continue in the maternity ward. The narrative made it easier for the maternity ward staff to remove themselves from accountability for the deaths that occurred and simply to continue to hold the districts, or individual women and their families, responsible for the woman's death. "Almost dead" women were also in this category, their trajectories before reaching the hospital predisposing them to death for which the nurses would not be responsible. While knowing more might have helped the nurses to understand the extent of the problem within their own facility, the lack of knowledge played an incredibly important role that facilitated the nurses' ability to continue working each day without being continually traumatized by these deaths. This complicated everyday ethical trade-off between knowing more to be able to (in theory) improve care and continuing to see deaths as predetermined in order to resist responsibility and lessen emotional burdens should not be underestimated. Deftly avoiding self-blame by not closely examining this narrative was a form of self-care and even care for shift-mates, that helped nurses continue working and providing care to all the women who did not end up dying. At the same time, the narrative perpetuated deaths by creating the cognitive space to not confront individual actions, ward or hospital responsibility. This narrative was yet another way in which the system protected itself and its inertia, resisting efforts at change to improve care.

SELF-REFLECTION AND REMEMBERING

In addition to talking about women as arriving at the hospital already dead, the nurses deployed other coping mechanisms to help themselves deal with the deaths of women under their care. While we were discussing deaths on the ward in the previous year, I asked Nurse Aneth how she felt about them. She explained:

> Of course, I can't feel good. It's a death that, okay, she died, and other people, on other wards, they died. Fine. But that death [of a pregnant mother] is one which is somehow exceptional, because if you tell me a man on [male medical] died, a woman on [female medical] died, obviously they came and they were sick, indeed that's the reason they came to the point of being admitted. But pregnancy is not a sickness. Pregnancy is not an illness. We usually depend on the fact that this mother comes when she's pregnant, she gets her baby, and she returns home. . . . Therefore, it's—of course, I always feel bad. It's not nice. . . . You really think about a lot of things. You will think this, you'll think this, you'll think this. But enough, it has happened.

When I had first arrived on the maternity ward in February 2014, there was a spate of deaths that month. I felt as though I could barely process one death before another woman died. I was still trying to gather the information to reconstruct the trajectory of the first woman's demise when another woman would arrive and subsequently die. It seemed like a flood. However, the nurses only once ever publicly showed that they too were moved by the number of deaths on the ward and in fact sometimes deeply so. From my outsider's perspective, it more often appeared as though the nurses were barely touched by the deaths of women and even less so by the daily deaths of neonates. Aneth's description of the thoughts that would swirl around in her mind after a death proved otherwise and also came to be representative of one of the main coping mechanisms the nurses described to me.

But, before talking about coping, in interviews, the nurses and I discussed why it might look as if, from the outside, the nurses were unaffected by these deaths when, in actuality, they told me they were all pained by the deaths of women on the ward, as well as the deaths of the babies. Nurse Sokota, who always had a no-nonsense demeanor, told me, "A nurse shouldn't, you know, shouldn't be really sad, to the point that . . . it's not that . . . maybe you're not hurt. Really, you're hurting. I don't show a lot . . . [because] the women will say the nurse has started to cry tears on the ward, now you, you're not a nurse. You see?" While several of the nurses told me that sympathy and empathy were important, they emphasized how letting the women see them struggling with the pain of a death could undermine their professionalism and be demoralizing to the women.

Crying in front of patients could also close the distance between the women and their providers, an undesirable outcome that could, in future encounters, undermine the nurse's authority in the ward setting. While it may have appeared that the nurses were not compassionate, their accounts reveal that they were, in fact, engaging in difficult emotion work to suppress their sadness or personal distress in order to inspire patients' confidence in their technical nursing care by appearing stoic and businesslike; emotion work itself became an act of affective caring.

In thinking about care, if we separate technical care from the affective care work done by nurses and other health care providers, we do a disservice to them. Likewise, this separation collapses some of the complexity of working in a busy, underresourced maternity ward. The interconnectedness of these two elements profoundly challenges providers' decision-making when they encounter ethically difficult or morally uncertain situations. Overlooking this interconnection reduces our understanding of how they arrive in the domain of everyday ethics. In the aftermath of deaths, the nurses may not have adopted the affect some patients or onlookers would have expected or desired. But they were engaged in a different, locally and professionally appropriate form of affective care work shaped by their everyday ethics.

Nurse Peninah confirmed Sokota's thoughts about a nurse's appropriate emotional expression, elaborating:

> Therefore, yes, the patient, when you are sad, don't show her a lot, that sadness, to take her there. If she loses the desire and you, you lose the desire, there's nothing that can be done to help. Therefore, you reach a time a person just takes that. Honestly it hurts a lot. But now, this mother, let's not show her so much that even I am hurting [because] then she herself won't be able to cope [with the fact] that "my child has died, the nurse, too, she is sad," therefore you find there isn't any help. Therefore, a person should be hurt, but she stays there at that time to help that other person who is doing what? Who has the problem.

Instead, the nurses saved the outward manifestations of their inner distress for other venues and more domestic, as opposed to professional, spaces.

Just as Aneth mentioned, many of the other nurses explained that the deaths of women on the maternity ward were especially painful because pregnancy was not an illness that ought to lead to death; these deaths were more exceptional and less anticipated. Nurse Happy explained the effect of this on nurses' emotions, as well as how news of these deaths found its way into nurses' domestic spaces, where they might more openly mourn:

> Honestly, it's really painful. Because a pregnant mother, honestly—it's not good if she dies. Nor her baby. Because a pregnant mother isn't sick. It should be that a mother comes, and she leaves safely. Therefore, this death, it takes us by surprise. Honestly, I worked on [male medical ward], and there they were dying just normally. We say, "This man came with his illness, it wasn't possible [to heal], and he has died." But for a pregnant mother, it really hurts, it hurts a lot. It's painful for us, all of us nurses, because even if I wasn't on duty today, like today I'm resting at home, there [at the ward] if a death happens, I find that the news spreads, you're called on the phone, "Today we have a death!" So it surprises every person.

The deaths also took nurses by surprise because of the sometimes-sudden onset of complications and the woman's rapid demise, which differed from the chronic or slowly progressing conditions of patients on other wards.

While they clearly were affected personally by the deaths of women on the ward, the nurses found it important to maintain their professional comportment in front of the patient or, in the case of her death, in front of her family. The nurses saw their stoicism in the face of a tragedy as part of demonstrating to the patients that they were in control of the situation and that they could be relied on for continuing care. The good nurse suppressed her own feelings and any outward show of them until a more appropriate, private time. Still, Nurse Peninah explained how lingering thoughts about a death could impinge on daily activities, escaping from the neatly stacked mental boxes: "People have become used to it because every day—let's say, what have people gotten used to? That every day you encounter deaths? You see people have died, babies have died, but . . . [when] [the nurses] are sitting . . . alone, for example, there in the tea room, they start, 'Why did this baby die? This baby, why did he die?'" Nurses mentioned that this type of reflection on prior deaths most often occurred as they went about their daily activities. Likewise, it could follow them home as they continued to think on the events that had transpired and what they might have done differently. Through conversations, it slowly emerged that this type of reflection was the primary coping mechanism for many of the nurses.

Partly because of my own efforts to process the maternal and perinatal deaths all around me for over a year, in interviews I pointedly asked the nurses how they coped with seeing deaths on their ward or of the women under their care. I asked them what they did in order to not lose heart, so that they might continue to work with other women in the days, months, and years to come. I also wanted to learn if their experiences with a relatively high number of deaths caused them to ever question their line of work or their desire to continue working in maternity care. Nearly every nurse related at least one instance of a woman for whom she had been caring who had died and whose death had stayed with her.

As we sat together in overstuffed armchairs in her sitting room, while other women quietly passed through the room on bare feet, going into the kitchen or fetching Faraja's daughter, a young and perpetually cheerful Nurse Faraja became thoughtful and began to tell me in vivid detail, "I feel really bad, you can even cry." She said a woman could arrive on the ward in good condition, engaging and talkative, and then "She dies because she doesn't get blood, postpartum hemorrhage [PPH], or her condition just changes, it really hurts a lot." I gently murmured, encouraging Faraja to continue. "I remember there is one day when all the nurses that were on shift, we cried. One mother came, she was in the second stage. She was a grown woman, healthy. So, anyway, she was delivered, she pushed out the baby. I mean, in the act of just pushing the baby, she straightened out right there and died. And she had come talking a lot and, really, we remained there asking ourselves, 'What was this thing?'"

As we continued to talk, Faraja told me of a second woman whose death was not easy to forget. Faraja had herself given birth to her daughter around Easter in 2014. Faraja recounted the case of another mother whose child was nearly the same age now as her own: "It was her first pregnancy, she had come and stayed two days on the ward. The third day her contractions increased, and she gave birth to a baby girl who weighed 3.5 kilograms. After that, we were talking with her like normal. Now she got PPH, yeah, and there was no blood in the blood bank, no relatives [to donate]. Well, we were talking with her, and then she said, 'Nurse, I'm feeling tired.' She had been sitting drinking tea, so I told her to lie down. I say! That lying down, it was silence right away." Faraja paused to shake her head and, looking into the distance, past the softly waving curtain at the open front door, finished with "It hurt us so much and her baby was crying so much, like she knew her mother had died. So that was last year in March. Her baby is still there, she's called Enjoy and now she's learning how to walk." Unlike the deaths of women after a slower decline or after showing outward signs of chronic conditions, such as advanced AIDS, these deaths that stuck with Faraja were of women who had suddenly collapsed and rapidly descended into death, without time to help them.

In response to my question about how the nurses were able to return to work day after day when they faced these deaths, Nurse Rachel described how she had been the only experienced maternity nurse, assigned to night duty with several new graduates who had not yet learned to deal with obstetric complications. After stating that she always felt bad when she heard of a maternal death on the ward because of her own experience failing to save a woman, she began to tell me what had happened. She described the never-ending night shift, saying, "Honestly, I struggled with that mother from admission until she passed away, and it was during my shift [that she died]. Honestly, I lost the desire to work. I felt totally like I couldn't do work after that mother died. Then she died around the time of midnight, so I felt the work was really hard until it came to be 6:30 a.m. [end of night shift]." Sometimes even a nurse's commitment to professional comportment was barely enough to carry her through a shift; the case would follow her home, with the details swirling in her head as she second-guessed herself and all others involved. Nurse Rachel suggested that she might lose the motivation to work because she was preoccupied with the details of what had gone wrong, emotionally frustrated by the lack of information she had and the lack of ability to more effectively aid the woman and to save her life.

In their explanations, it is clear that these cases often stayed with the nurses and caused them to ruminate on the details of the woman's care and illness or the events leading up to her death. Many nurses explained that this was their coping mechanism for coming to terms with the deaths of women. The nurses consistently worked in this same environment that hobbled along as best it could. Most women, who did not have any complications, were able to give birth and leave the hospital without any adverse events; they received care that was *good enough*, and the system operated similarly. However, the cases of complex problems or emergencies exposed the ever-present fault lines and weaknesses of the maternity ward and resulted in deaths.

TO FOLLOW UP

The nurses nearly all told me that they had tried to *fuatilia*, or follow up, when they saw there had been a death. They mostly did this in the case of a stillbirth or neonatal death, but the nurses nearly all mentioned following up as something they did in the wake of any death. In talking about maternal deaths, Nurse Rachel said,

> Me, I always really try to do that follow-up, like what did I miss? What mistake did I make? What should I correct? Maybe for that mother, what should I have given her so that she didn't die? Like that day I was supposed to give her hydrocortisone but there wasn't any. I sent a person to the pharmacy but there wasn't any, but I was feeling that if I could give this mother hydrocortisone it would be able to support her. I mean, I really worried about all her treatment, but it wasn't possible [*imeshindikana*]. Therefore, another challenge for maternity is supplies. . . . It should have all the important medications and everything that has to do with care, I mean, we would at least be able to save lives.

One important linguistic note: in many of the original transcripts the nurses used the word *imeshindikana*, which I have translated as "it was not possible." However, this translation does not effectively capture the nuance and the sense of the original Swahili. In the original Swahili construction, the sentence does not indicate a subject or responsible entity. This is perhaps indicative of another move on the nurses' part to remove the locus of control from themselves and onto some external entity, be it chance, bad luck, the will of God, or some other force. I prefer to think that this turn of phrase reflects the general state of the system. In some of these narratives, it was not something such as luck that prevented the woman's life from being saved but instead the broken health care system itself that impeded her treatment and possible recovery, together with the bureaucratic, underresourced environment of the hospital. Rachel specifically mentioned that the poor availability of supplies had caused her to be unable to resuscitate the woman on her deathbed.[5]

Nurse Aneth, when talking about the deaths of babies, started by saying, "Mm, well here, really the thing to do is—you know, a lot of people, these questions that you're asking me, I don't think that my colleagues, how they answered you but I think a lot maybe have answered you theoretically. She just thinks, 'I can do—I can do—' but that thing, has she ever done it even once? The thing that you do, first, you follow up." She went on to give me an example of what she would do to try to make sure a woman got some answers about why her baby had died in utero, including suggesting testing for the woman and her partner. This explanation about following up was nearly universal for the nurses with whom I discussed this topic. Problematically, because most of the nurses were not included in the maternal death audit meetings, most often they did not even have the opportunity to go over the case of a woman's death with the physicians or their fellow nurses to compare their interpretations of the problems.

ACCESS TO INFORMATION

While the nurses were left ruminating on the deaths to which they may or may not have contributed, the physicians and administrators were holding maternal death audits every seven or eight months, including only a couple of nurses from the ward, and not returning a report of the results of the audit to the full ward staff. In the absence of answers or other mechanisms for discussing or debriefing cases of deaths, the nurses almost universally told me that their coping strategy was to go over the details of the cases alone, in their heads. In this context of little to no information about the details of women's cases or the results of the maternal audit meetings' analysis of these cases, it is easy to imagine how nurses could become demoralized and lose motivation as they continued to encounter the deaths of women and babies on a regular basis. Without the necessary information to confirm the ideas they had worked out in their mental walkthroughs of the cases, they were less able to act on their ideas for improving outcomes in similar cases, even if they had come up with practical and concrete ways to do so. Alternatively, without confirmation of their own culpability that might have been a result of the maternal death audit meeting discussions, the nurses may also have personally benefited from their lack of inclusion and information.

The poor communication back to the rank and file on the maternity ward after these audit meetings was another way in which the institutional environment of the hospital inhibited efforts to improve care and prevent maternal deaths. Nurses did not change their behaviors because the administration did not empower them with the necessary information to affirm their individual analyses of the problems that led to women's deaths, nor did the institution support single-handed efforts to change routinized practices, even those the hospital identified as inhibiting better care. The lack of communication in these cases also supports the idea that the hospital and regional health leaders were primarily using the maternal death audit meetings to fulfill biobureaucratic requirements and that they considered the purpose fulfilled when the paperwork was complete. This perspective created no expectation for actions beyond the bounds of the paperwork, which was why the information stopped at the administrative level. These results of the audit meetings were yet another example of how top-down, technical approaches to solving complex health service challenges were ineffective in this setting. Overall, the nurses expressed frustration with their lack of information, not just about maternal deaths, but also about institutional goals and policies of the hospital.

CARING FOR THE CARERS

In a meeting on respectful maternity care held in Dar es Salaam in July 2015, one of the presenters, Dr. Brenda D'Mello, talked about "caring for the carer." In a large hospital in Dar es Salaam, on the other side of the country from Mawingu Regional Hospital, she had been working to implement a program for the nurses on maternity to be able to discuss cases and express concerns, frustrations, and challenges within their environment, emphasizing "no shame, no blame, no name." Giving the nurses a formal mechanism for voicing their struggles with grief due to encountering deaths or due to working in high-pressure/high-volume work environments was one way in which Dr. D'Mello and her teams had been trying to grow hospital staff support programs. At Mawingu, as of the end of 2015, there were no such support mechanisms for the nurses and physicians working on the maternity ward. In the absence of formal avenues for coping with the stress of seeing women and babies die on a regular basis, combined with the under-resourced work environment and an overall poorly functioning health care system, the nurses often comforted themselves through narratives of hopeless cases, women arriving "already dead" from far-off villages. They comforted themselves by repeatedly examining the trajectory of a woman's care and subsequent death in the hospital, turning to narrative as a way of creating order and understanding around these tragic experiences.

It was not as though the hospital had to choose between either fulfilling bureaucratic reporting requirements *or* providing information to and supporting its nurses. But in the hospital-as-institution's everyday ethical calculations, as engaged in by its administrators, there were greater incentives for filling out the paperwork, or rather, there were greater disincentives for *not* fulfilling those duties. Consequently, the nurses' needs dropped out of sight. The hospital missed an opportunity to care for its employees as they continued to confront the deaths of both women and babies. The administrators could have improved communication to provide the nurses with reassurance that a death was not a direct result of their care or confirmed the nurses' individual assessments and responsibility regarding what had gone wrong. While the nurses sought to do what they could in the event of an obstetric emergency, the institutional forms of care—supplies, supportive supervision and mentoring, protective equipment, timely and responsive communication—all continued to be lacking, further demoralizing and demotivating the nurses, who were left with narrative as their primary coping mechanism.

BEYOND THE HOSPITAL WALLS

If the nurses had little control over what happened within their own ward and hospital, then what transpired in women's lives outside the hospital was entirely outside their sphere of influence. Yet, it always affected the nurses' work. When I made my first visit to Mawingu in 2012, it had not been my intention to study maternal mortality, and it had certainly not been the focus of my early pilot study the following year. However, in 2013 I came to fully realize it was the nurses and doctors who seemed to have stories they wanted and needed to tell. These stories were largely about their work environment, about the difficulties of working in a forgotten and long-ignored region, and about the inequities their patients struggled against on a daily basis. The stories were also about their own professional goals, aspirations, and ethical commitments. I was fortunate to find open-minded doctors and administrators who, instead of being threatened by my subsequent suggestions to research maternal death in their setting, saw in this research an opportunity to learn more about their own practices and improve care. The nurses, lower down the hierarchy, had had no similar say in granting me permission to conduct research on their ward and in their working lives. Instead, they initially accepted, in some cases begrudgingly, my presence as an imposition placed on them from the top.

My first days back on the ward in early 2014 included many conversations in which I tried to introduce my research while maintaining a neutral tone, emphasizing that I was not there to blame people or attempt to hold them in some way accountable for the deaths that continued to occur. I repeatedly told anyone who would listen that I was going to spend time at the hospital but also planned to go to villages to speak to women, community leaders, and rural health care workers. Some nurses gave satisfied nods upon hearing this part of the explanation, convinced that that was where I would find my answers. I still, more than five years later, distinctly remember Nurse Peninah bristling as I scuttled behind her on the ward, answering her demanding questions while she went about her work. She grumpily said, "You know, most of the problems are because those mothers, they stay there with the *mkunga wa jadi* [traditional birth attendant] there at home for a long time. They delay there at home until there is a big problem, and then, then they come here. They come with impending rupture of the uterus. You see, a large number of them, they die because of ruptured uterus." I nodded, not wanting to disagree but also not knowing if what she said was accurate, new as I was. She continued in the same accusatory tone, "If you say that it's mismanagement that is causing maternal deaths, *siwezi kukubali,* I can't agree!" I hurriedly spluttered, "No, no! That's why I am also going to villages, to talk to those *wakunga wa jadi* and to those working in the dispensaries and health centers, because they first see those women who are coming from home with problems!" Somewhat placated, she said, "Okay, then you will get good data."

Similarly, when I was applying for grants to fund this research, some reviewers and granting agencies suggested I needed to do more work in the community, focusing less on hospitals because these institutions were unlikely to be the main contributors to these maternal deaths. Truly, women's lives beyond the hospital walls deeply and indelibly influence their likelihood of survival during an obstetric emergency.[6] But it is also true that these same obstetric emergencies revealed the always-and-already present weaknesses in a biomedical system of care that was continually a bricolage. The ragged edges were hidden from sight for most women and their families because most births went smoothly. However, when a problem arose, it was easy to see the many pitfalls in the path to good health that threatened to swallow a woman whole.

Women's lives outside the hospital could either help them bridge the threatening gaps in the system or work synergistically with systemic scarcity to hasten their descent into death once they had arrived at the hospital. Early in my fieldwork, my good friend Japhet and I sat on the tiled steps of my newly rented little house in Sumbawanga Town. He charged me with an important task: "You will have to look, I know it will be the poor women and the ones from the village who will be dying the most. I'm sure of it," he said. A month or so later, I held a group discussion with women who attended the church Japhet and his family also frequented. I had only a few questions, and as the rain pelted down on the metal roof, threatening to drown out the voices of the women huddled together in the narrow seats of children's school benches, I listened to what they thought could cause a woman to die. I asked the women to each make a list, and one of the most commonly cited causes was "*Manesi kuangalia hali ya mtu mwenye pesa,*" the nurses look at the condition of people with money. Time and again, women were convinced that if they did not look as if they had money or did not know someone who worked at the hospital, the nurses would ignore them or forget them, a situation possibly leading to their death. In 2019 interviews with two of my longtime friends, both told of how they would have received worse treatment, or none at all, had they not had connections to hospital staff members.

In pointing to nurses' evaluations of patients based on perceived wealth or personal connections, the women were invoking the concept of stratified reproduction. Shellee Colen defines this concept: "Physical and social reproductive tasks are accomplished differentially according to inequalities that are based on hierarchies of class, race, ethnicity, gender, place in a global economy, and migration status and that are structured by social, economic, and political forces."[7] Colen goes on to say that stratified reproduction itself reproduces inequalities and differential access to material and social resources. For women giving birth at Mawingu, their lives before the hospital established these inequalities and converged with the nurses' treatment of them.[8] Nurses' calculated disbursal of care along perceived class or ethnic group lines, or on the basis of their judgments of who ought to be reproducing (often related to age and/or marital status and number of previous pregnancies), undeniably colored women's experiences of care, even when this differential treatment did not result in death or severe morbidity. Nurses themselves saw their employment status at the health facility as an important source of capital that, while not monetary, nevertheless enriched their kin and strengthened the nurse's position in her family and community. Surely, the nurses would argue that they did not favor some patients over others, but I saw this differential treatment many times, including abrupt changes in behavior as nurses finished with a woman who had arrived from a village and turned to assist a fellow nurse's relative. The difference in expressed compassion and level of cordiality was like night and day.

In the end, my research assistant, Rebeca, and I spent three months traveling to eleven different, randomly selected communities throughout the region in order to hear from women, their husbands, their community leaders, and their village health care workers. From nearly one hundred hours of conversations with hundreds of participants, the road to death for pregnant women in Rukwa began to become clear. To be sure, some women faced nearly insurmountable difficulties in obtaining transportation to health facilities or faced other delays in reaching care, so that they indeed arrived nearly dead. Others arrived early but uncertainly, scarred by previous bad interactions with the biomedical system and lacking the confidence to speak up about their needs.

Clearly, women did not arrive at Mawingu in a vacuum. Instead, before their arrival, they might have already been subjected to a number of factors that could predispose them to poor health and biomedical risk during pregnancy and the postpartum. Starting from a young age, girls might not have had equal access to education, might be married or might have gotten pregnant at a young age in order to meet the financial needs of their families (through bridewealth payments) or because they lacked other activities to fill their time, bore the largest burden of work in the family, and might not be involved in family decision making, in addition to sometimes being victims of intimate partner violence. The next chapter follows women's journeys in their communities as they grow, enter into marriage, become pregnant, and navigate their options for care. Their logics of risk and care drew on an ethics of interdependence and reciprocal care often unfulfilled in biomedical spaces.

The public health literature often attributes indirect causes of maternal death, as one article from 1985 states, "to the patient, the environment, cultural beliefs or to defects in the health services."[9,10] Within public health, the three-delays model continues to structure analyses of maternal death. This model cites three types of potential delays for receiving care during an obstetric emergency: (1) delay in deciding to seek appropriate medical help for an obstetric emergency; (2) delay in reaching an appropriate obstetric facility; and (3) delay in receiving adequate care once at a facility.[11] This model provided an underlying logic for clinicians, policy makers, and public health practitioners and continued to influence discussions of maternal mortality in Rukwa. Its pervasive influence was particularly apparent in discussions during maternal death audit meetings when providers had to decide when delays had occurred, with blanks on the form for each of Thaddeus and Maine's three delays. Both the broader public health literature and the health care workers with whom I worked often blamed women's decisions to seek care from a local midwife or other indigenous healing expert for delays in reaching biomedical health care services when an obstetric emergency was underway.

But the three-delays model significantly flattens women's experiences, disallowing many other variations and all the intermediate steps at which delays often occur, as well as nearly all the socioeconomic and structural factors that have shaped her life before and during her pregnancy. The model also does not incorporate any discussion of when or why a woman might *choose* to avoid a biomedical facility, assuming only that every woman would be best served if she could make it to a facility soon enough. While the regional hospital employees and administrators often appeared keen to concentrate on improving those items over which they had immediate control, they did acknowledge that many circumstances of a woman's life could predispose her to delays in seeking care or even reduce the likelihood that her body would be able to hold out against an obstetric emergency long enough for her to get effective treatment and recover. If a woman did not choose to immediately report to a biomedical facility, the health care providers and administrators often attributed this to ignorance, backward beliefs, or some other failing on the part of the woman and/or her family. What the audit meetings rarely discussed were women's previous interactions with biomedical care and how these might have convinced them to avoid their local facilities.

When women were able to access care in biomedical facilities, there was the potential for numerous other conflicts between local and global maternal health logics. Understaffed dispensaries, with providers concerned with sustaining their own families on low salaries and working in remote areas with little support, often led to poor quality of care and interactions in the care setting that left much to be desired. It is no surprise, then, that many women with economic means and the money for transportation sought to bypass their village facilities, or even the district hospitals, in favor of Mawingu Regional Hospital. In other cases, repeated encounters with poorly stocked facilities led women and their family members to suspect providers of corruption and extortion.

Against a background of complicated care pathways, poor infrastructure, lack of transparency, and corruption or negligence, which I discuss further in the next chapter, it may seem harder, at first glance, to discredit the nurses' narratives of women arriving at the regional hospital on the verge of death. However, the story is not this straightforward. This line of thinking has led to an anthropological research focus on communities and women's experiences in order to understand maternal death. In contrast, the nurses themselves, in their accounts of how they went over the details of cases in which a mother died on their shift, described how the hospital environment, interactions with other providers, and their own actions could contribute to a woman's death. Even in cases in which they were uncertain about the ultimate cause of a death, the nurses repeatedly searched for points of weakness, breakdowns in care within their own environment, not out in remote villages. However, when confronted with official prompts for auditing and accountability, the nurses and doctors preferred to fulfill bureaucratic requirements without drawing too much attention to their own culpability. In this way, they quietly resisted the new subject formation and self-disciplining that these global systems of auditing would require. In the more informal, private spaces of hospital break rooms, homes, or the corners of their own minds, the nurses and doctors searched, combing through their own (in)actions in search of causes of death.

Engaged in a personal ethic of care that accorded the nurse-patient relationship a quasi-sacred status, many of the nurses found it deeply disturbing when those in their care died. They held themselves accountable through their ruminations and lingering doubts about causes of death. The health care workers created yet another informal system of accountability that adhered to their morals and personal ethics of care and demanded answers about the deaths they witnessed. But when presented with formal modes of accountability, the health care workers often protected their own instead of "telling the truth" to its full extent on forms. These actions too were part of this local ethic of care, deeply shaped and patterned on existing social norms in Rukwa, and in Tanzania more generally. In the absence of other information, nurses formed and re-formed hypotheses and trajectories, hoping to create a better outcome in the future. Ultimately, self-preservation and the need to work another day to provide for themselves and care for their families, as well as for future pregnant women, led many of the nurses to quietly avoid engagement in meetings or audits that would name themselves or their colleagues as responsible parties in a woman's death. Instead, they bore these deaths as integral, but concealed, parts of their nursing identity. The official records kept at the hospital for years or sent on to the regional and national level condensed the high-stakes events upon which the nurses ruminated long after the fact. Incapable of containing and accurately representing the unknowns, uncertainty, messiness, concealments, fears, and hopes of a woman's care trajectory, the simplified story documented on forms and in files turned truncated representations of life into objective facts.[12] In the process, other true causes and contributors to maternal death in the hospital were allowed to remain hidden, just out of sight, beyond the bounds of official knowledge and fact.

8

"Pregnancy Is Poison"

The Road to Maternal Death

Within public health generally, and at Mawingu Hospital, maternal mortality has often been reduced causally to women coming from villages and lacking trained assistance, or to a lack of women's empowerment and vague attributions to harmful "culture." While I disagree with this reductionism—both biomedical and cultural—social relations, meanings of pregnancy and risk, and expectations for local midwives within communities did shape the strategies and decisions of pregnant women and their families. However, as many others have suggested within medical anthropology, some public health practitioners and policy makers use culturalist explanations of increased morbidity and mortality to deftly mask entrenched political economic forces, which are extraordinarily hard to address.[1] Likewise, culturalism often views culture as bounded, static, and homogenous.[2] In contrast to deep structural problems, perceived harmful, static cultural practices are easy to address through education campaigns, just as the maternal death audit action plans attempt to do. Both cultural and biomedical reductionism conceal a number of other important questions such as: What factors might cause a woman to arrive at Mawingu Regional Hospital "already dead"? What might lead her, through either choice or circumstance, to give birth with a local, nonbiomedical birth attendant? Are there really only three delays? The following story of Pieta involves more than the gaze of biomedicine can reveal. Her story complicates the dominant global health model of the three delays and its attendant logic of risk and care for pregnant women by showing the complexities of local logics of reproduction, care, and risk in pregnancy in Tanzania.

After Pieta's story, I present some of the underlying experiences, logics, and structural forces that shape women's lives before they arrive at Mawingu Regional Hospital pregnant or in the midst of an obstetric emergency in order to demonstrate how a woman might come to die at the hospital. Ultimately, women's previous interactions with biomedicine work to erode community members' trust in the health sector's ability to actually mitigate risk for pregnant women using an ethic of care that matches their desires.

PIETA'S MALPRESENTATION

At the end of the rainy season, as I navigated mud-slick roads with the windshield wipers on their highest setting, white knuckles gripping the steering wheel, on the way to Kizi village, the district ambulance sped by in the opposite direction, taking a patient to Namanyere District Hospital. When my research assistant, Rebeca, and I arrived in Kizi, we first went to the dispensary (figure 13) and, once we began talking with the staff members, discovered they had called the ambulance a couple of hours earlier. They had been trying to help a woman in labor since the middle of the night, around 3 a.m., when she had arrived from home complaining of problems. When the nurses had examined her, they found Pieta's baby was transverse and the baby's arm was the presenting part; she would need a C-section in order to give birth. She was twenty-five years old and pregnant with her third child. Pieta's relatives had taken her back home from the dispensary, refusing help from the nurses but asserting that her father-in-law would be able to "say some words" to resolve the social conflict in the family and the malpresentation, making it so she could give birth without an operation. They refused to let the nurses call the ambulance. Eventually, the nurses from the dispensary went with the village executive officer to her house and were able to convince the woman's family to bring her back to the dispensary again several hours later, now around 9 a.m., so they could finally call the ambulance. Though they wasted no time calling for the district's one ambulance, the car did not finally arrive until 1:30 p.m. because of the trip to another village and then back to Namanyere, the district seat and home to the district hospital, which was when we had passed it, and then back again to Kizi, many miles to the north of the district hospital.

While we were waiting for the ambulance to arrive, I looked in on Pieta and saw that she had a full bladder and that the nurses were trying to keep her hydrated with IV fluids. I asked if she had been able to urinate, and the nurses said no but that they did not have any catheters. At any rate, the baby was compressing the urethra, which would have made it difficult to insert a catheter even if they had had one. Pieta was confused, exhausted, and barely able to answer questions. She was also in pain and extremely uncomfortable as the baby's now-bluish arm protruded from her vagina. When the ambulance arrived, the dispensary nurses, and those who had arrived with the ambulance, loaded her into the back, along with two male relatives to donate blood, in case she would need it, and two of her female relatives. Her husband planned to go ahead on a motorcycle. As we waited for Pieta and the relatives to settle into the ambulance and for the nurses to hurriedly fill out a makeshift referral form, I spoke with her husband. He told me

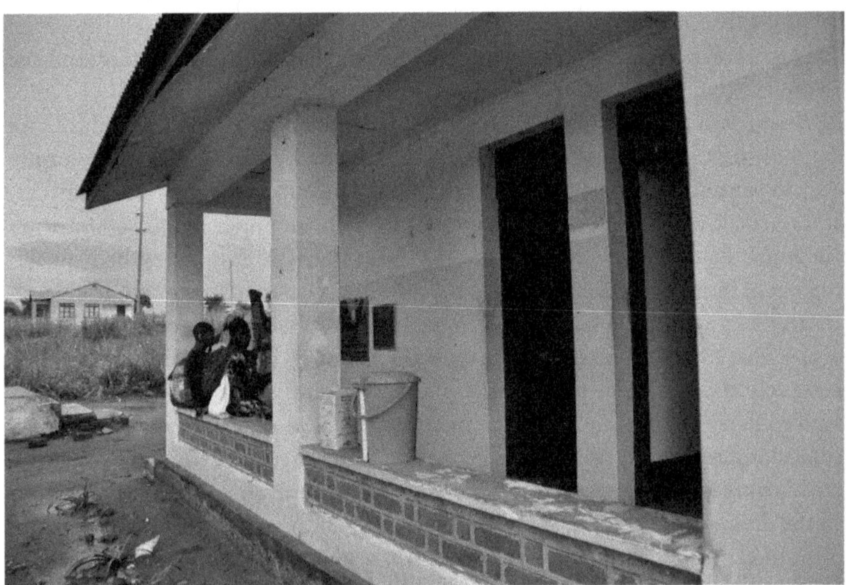

FIGURE 13. The exterior of Kizi dispensary. Photo by author, 2015.

that Pieta herself had asked to go back home, refusing to let them call the ambulance. When I pressed for further details about the family problems the nurses had mentioned, he was noncommittal and vague. After they left in the ambulance, I talked with the nurses about the situation again, and they accused Pieta of lying about when her contractions had started. They were saying that maybe this lying was because Pieta had planned to give birth at home and did not want the nurses to know she had been in labor for some time already before arriving at the dispensary. The nurses told us that it was not uncommon in their village for women to report having had fewer pregnancies so that they would not be told to give birth at the district hospital.[3] People in Kizi believed any referral to the hospital meant the woman would have a C-section.

Before returning to Sumbawanga Town that evening, Rebeca and I stopped at the district hospital in Namanyere to see Pieta. She had had a C-section, and she'd had a baby boy, weighing 3.0 kilograms, but he was stillborn. She also had received a blood transfusion, and drugs were in such short supply in the hospital that she and her relatives were told she had to buy them, but they had not brought enough money. In the end, the family's financial circumstance forced them to go to the district nursing officer herself to request the money for her medications (facilitated by the hospital), which was exactly what many people in the surrounding communities feared when they were told to go to a hospital for surgery—having to spend money on supplies or medications. Pieta also told me multiple times that she was glad we had been there because she felt that the nurses at the dispensary *walinishangaa tu* (they were just shocked by me). She told me she felt the nurses had not known what to do with her case, and she said she had been confused and so tired.

Despite what Pieta thought, the nurses had known the proper procedures, for the most part, but, again, circumstances brought on by a lack of supplies (a catheter, for example) and only one district ambulance forced delays in Pieta's care and referral. Faced with caring for a patient with a complicated case and without immediate referral support, the nurses at the Kizi dispensary had quickly run out of the techniques with which they were familiar and, in the end, could only watch Pieta, which she had perceived as the nurses being shocked by her condition. Pieta's case illustrated many of the ways in which community and biomedical perspectives could come into conflict; she was just one woman of many who experienced delays during an obstetric emergency because of complex interactions of clinical, social, and infrastructural factors. When we received women like Pieta at the Mawingu Hospital maternity ward in town, we rarely saw, or even heard about, all the events preceding the woman's arrival, but all these events, and the woman's prior life, indelibly influenced her decisions, conceptions of risk (biomedical and social), and, ultimately, whether she (and her baby) lived or died. While most women and health care providers with whom I spoke did not necessarily view pregnancy as an illness, it was an inherently risky time in a woman's life. Following a spate of maternal deaths at the regional hospital, one nurse said, "Who said pregnancy is not an illness? Pregnancy is poison!"

However, the global public health constructions of the problem of maternal mortality have been built on logics of risk and care that sometimes differ from the logics that circulate and guide actions and practices within communities. These logics, and how they portray women, have likewise shifted since the inception of the Safe Motherhood Initiative.[4] The World Health Organization's recommendations, which permeate policy making at national and local levels, are based in a particular version of the world in which pregnant women *have the potential* to be agentive, rational neoliberal subjects who, with the right amount of information and health education, will make choices during pregnancy and while giving birth that will help them to be healthy and safe. This neoliberal subjectivity then becomes another linchpin in the global health community's quest to continue reducing maternal deaths,[5] and it is embodied locally in Tanzania in the discourse around *maendeleo* or development, which extends to responsible, "modern" personhood, including appropriate, effective, and timely use of biomedicine.[6] An underlying premise here often seems to be that women can become these ideal actors when they overcome their culture, a vague barrier to realizing women's empowerment, gender equality, and ideal use of biomedical institutions. However, these logics of risk, care, and neoliberal subjectivity differ, sometimes drastically, from the gendered, social logics operating within communities that work to guide and influence women and their larger networks through more complex decisions related to care, medical pluralism, and the sociality involved in reproduction.

PATHWAYS TO DEATH

To arrive at Pieta's point, a crisis situation that culminated in the death of her baby and an expensive surgery, women first walked a long road extending back into their childhoods and adolescence.

One global effort, reflected in the SDGs and MDGs, to increase women's empowerment centers on improving girls' access to education.[7] Several studies show that education for girls, even just through the completion of primary school, is a predictor of lower maternal mortality levels.[8] It is not so much the book knowledge girls gain in school as "the knowledge to demand and seek proper healthcare,"[9] through more general empowerment, confidence, and skills needed to navigate information or bureaucratic systems. Women who have been to school may also have access to better employment or income-generating activities in both the formal and informal sectors, which can strengthen their position within their families.[10] Studies have found that health messaging and education alone increase women's knowledge of health problems during pregnancy but are not capable of fundamentally changing women's social environment during pregnancy.[11] This finding suggests there are other structural factors affecting women's "social environments," for which education is not the answer. Globally, more and more girls are entering and staying in school, sometimes even surpassing the number of boys enrolled. However, in Rukwa, many girls ended their education when they were in their early teens. Others, because of the poor quality of instruction, completed primary school but were functionally illiterate.

Though primary school became free to all Tanzanian students starting in 2011, it was not until the very end of 2015 that the government abolished all fees for the lower levels of secondary school, the Ordinary ("O") Levels.[12] At the time of my fieldwork in Rukwa, all children who passed the primary school exams were allowed to continue their schooling, but only those who did very well received low-cost spots in government schools. This meant that many children ended their educational journey after primary school, at around thirteen to fifteen years old. Parents insisted they would educate both their male and female children, but when I pressed them to choose between a son and daughter if they had the resources to educate only one, many people responded they would send their son for further education. Community members said this was because they were concerned a girl would get pregnant while in school. However, this choice was predicated more on economic calculus, in most cases, than on lingering beliefs that it was better to educate boys; in fact, many parents suggested daughters were more likely to take care of their families if they succeeded economically, thereby making them better long-term investments, so long as they escaped early pregnancy.

Despite increasing access to secondary school education by abolishing fees, the Tanzanian state falls short of policies that would support gender equity, or even equality, in education. In June 2017, Tanzanian president John Magufuli announced at a rally that girls who got pregnant while still in school would never be allowed to return, citing them as "bad moral influences" who would teach other girls how to become pregnant.[13] Though the law enabling expulsion of pregnant schoolgirls under "offences against morality" passed in 2002, many teachers allowed girls to continue their studies after giving birth.[14] Now that future for girls is even less certain.[15]

There were few options for a girl who stopped her education after primary school. In Songambele village, as well as many others, parents told us there were no formal mechanisms for teaching sex education. There had, at one point, been rituals surrounding adolescence and marriage that included an element of sex education, but the Wafipa in the villages I visited no longer observed these practices. No other institutions, such as the clinics or schools, had yet picked up this slack in a way that reached a wide population, and the result was young people, out of school but unready to settle down to a life of backbreaking farm work, who sought out amusement in the company of the opposite sex with little knowledge of safe sex practices or how to prevent pregnancy. As Augustina in Songambele told my research assistant, Rebeca, and me, "You find like that ability to take her to another school, you don't have, so she just stays at home, and the results are that she gets married. I mean, she doesn't have anything else to do. Therefore, even if you forbid her, it just is that way, or she gives birth at home [unmarried]."

One of the first things I had noticed at Mawingu Hospital in 2012 was the high number of very young girls giving birth at the facility. At that time, I had asked Dr. Charles if, from his observations women in the region commonly gave birth at a young age. He confirmed, "Yes, even me, I was surprised to see such young girls here. I even once saw a twelve-year-old, you can't believe. Yes, there are young girls coming here to give birth in this region. More than other places." Clinically, girls who have not finished growing have a higher chance of developing severe complications, such as cephalopelvic disproportion, necessitating surgical birth.

These unintended, early pregnancies also put young women in a more socially precarious position. For example, one young woman whose case I followed at Mawingu came to give birth, only to discover she had a phantom pregnancy.[16] Instead of waiting for further test results or counseling, she absconded from the ward without discharge. When Dr. Charles and I had spoken to her, she told us her family had been unhappy with the news of her pregnancy and that conflict had ensued between her family and that of the man who had gotten her pregnant. They had only resolved the dispute when he agreed to pay bridewealth and marry her, solidifying his obligations to the woman and ensuring that the baby would be counted as part of his family. Now, in light of the nonexistent pregnancy, her status was once again uncertain. This uncertain social position could also severely limit the support a woman would have available should she develop a complication during her pregnancy, or while giving birth, and need financial resources. In describing the effects of early marriage and pregnancy on families, another woman from Songambele explained, "Really, this has a lot of effects because your child, if she gets a child, okay, it's your grandchild, but both are children and the burden of raising them is yours, as the mother, because a time will come when she will be defeated by life there where she has gone [to the father of the baby] and she will return home." In this case, if a young woman returned to her parents, she might be unable to draw on the baby's father's family for financial or other support, particularly for needs requiring cash, such as health care services.

Tanzania has a law forbidding marriage for anyone under the age of eighteen, but poverty and a lack of other options for their children often pressure parents into accepting or demanding an early marriage so they can collect the bridewealth payment. After our group discussion in Songambele, the village chairman's wife Susanna pulled my research assistant aside, entreating Rebeca to talk to her husband on her behalf because he had agreed to the marriage of their fourteen-year-old daughter as a second wife to a much older man who had impregnated her. In desperation, Susanna had gone to the man's house, breaking the lock on his door, to physically remove her daughter from the situation. There was a court case underway because the man had accused Susanna of destruction of property. Legal recourse against the older man and prospective husband was, however, out of the question; Susanna's husband refused to bring charges against the man because he had already paid for the marriage. While on paper the Tanzanian state protects minors from early marriage, once again the lives and structural constraints on the ground reflected a different reality, one that continued to endanger girls through early childbearing.

BRIDEWEALTH, MARRIAGE, AND DECISION-MAKING

Once a woman of any age enters a marriage, bridewealth, gender dynamics, and household work all affect her health, her decision-making autonomy, and, subsequently, her ability to get lifesaving care at a health facility in the event of an obstetric emergency. Bridewealth is a long-standing institution in many parts of sub-Saharan Africa and includes the exchange of goods between the groom's family and the bride's family. Here the flow of goods is opposite to that in a dowry, when the bride's family must pay the groom's family. For most ethnic groups in Tanzania, bridewealth is paid in cattle or smaller livestock, such as goats or even chickens. Currently, many families will also accept the cash equivalent of the livestock in lieu of the animals themselves. In patrilineal groups like the Wafipa, and the Wasukuma, who make up a sizable minority population in some villages in Rukwa, the woman joins the groom's family. A man in Kizi village during our group discussion explained, "I should just say, you know the basis of the difficulty is that you find you have educated your daughter, she has gone there and gotten married. Now the motive is always bridewealth, I mean that is the problem because, for example, a Sukuma, he always gives really a lot of cows. Now, he is believing that 'her, I have bought her.'" The other men in the room listened attentively, waiting for him to finish, "I mean, it would always be just like a person is giving [bridewealth] like a gift. But the question of this bridewealth, it makes people feel like they have bought other people, again like me, maybe I take ten cows to [my in-laws], then today you [my wife] have done something at your home place without asking me, weee! It will all erode! [i.e., the marriage relationship will break down]." Several of the men in the room chuckled or nodded, acknowledging that this sometimes happens. Another, though, spoke up thoughtfully: "You know, we Africans, the question of giving bridewealth, there is something there in between. First, it brings a good relationship between two sides, then it brings respect" to the man because he can say he officially married a woman and had the financial resources to do so. The men noted that if a man chose to abuse the covenant of bridewealth, used to establish this goodwill between families, he could wield it as a weapon to punish his wife and limit her freedom or autonomy, keeping her in a subordinate position in the family.

From speaking to men in Kizi and other communities, it became clear that women whose families had received a large bridewealth payment were not supposed to disobey their husbands or, in fact, contribute much to any sort of decision-making in the extended household. These large bridewealth payments were more common among the Wasukuma people, who paid sometimes ten times as much in bridewealth as the Wafipa. One Sukuma man said, "I mean, if I give a bridewealth for a light-skinned girl, I mean it can be sixty or forty cows. Therefore, she must submit to me a great deal because you have given for her a large bridewealth." This mode of thinking had ramifications for health care, particularly for pregnant women, because their position in their marital home could make it difficult, or impossible, for them to choose when to seek biomedical (or other forms) of care during their pregnancy or at the time of giving birth. Yet although this was ostensibly a cultural norm and seemingly monolithic, the practices varied widely depending on individuals and their choices about how to interact with the institution of bridewealth.

When women could not voice their need or desire to access biomedical services because they were not the primary decision makers and were subordinate to men who felt they "owned" them, they could suffer from life-threatening delays, reaching Mawingu Hospital, for example, only in time to die on the hospital's doorstep. In Mkamba village, a Sukuma man told me that even if there was an emergency in the family, a Sukuma woman would not sell a cow, or anything else, to raise money for emergency transportation to medical care. Instead, she would have to wait for her husband or other male relative to carry out those procedures, thereby possibly resulting in delays.

Among the Wafipa, there was not as much consensus on these issues of bridewealth, and men generally put forth a range of thoughts on the topic of women's roles in the family, some saying they involved their wives in decisions. In Songambele village, women said that men often refused to listen to their opinions or input because men feared that listening or submitting to women would make them look weak or seem as if they had allowed themselves to be dominated by a woman, which was socially undesirable. One woman said, "They will always say this, men, I mean, [they say], 'Me, I should give bridewealth, then you make yourself to answer me, isn't it that I have married you?'" In Swahili, men marry (*kuoa*) and women are married (*kuolewa*). For women, it is always a passive verb and for men it is an active verb, which was reflective of how many men saw their roles. They often used this linguistic difference to remind their wives that they, as the husband, were in charge. Therefore, these dynamics, influenced by bridewealth and socially constructed gender roles, also contributed to what men were willing to do and to what degree women were able to make decisions, particularly about their own health care needs.

In Kalumbaleza village, the topic of decision-making came up directly in relation to health education, pregnancy, and the prenatal clinic. One of the health care providers in the village had told me that he was frustrated because he often advised women to plan ahead in order to give birth at Mawingu Hospital, for example if they were in their first pregnancy, were very young, were very short, or had had many previous pregnancies, all risk factors for various complications. I asked women in a focus group why they might not be able to follow the advice of the clinician if he instructed them to give birth in a larger hospital. One woman responded: "Because men, if they were attending the antenatal clinic, they would know a lot of things. But now, because they don't attend, that's the reason they don't know that there is an importance to going to give birth in Sumbawanga. If you tell them, they become argumentative. For example, if you leave the clinic, if you tell him, your husband, that you are supposed to go to give birth in town, he doesn't understand you at all. Now, as a woman, you don't have any way out, you just have to stay quiet." Here, in these villages, if a woman did not have any access to cash herself, there were few options for her to arrange for travel to the hospital in Sumbawanga or even to the relatively nearby health center. She was often dependent on her husband for the financial resources, as well as, in some cases, for permission to travel. Because men did not attend the prenatal clinics with their wives, they did not learn about danger signs in pregnancy or the reasons why the dispensary workers might refer a woman to a higher level of care. Instead, they might assume their partners were simply angling for a trip to town or that they preferred to not give birth in the small, underresourced dispensary.

The nurses at Mawingu tended to be from families of higher socioeconomic status than the farming communities in these outlying villages. However, they were not very far removed, in many cases, and several had come from families in the region. This meant the nurses were, on the whole, familiar with what women's lives might look like before they arrived at the hospital. It was easy, then, to point to many of these other social issues, particularly those widely perceived to be due to "backwards thinking" or a lack of education, as the cause of a woman's late arrival and precipitous death at the hospital.

PRONATALISM AND THE VALUE OF REPRODUCTION

Once married, couples face a strong social imperative to reproduce. While women in more urban areas in Tanzania appear to be verbalizing a desire for smaller family sizes, women in rural areas often still express a desire for larger families, for a number of reasons.[17] One of these reasons is simply the fact that under-five mortality is still quite high in the country,[18] and many families expect to lose at least one child. Having children solidifies a woman's place in her marriage and in her husband's family, and being unable to conceive, regardless of which member of the couple might be the source of the infertility, often results in social precarity for women.

Gender relations in Rukwa highly influenced the extent to which women were able to contribute to choices about birth spacing, family size, and family planning. A woman told me that while she, as the wife, might prefer to stop having more children, her husband did not know about the potential dangers of having many children and simply saw a large family as an expression of his masculinity and a societal ideal. In every focus group discussion in communities, women complained that their husbands did not support them through the difficulties or complications associated with using various forms of contraception. Women often felt alone in shouldering the burden of limiting family size. In this context, I asked men in Songambele village about family planning and who decided when or how many children to have. One participant told me, "This decision takes place between the husband and wife. Now, a problem, you find, inside the home, a wife can say, 'Let's use family planning' and instead that is her strategy to find a lot of men. . . . She starts to annoy me, saying that that family planning is a really good idea. But many [women] use it for another purpose." If there was this lack of trust between the woman and her partner, it became exceptionally difficult for her to negotiate the use of contraceptives to space pregnancies or to limit the number of children she and her husband would have. While this man from Songambele started out by making it sound as though the man and woman both had equal say, an inherent suspicion about women being unfaithful colored his view of contraception. Such opposition could lead to maternal depletion and increased danger of developing severe obstetric complications if a wife were to carry more than five pregnancies.

GENDERED CARE AND WORK DURING PREGNANCY

Children, especially girls, are often a great asset to their families when it comes to additional labor. Early contribution to the household economy persists and only intensifies throughout a woman's life. In many societies, women bear a "double burden": they are responsible for household work as well as a large amount of agricultural labor.[19] Historically, women played an important part in agricultural cultivation of key crops that were essential for the family's survival.[20] Colonialism changed the gendered structure of labor in ways that largely excluded women from involvement with cash crops, relegating them to kitchen gardens for domestic use. This gendered involvement in cash crop production had a substantial impact on women because many households did not pool money and other resources; women could no longer bring in equal resources as subsistence farming lost its value in the colonial, capitalist economy.[21] Men began to occupy the position of economic providers for the family, an arrangement that followed models imported by colonial rulers from their own countries and largely continues in Tanzania to the present day. In communities in Rukwa, many men related a common narrative about economic provision as care for their families and their wives and as a man's primary role in the family. Women, on the other hand, engaged in large amounts of domestic labor without being exempt from agricultural labor needed to sustain their families.

As becomes immediately obvious, while women do incredible amounts of work, very little of it takes place in the formal economy. Women in rural areas have very little leisure time and are often unable to rest, even when they are pregnant, because of their responsibilities. What also becomes clear is that the labor and economic contributions of women often go overlooked, even by their husbands: "Partly because so much of their outside labor is unpaid and therefore 'invisible,' women are rarely relieved of any of their housekeeping duties by their menfolk,"[22] a pattern as true today as in 1989, when the WHO published the report quoted. Many women, over the course of my time in Tanzania, have told me that ideally they would reduce their workloads during pregnancy, but only some women had the resources, social or otherwise, to be able to do this.

Once, while on a supervision visit to communities in the Nkasi district, we were riding in the car past people coming back from the fields. One of the district health administrators commented that you always see women with water or firewood on their heads, babies on their backs, a hoe in one hand, maize in the other, and another baby growing in their belly. And the men are walking behind the women, maybe with a couple of ears of corn or a hoe. She said that women were like the donkeys of the community, doing all of the heavy lifting (figure 14).

Women often told me that even during pregnancy, if they expressed a need for help with their work, their husbands simply said, "What, are your hands pregnant that you can't work?" A woman in Songambele described women's typical daily tasks and their husbands' contributions: "If you wake up, you sweep, you wash dishes, you cook. Another time there's no firewood, so you go to collect firewood.

FIGURE 14. Women carrying firewood and water. Photo by author, 2015.

You go to the field, and there you are pregnant and there you have a baby on your back, and if you tell your husband, he tells you, 'What, is the pregnancy in your hands?' Even to sleep at night, he says, 'Let's sleep together,' and there he doesn't care if you are tired. Honestly, the work exceeds us, women from here." Women overwhelmingly explained that men did not help with domestic tasks even if they, the women, were sick or pregnant. Instead, it was most often other women who would help a pregnant neighbor or relative in a communal sharing of tasks. Women could also rely on this help only if they maintained good social relations within their community and were not, for example, from outside the area or from a minority ethnic group.

Men viewed their own roles as the family providers. While frequently it was only men who were to be found with the leisure time to hang about playing cards, checkers, or the board game *bao* under shady trees in the afternoon, or drinking and taking meals in bars, men described how a husband was responsible for always searching for the materials or money needed to meet his family's needs. Ultimately, this searching, the man's role as the "finder," was a key responsibility in caring for the family despite the more nebulous form of this work.

The gendered logics at play in the communities did not cleanly map onto the policies laid out by top-down approaches to interventions aiming to involve men in women's health. Global trends, taken up by the Tanzanian government and enacted by local village leaders and NGOs, often drove policies recommending (or mandating) that men attend prenatal visits with their partners, sometimes even causing dispensary workers to fine women or turn them away if they arrived for care unaccompanied. These types of mandates overlooked how men, to different extents and with vastly differing levels of enthusiasm, were already engaging with their partners' pregnancies and health through other, less obvious tasks. These tasks were, nonetheless, socially valued masculine tasks, deviations from which (such as early adoption of other, externally imposed activities) were socially sanctioned. One man, George, in Kizi village explained why a man might not engage in the same tasks as his wife: "Another time you can find that a man, he wants to help his wife. Now, other people, if they pass by, they say he has been ruled by [*tawaliwa*] his wife, so to remove that, the man he decides to change because he is afraid they will tell him he is being ruled by his wife. So then even if his wife gets sick, he says she has done it to herself and says, 'Get up, cook,' just so to protect against what's being said on the street."

After George had finished speaking, Boniface presented a slightly different picture of what some men in the community might do when their wives were pregnant:

> I think when we say the question of helping our wives, it's not necessary that you carry a bucket of water on your head [like a woman], you can even borrow a bicycle from your neighbor and go to fetch water. Cook a little *ugali*, you and the two children, you just stir it around a couple times, you all eat it, and you give some to your wife. Because when women are in that state, they always want to see their children, they want their family to be close. Because that pregnancy, they share with each other, it's of both of them, so therefore it's necessary that the husband also should be pained, he should think about how his wife will give birth, why should she suffer with work while he is there?

In this conversation, men elucidated a number of ways in which they sought to care for their wives, though they did not explicitly use this term. In Mkamba village, the community leaders, primarily men, also described how they would enlist their female relatives to help their wives with household tasks during pregnancy, clearly presenting this as a form of caring for their wives. Men sought to engage in this care in gender-specific ways that would be accepted by the broader community.

In other situations, too, men did not want to be seen to be doing so-called women's work. In Songambele, we were told that some men would accompany their wife to the dispensary when she was in labor only if it was during the night. Slightly surprised by this, I asked for further explanation, thinking it might be due to fears of more danger at night. No, in fact, I was told that it was because men were embarrassed to be seen because it was not considered "manly" to go with one's wife when she was in labor. Pregnancy was still very much women's business. Instead, many men preferred to find a female relative to accompany their wife to the health facility when her contractions began, and the men might follow along later. Men, however, as the "finders," were nearly always responsible for securing transportation when their wives needed to go to a health facility or received a referral to another level of care. Procuring transportation might include selling family assets, collecting contributions from neighbors and relatives, or negotiating to use a car on credit. Poverty could make these processes painstakingly slow, exacerbating delays and threatening a woman's life even further. These complicated, gendered interactions and negotiations surrounding care seeking often determined where a woman gave birth and how quickly she reached care during an emergency. Sometimes, because of delays in marshaling resources, precipitous labor, or maybe her husband's refusal to accompany her to a health facility, a woman gave birth at home with the help of a local midwife or *mkunga wa jadi*.

LOCAL MIDWIVES AND PREGNANCY

Speaking in Kifipa, a wizened old woman surely at least in her eighties, Bibi Mbalazi, spoke slowly and with authority, explaining, "Me, I always know, by looking at the umbilical cord, that this mother, she was bound by some person so that she would die from her pregnancy. You find the umbilical cord has already been tied, tied like this, but God helped her, and the midwife delivers her safely." I had asked her about the rumors I had heard about powers traditional midwives had had in the past either to use witchcraft to bind women to them or to detect the malicious intentions of others toward a pregnant woman. In this case, Bibi Mbalazi explained, the knotted umbilical cord could be evidence of witchcraft. The rest of the room was silent until one of the other women translated the response into Swahili for me. After this, Bibi Mbalazi resumed, telling me how, in the past, women had brought gifts of flour and beans to their midwife, entering into a contract with her to deliver the baby when the time came. But sometimes a woman would end up going to a different midwife for the birth and then not pay or not finish paying the original one. Then, Bibi Mbalazi said, the two midwives might fight over the right to deliver the woman, and the midwife who felt cheated of payment might interfere with the birth through witchcraft and harm the woman or her baby, thereby corrupting the goals and reputation of midwifery. She continued: "People are fighting over the mother, therefore they are doing everything top to bottom [in their power], so she doesn't give birth, [thinking] 'For this one, [I will do this] so she knows to come to my place.' Therefore, another time, there is a death of a pregnant mother or even one midwife among them." Women and local midwives all used to know who would help the woman give birth, entering into a relationship with that person early on. These relationships no longer existed with the local midwives and often were not possible with biomedical health care workers. Such contemporary distancing between pregnant mother and (biomedical) midwife might reduce the potential for jealousy and witchcraft, but it also limited the social embeddedness of giving birth. Unlike the *mkunga wa jadi*, who could diagnose malevolent witchcraft intentions by looking at an umbilical cord, biomedical nurses tended to operate in a different world. Though often products of a similar environment, nurses, through training and practice, came to inhabit a slightly different ontological world, in which knotted umbilical cords held biomedical meaning first, before becoming signifiers of witchcraft.

Though local midwives, who conduct deliveries at women's homes, continue to practice in many communities, most women, particularly younger ones, now express a desire to give birth in biomedical facilities. In ten out of the eleven villages in which I conducted focus group discussions, women stated it was now more common to give birth in the village dispensary or another biomedical facility than to use the services of a local midwife at home. Strictly speaking, in these communities local midwives did not provide any care for women before the time of labor and delivery, in the past or present.

These *wakunga wa jadi,* called traditional birth attendants or TBAs in public health literature, often fill gaps in the biomedical system. In the maternal death audit meetings and other biomedical spaces, administrators often blamed TBAs for delaying women's arrival at a biomedical facility. They imagined that these TBAs detained women in their homes, allowing them to labor for long hours before referring them to facilities. Likewise, in the biomedical imagination in Rukwa, administrators and providers, drawing on culturalist reasoning, often envisioned women seeking out TBAs, actively avoiding facilities out of *imani potofu,* or backward beliefs. However, this is much too straightforward an explanation for how women sought to patch together care when they went into labor early, or in the middle of the night, when in the fields farming, or when their husbands or other relatives were far away. *Wakunga wa jadi* stepped into these gaps and assisted women, often in ways women found to be more comforting and supportive than in hospitals, though both women and the *wakunga* themselves acknowledged it was preferable to go to a facility where emergency care was available. Most commonly, women and *wakunga* gave the example of blood transfusion and IV fluids or oxytocin to augment labor as care that was unavailable at home but could be lifesaving and desirable. Often, if a woman gave birth at home with an *mkunga wa jadi* it was because she lacked the resources or transportation to go to a biomedical facility.

As biomedicine continues to reach into ever-further corners of the world, biomedical knowledge has become the proverbial gold standard in many locations. However, the arrival of biomedicine did not preclude the continued utilization of alternative forms of healing or health care. The ongoing presence of coexisting systems proved time and again to be at the root of contestations over "truth" and "lies" on the maternity ward, as when nurses accused women of killing their babies by drinking local herbal medicines or using other nonbiomedical treatments. Nurses might look down on a woman as being uneducated and "from the village," in a derogatory sense if they thought she was resisting biomedical interventions, authority, or methods. By extension, biomedical health care workers largely scoffed at the methods and knowledge of "traditional" healers and birth attendants, at least in public settings.[23] At their heart, these were contestations related to power and authoritative knowledge within the walls of the regional hospital. As certain ways of knowing, and the attendant practices, are discounted, others gain ascendance and are thereafter sustained and reproduced.[24] The WHO and the Safe Motherhood's shifting targets and priorities throughout the 1980s and 1990s also helped to create and perpetuate the power of biomedicine in many low-resource settings, as these organizations and programs first created the category of "traditional birth attendants,"[25] invested in training them, and then reversed course, recommending only "skilled" (as these women were not) attendants at birth in biomedical facilities.

In Lowe village the *wakunga wa jadi* informed me that they were practicing more than they had in the past because the village had recently chased out one of the government dispensary nurses and because the other providers had been away for some time. Villagers reported that this nurse had allowed women to give birth unattended, alone on the dispensary doorstep in the middle of the night. In an act of resistance, and in an effort to demand the health care services that they felt were their right, the community finally reported one of the nurses and kicked her out of the village after people died on account of her negligence. In the absence of biomedical providers, women had once again turned to *wakunga wa jadi* for care. The most senior *mkunga wa jadi*, Bibi Mbalazi, was able to describe, in detail, how she would deal with various obstetric complications. Her level of skill and knowledge surpassed that of many so-called skilled personnel employed in village dispensaries. She reported that she had never once lost a woman to complications. Traditional midwives throughout the region told me younger women were not interested in learning more about the practice and were not entering this line of work. Even though women with whom I spoke were expressing stronger and stronger preferences for biomedical care, this preference was also shaped by the foreclosing of alternatives.

Many villages in Rukwa had implemented a system of fines for women who gave birth someplace other than in a biomedical facility. One man in Ngorotwa village explained, "Also you find other [women] who give birth at home, then even they don't go to the facility. Her outcome, if she gets problems, is a challenge, and others are afraid to go [after giving birth at home] because they are afraid of the 10,000 shilling fine [for giving birth at home]." This fine is yet another example of biobureaucracy, meant to curb what is constructed as the deviant, dangerous, or abnormal use of the *wakunga wa jadi*, regardless of the circumstances surrounding the need to resort to nonbiomedical assistance or a woman's prior plans to do otherwise. Instead of encouraging the use of biomedicine, the fine became, for the poorest women, a structural impediment to achieving biomedical care. Knowing she did not have cash to pay the fine, a woman who was unable to reach a facility delayed visiting the facility even if she experienced a postpartum complication or wanted to have her newborn checked and given vaccines.[26] Such bureaucratic technologies do not prevent "culture" from leading women to TBAs but instead further entrench existing inequalities in access to care. To avoid these fines, and in order to be ensured service in the future when they took their newborn to the dispensary for vaccines or when women later sought contraceptive advice, many women allowed themselves to be integrated into the biomedical system. In fact, this integration was inevitable if women wanted other care or benefits in the future, such as the legitimacy provided by documents like a child's clinic card or the paperwork necessary for a birth certificate application.

The people in the Rukwa region were still widely relying on the *wakunga wa jadi* until relatively recently because of the slow development of health care services and facilities in the region. Sometimes women would go first to their local *mkunga wa jadi* before heading to a biomedical facility because there were certain aspects of care that the biomedical system could not provide. For example, as in Pieta's story that opened this chapter, sometimes people believed that prolonged labor was caused by social problems within the family and that biomedical personnel could not address those causes.

In other instances, the *wakunga wa jadi* provided herbal medicines that women and their families believed would increase the contractions and result in a fast birth. Many of the biomedical personnel complained about the use of these herbal medicines because they were convinced that large numbers of women in the region used them and that the medicines caused problems such as ruptured uterus or stillbirth. The regional reproductive and child health coordinator told me, "And they use a lot of those local herbal medicines. Up to right now, here where I am talking, even there in the labor ward a lot of times they are confiscating those herbal medicines." The use, or even suspected use, of these herbs led to repeated conflicts between women and biomedical providers, particularly at the regional hospital. Because of the lack of privacy, no option for having a relative remain with the woman in labor, and the prohibition of herbal medicines, the biomedical facilities did not generally meet some of the locally valued requirements of a good place for giving birth.

Home birth fines and the complicated paper-based procedures for proving an accidental delivery outside the local biomedical facility served to deteriorate relationships between some *wakunga wa jadi* and the biomedical facilities even further. But the ones most often caught in the middle, bearing the brunt of these struggles for legitimacy and control over birth, were pregnant women themselves. These are not new concerns; this conflict has deep roots and a long history in Tanzania. There have been policy debates about the merits of home versus hospital or institutional births since the colonial period, representing a deep agnosticism related to the relative cost/benefit of each location in this low-resource setting.

TRANSPORTATION TRAVAILS

When women did try to access biomedical services, transportation was one of the most frequent impediments to timely arrival at a facility because of poor roads and a lack of public transportation. Ilambila village had particular difficulties transporting ill community members and pregnant women to the nearest health center. The dispensary providers told us that the district government ambulance had never once arrived when they had called it; they no longer even tried. Now they preferred to arrange alternate transportation to expedite arrival at the health center. The result was, as one of the village leaders explained, "You will find maybe that a patient needs to be taken to [the health center], you find that the patient's husband must sell maybe a cow or a plot of land to get the money for the expenses of the transportation." Rebeca asked the assembled group of leaders what would happen if a woman and her family didn't have any resources to hire a car. Another man in the group responded, "You just die."

One of the village chairmen, Jobu, continued, "I should add another challenge. You find that other people don't have the means at all even to rent a car, they have to be carried by bicycle and that mother can die on the road. We return the corpse to be buried. If she gets lucky to maybe pay for a motorcycle, then that gets her there." Curious about the specificity of his answer, I asked, "Has it ever happened that a mother tried to go [to the health center] but then she died on the way?" Jobu replied, "Yes, it was by motorcycle, three years ago." I prompted the group further, wanting to know what had happened. Danieli cleared his throat and began to speak: "I transported her by motorcycle. . . . We were on the road and she died. I had to return the body. So it's a problem. Yeah, transportation by motorcycle is problematic, I mean if a person has already died on the motorcycle, you have to tie the legs, I don't know what all, I really got problems." Danieli had tied the dead woman's arms and legs to his in order to keep the body from sliding off the motorcycle as he painstakingly drove back to their village.

Many other communities faced similar challenges, and health care providers working in village dispensaries related stories of very sparse and unreliable district ambulances, long waits, or struggles to find transportation. In some villages, they did not have working cell phone networks or radio call systems, and the providers would have to climb a hill to reach a spot with reception before being able to call for the ambulance. The walk itself could take at least forty-five minutes, further delaying the referral. As one man in Ngorotwa said, "And another thing, you find that maternal deaths and those of children are many because we are told that we have a car for the health center, but we haven't seen it. Therefore, this promise of transportation for patients is still ongoing."

In several of the communities Rebeca and I visited, the community members described how Parliamentarians swept through the area during campaign season. They would make grandiose promises of new ambulances as they acknowledged the dire need for better emergency medical transportation in the region. And yet these ambulances rarely materialized. The district and regional medical offices did not have the capital needed to purchase appropriate vehicles that were equipped as ambulances either. In one case, I saw the ambulance for Ngorotwa

Health Center, donated by one of the aforementioned Parliamentarians, driving around Sumbawanga Town and could not help but wonder to myself why it was there instead of parked at the health center several hours distant.

In another instance, I was on the maternity ward at Mawingu when we received a woman had been referred from a dispensary many miles away, close to a neighboring region. She arrived exhausted and dirty, telling us that in the middle of the night she had walked for hours in the rain after the car that she and her relatives had hired had broken down. She collapsed onto a bed in the maternity ward with mud caked on her legs up to her knees and with the umbilical cord protruding from her vagina—a cord prolapse that caused her stillbirth, which probably would have been preventable had she reached care sooner. She had arrived without a formal referral letter or an accompanying nurse, making it easy for the harried nurses at Mawingu to assume she had arrived from home and did not have a serious condition. The ongoing challenges of poor road infrastructure, lack of transportation, and a weak referral chain were all important contributors to maternal and neonatal deaths and powerfully shaped women's experiences before their arrival at the regional hospital when they were referred there for further care. These challenges, too, were all highly visible reminders of how the state failed to care for its citizens and allowed pregnant women and others to die while in the throes of a medical emergency.

INTERACTIONS, NEGLECT, AND THE QUALITY OF BIOMEDICAL CARE

Once a woman arrived at a biomedical facility, the quality of services provided, and the appearance of the facility itself, became of the utmost importance, influencing her future decisions about where to give birth in subsequent pregnancies. Both in women's minds and in guidelines, quality care required material goods and physical infrastructure but also respectful, responsive health care providers. Breakdowns or deficiencies in any of these areas eroded women's trust in their local biomedical services. Even if she chose to return to her nearest biomedical facility after a bad experience, a woman might no longer honestly share with nurses her medical history, her previous attempts to access various forms of care, or her desires. Secrecy was often a result of past instances in which nurses had accused a woman of lying or of being noncompliant, a problem patient. In other cases, a woman had seen that no matter what she said or did, the nurses ignored her and, in moments of need, demanded money for supplies, a bed, or documentation to which, legally, the mother had a right for free.

These types of past experiences could then create a cycle in which women no longer trusted the recommendations of their providers. Poor relations between village health care workers and their pregnant clients could mean women did not receive adequate explanations for referrals. Bennet, a village leader in Mkamba,

FIGURE 15. Foundation of an unfinished addition to the dispensary in Songambele village, March 2015. Photo by author.

told me, "Then another thing, women are embarrassed, I mean if she is told then, for example, that she should go to town, right away she knows she is going to be operated on. Really the goal is for her to get the best care that she needs, but she remains there at home, embarrassed. . . . But, on the other hand, care should be improved, and these providers of ours should be given training." He felt that women misunderstood the reasons for their referrals while, at the same time, acknowledging that the quality of care in their dispensary needed to be improved.

In Songambele village, located high on the Ufipa Plateau, the dispensary had a common problem of not enough beds for mothers in labor or after giving birth. The foundation of an expanded maternal-child health building stood uncompleted near the existing dispensary building, which remained unfinished in 2019 (figure 15). Nurses often told women to return home almost immediately after delivery to save space. In this community, I asked women if they knew of anyone who had developed complications after giving birth, while on the way back home from the health facility. Mama Rajabu told me, "I myself, I remember it happened to me! When we were on the road, a lot of blood started coming out and I had to lie down at a neighbor's. We were with my in-law, and she made the preparations to return me to the dispensary and there they gave me a shot. I was admitted and later they came to get me [to take me back home]." Another woman jumped in and said, "Even my daughter, it happened to her, too, just like that!" Bleeding after giving birth is relatively common and can sometimes be severe, requiring additional oxytocin to help the uterus contract or, in other instances, may entail manual removal of retained portions of the placenta that broke off during the birth. Most often, protocols for best practice recommend a twenty-four-hour observation period to make sure the woman's uterus has contracted and she will not hemorrhage. This is also a crucial time period to monitor the woman to make sure she has not developed a problem such as pregnancy-induced cardiomyopathy, eclampsia, or infection. Poor infrastructure combined with low levels of provider knowledge or a lack of communication could cause some women to begin viewing biomedical facilities as places that caused problems instead of solving them.

In nearly all of the villages I visited in Rukwa, we found at least one provider absent, often without notice or explanation. The reasons for the absence ranged from annual vacation leave, to participation in seminars, to three of four nurses in one village all being out on maternity leave, to providers being away while they traveled four days, round trip, to collect either supplies or their salary from the district medical offices. Other times providers simply left work to engage in other income-generating activities or had worked overnight, in the case of births, and were resting at home. Finding their providers led to delays in care for people in many communities.

Even when providers were present, community members cited a lack of supplies and suspected corruption as deterrents to the increased use of the facilities in their villages. The women in Ngorotwa outlined some of the problems in their community health center. They complained that if a woman did not have any money she would not get her prenatal clinic card (which, legally, was always supposed to be free) or medication and might be charged a bed fee after giving birth there, also an illegal practice. In a group conversation, Mama Malaika told me, "If you don't have any money, you won't get medicine!" Interjecting, Mama Grace explained, "The medicines are there, but they tell you you have to buy them. For example, you have a pregnant child. Now, while you are taking her there, maybe she gives birth on the way. Now, if you take her there to the facility, you are charged money," the home birth fine. Mama Noel picked up the thread and continued: "Another challenge is a mother, if she has already given birth, to let her get out of the bed, you have to give money. Even for a pregnant mother. They ask for 12,000 shillings, for soap or something, they say. I don't know." Surprised, I told the women, "Me, I don't understand, because health care for pregnant mothers is supposed to be free." Mama Grace explained that they knew care was supposed to be free. But it was difficult to hold health care workers accountable. She explained, "If you ask them, they will tell you that not even one day have they ever charged a pregnant woman. Even if you call [the nurses] to a public meeting, they refuse, they say they have never done that. If they say to ask the women, the mothers are afraid, so there isn't even one who says because she is thinking, 'If I say, then the day I go to the health center they will chase me out,' so that is what is restraining the women."

The women in Ngorotwa were unable to report their health care providers for bad behavior or for imposing illegal fees for fear of retribution the next time they needed health care services. These accounts in village biomedical facilities illustrate the reasons women often decided to seek care in other, higher-level facilities, thereby increasing the burden on the regional hospital. On the other side, rural health care providers reported that they charged small fees for antenatal clinic cards or other services sometimes as a way of raising funds to pay for a security guard at the dispensary or other such initiatives. This is not to say that sometimes they were not also charging women to line their own pockets, but only to acknowledge the fact that providers sometimes were unaware they were engaged in an illegal practice or found ways to justify the fees they imposed with rhetoric about using the money to improve services.

Seeking better-quality, more comprehensive care through either self or health care provider referral, women often arrived at Mawingu Regional Hospital after days, months, or years of struggle, trying to extract sufficient care from a reluctant and overburdened, undersupported system. Sometimes they did indeed arrive from distant locations, in bad condition, exhausted and physically depleted, hoping beyond hope that the regional hospital would be able to save them where others had failed.

BROKEN PROMISES OF CARE

Both at the community level and within health care facilities, women experienced varied forms of care and, often, a lack of it. Just as policy makers suspected, some of this lack of care was rooted in gender inequities or cultural practices like the exchange of bridewealth or beliefs in the value of herbal medicines. However, as becomes clear from talking with groups of men and women, culture is not static nor homogenous; men and women make space for care during pregnancy within and beyond the bounds of existing practices or "traditions." Just as cultural practices could not explain away the structural factors shaping high rates of maternal death, neither could biomedicine solve all of a pregnant woman's problems, even when she arrived early to a facility. Communities expressed dismay, frustration, and feelings of betrayal when they perceived a lack of health care resources and poor quality care. In rural areas of Rukwa, village leaders told me with pride about how Nyerere had once visited their community to look out over the Ufipa Plateau. Nyerere presented Songambele village with a certificate for their excellent collective farming practices as a model Ujamaa village. While, to outsiders, Tanzania's socialist era feels like the distant past, many community members hold on to an expectation of collectivity and support extending to the state level. People often expressed disappointment in health care services because they thought the state had a responsibility to provide medications and health care to its citizens, a vestige of the socialist era and a testament to its enduring legacy.

Negligent, abusive, or corrupt care in their communities conditioned women and their relatives to mistrust the biomedical system even before they arrived at Mawingu. Their locally constructed, gendered logics of care and ideas of risk (social or, less often, biological) informed their comportment and interactions in the hospital setting. These views, combined with past life events, sometimes paved the road to late arrivals, medical complications, or even death.

I want to emphasize once again how the growth of biomedicine has come to disallow other forms of caring during pregnancy and childbirth. This outcome has been accomplished, in part, through the expansion of biobureaucracy across levels. WHO-led logics of rational actors and rights may, at times, conflict with the goals, needs, and conceptions of risk present at the local level in Rukwa. Biobureaucracy continues to expand through fines, forms, referral procedures, and guidelines of best practice that structure whom biomedical health care providers view as compliant health-seekers, men and women both, when they go to biomedical facilities during a woman's pregnancy or when she is about to give birth. The biobureaucracy has also expanded in a way that makes it difficult for village dispensaries to maintain supplies and to provide the high-quality care that women desire. Instead providers who are underpaid and left without support sometimes resort to negligence or extortion to make ends meet in their own lives.

Just as biomedicine obscures a large portion of women's experiences leading to maternal death, a focus on something uncritically and homogenously deemed culture leads to the same result. Culturalism obscures how enormous systems—the biobureaucracies of safe motherhood, global policies, national budgetary problems and priorities, and poverty—affect women's and health care workers' decisions, actions, and experiences. In the end, long histories of fraught interactions, persistent supply shortages, rumors of corruption, and extractive biomedical practices all reduced the trust between women or their relatives and biomedical institutions. Because of an intricate combination of these factors and failed promises of state care rooted in Tanzania's socialist past, the death of a pregnant woman comes to contain much more meaning than the death of an individual.

9

The Meanings of Maternal Death

Why is it that maternal death so offends our sensibilities? Our collective sense of justice is violated when we think about women dying as they are bringing life into the world, even if we do not personally know anyone who has died this way. In Tanzania, and globally, a maternal death is not simply a straightforward event in which one woman, and possibly her child, die. The deaths leave traces on families, on health care providers, and on communities that continue to retell the most gruesome or heartbreaking accounts long after the woman herself is gone. These narratives that were discussed in the hospital ward, sanitized and transformed in the meeting room, and lovingly kept alive in homes as memories of women lost intersect with policies, documentation requirements, and care to make their marks on the minds and bodies of all those whose lives they touched. These deaths play across registers and levels, extending far beyond the individual and her family to local society, institutions, regions, the state, and the global community. They not only expose the weaknesses in a health care system but also highlight structural inequities that disproportionately affect the poorest and most marginalized in any country. In this concluding chapter, I trace how maternal death affects individuals and communities, as well as health care workers and institutions, including the hospital and the state. At a global level, there has been laudable rhetoric in support of reducing maternal mortality, but the effects have been mixed. What do persistently high levels of maternal deaths in certain regions mean for the world today? What can we learn from a poor hospital in a peripheral area of Tanzania that might help us ensure that fewer women continue to die? For Tanzanians, at each of these levels, deaths of women due to pregnancy-related causes represent a range of broken promises and hold different meanings.

MEANINGS OF MATERNAL DEATH FOR FAMILIES AND COMMUNITIES

In Tanzania, as in many places worldwide, women are the cornerstones of families and communities. Their domestic and agricultural labor, ingenuity, and tenacity are vital inputs that keep households together and surviving. Women often undertake backbreaking work and may struggle to procure subsistence needs for themselves and their families. But their role as mothers is often a source of great joy for them, with many expressing a desire for multiple children as sources of, and repositories for, love. Reproduction is a social imperative that also provides women with a more concrete form of security, tying men to them in ways that invoke interdependence and support, if not always affective caring. These moments of reproduction can also be highly tenuous and speculative, engendering a sense of danger during this period in which people take no outcomes for granted.

At this, the most personal and proximate level, the death of a pregnant woman can mean her children are orphaned or become neglected. Her husband mourns her death, and her female relatives prepare her body for burial. Even years later, they remember a woman lost. Some relatives search for reasons for the death in health care provider actions or negligence. Others speak of "bad luck," malevolent witchcraft, the will of God, or, for Muslims, a woman's *ajal* or appointed time of death. On a broader level, these deaths signify broken promises of state care that have a deep history in the socialist Nyerere era in Tanzania and still profoundly shape Tanzanian citizens' ideas about state responsibilities toward all members of society.

Supernatural Deaths

In the moral and ethical world of everyday Tanzanians, social relations and interdependence assure mutual support and survival through reciprocity and equitable distribution of resources. When social relations become imbalanced, often because of jealousy or resource accumulation, accusations or suspicions of witchcraft can proliferate.[1] In the case of reproduction, there are many stories of jealous co-wives who seek to keep their husband's affections for themselves, placing magic under the beds of other wives to prevent them from becoming pregnant. In other cases, a witch may steal a woman's menstrual cloths from the clothesline to use any remnants of blood in magic against the woman. Likewise, in Rukwa, placentas are known to be a magically potent item that ill-wishers can use against a woman. Other community members throughout Tanzania told me of the importance of keeping a pregnancy hidden, never talking about it openly until it was impossible to physically hide it any longer. If others knew about the pregnancy early, they might cause harm to the developing fetus or the woman herself. Similarly, women and their close, trusted family members were careful not to advertise too widely that the woman was in labor and had gone to the health facility to give birth, lest an evil person try to use witchcraft to cause the baby to be stillborn or even threaten the life of the mother herself.

While in the hospital, women and their relatives often spoke of "bad luck," but it is likely that at least some of them suspected other forces were behind bad reproductive outcomes. For some, this other force was witchcraft; for others, it was the will of God or Allah. Those whose religion helped them to exclude witchcraft as a likely causal factor were apt to say that God had not seen fit for the baby to live or that it was not the right time for the child to come into the woman's world. In the case of the death of a woman, family members also said it was God's will. For some Muslim families, belief in an *ajal* or *ajal musamma*, or appointed time of death for every person, led them to believe it had been the appointed time for the woman to finish her earthly life. At other times, it is likely that relatives spoke of bad luck while suspecting the hospital or health facility of some form of negligence or malpractice. They may have been too uncertain of reporting or accountability procedures to report their suspicions, or their previous interactions with other health facilities may have left them cynical about any possible effect of reporting or made them afraid of retribution.

Failure of State Care

For individuals and communities, maternal deaths also carry with them resonances of the failure of state care. Particularly in a country with rich ideological ties to socialism and state responsibility for collective well-being, the poor functioning or absence of structures needed to prevent maternal deaths means an ultimate lack of caring, or an inability to care. These state structures include, among many others, roads and public vehicles, supply chains, and the number and quality of health care facilities and trained providers. Breakdowns in any or all of these can further open the door to a preventable death. To Tanzanian citizens living in rural areas, a maternal death in their family or community holds within its broader meaning an image of the state's lack of care for them and for their very lives.

MEANINGS OF MATERNAL DEATH FOR THE HOSPITAL

Through discourse and attendant regulations that have imposed fines on women who give birth outside the biomedical system, the power of biomedicine is instantiated over and over again, effectively creating these facilities as the only safe place for a woman to give birth. However, the increased demand for these services has outpaced the supply of skilled providers and the material goods—medications and equipment—needed to sustain biomedical practice. When Mawingu was unable to keep up, women's care suffered, effectively making the safest place increasingly less safe, in an ironic perversion of government and public health goals. Beyond just unintended consequences, increased demand without the necessary increase in resources made the hospital dangerous in cases when women arrived without money or relatives and when catheters, antibiotics, sutures, or anesthesia were out of stock. The maternal deaths that occurred at the hospital were not just, or only, clinical failures but administrative ones as well. Poor supply availability, inadequate staffing levels, improper supervision, oversight, or management of lower-level health care workers, and tenuous electricity or water supplies all undermined the hospital's authority. On the one hand, the regional medical officer (RMO) saw the increased numbers of patients as a testament to the hospital's improving quality of care and thus its reputation. On the other, the influx of pregnant women, even those without problems, combined with women who had complicated pregnancies, put great pressure on the hospital's resources and contributed to the maternity ward's ongoing high rates of death and severe morbidity.

The burden of maternity services often overwhelmed the hospital and its meager operating budget. The maternity ward was the problem child of the hospital, as represented by constant reprimands related to standard reporting and documentation violations and by accusations of vulgar or abusive language, disrespectful behavior, mismanagement, and improper comportment among the nurses. The maternity ward is a ward of exceptions, prompted by the unpredictable and unique nature of every woman's labor and birth. But the hospital administration often tried to run the maternity ward in the same way as the others. As a result, the staff members on the ward, the nurses in particular, constantly received criticism. This environment led many of the health care workers to question their value to the institution, as well as the relative merits of continuing to work at the regional hospital. Several of the nurses repeatedly spoke about a desire to transfer to new work locations in other parts of the country.

The administrators themselves faced an onslaught of new guidelines and regulations from a variety of national and international bodies and organizations. Planners and policy makers intended all of these programs to help improve clinical care, but their unintended side effects were the vast and rapid proliferation of paperwork, documentation, and bureaucratic procedures. All this biobureaucratic expansion served to shift the focus away from care work and onto paperwork, away from root causes and onto technical interventions.[2]

In other instances, the accountability and monitoring systems the hospital and the Tanzanian government put in place to help ensure high-quality care that met international standards actually helped to undermine care and were subverted for other, social purposes or used merely to perform effectiveness. Often NGOs or the central government imposed these monitoring or accounting techniques from above, and the health care workers on the ground at Mawingu tried to make space for themselves and their lived realities in between the lines of the graphs and in the blanks of the forms and logbooks. In the end, the data making their way to the central government were highly unreliable, produced by important social histories that were concealed by the "objective" numbers on the page.

This evidence suggests that institutionalizing birth is not, in and of itself, the solution to reducing maternal deaths in any setting. Clearly, many of the ways in which the system in the Rukwa region and Mawingu Hospital was undermined and perverted, to the detriment of high-quality, guideline-compliant care, concerned a level of scarcity that was deeply engrained in and entangled with the rapid expansion of biomedicine in Tanzania. Through efforts such as reducing the training time for enrolled nurses (ENs), the government sought to improve services by increasing the absolute number of skilled providers. However, the real result was the proliferation of new graduates who had official certificates, book knowledge, and little else in the way of problem-solving skills or training in handling obstetric emergencies. In a similar move that privileged certificates and official qualifications over hands-on experience, President John Pombe Magufuli ordered a certificate verification exercise in 2017 that resulted in many health care personnel being fired for fake qualifications. The government's fetishization of certificates resulted in an even greater shortage of skilled health care workers throughout the country. The wrong targets often became the point of focus because of their easier accessibility. It often appeared that for the government doing *something* took precedence, regardless of the action's unintended consequences. In the same vein, the ongoing fines for women who gave birth at home, and levied against those who assisted them, again reinforced the government's emphasis on and fetishization of papers—training certificates—despite the demonstrable knowledge of local midwives and the lack of knowledge of many new ENs who had made it through the government's expedited training programs. Quick fixes such as these continued to undermine the system and the care available to women.

The government must advance beyond rhetoric and draconian punishments that prevent women from accessing plural forms of care when the proposed alternative, birth in biomedical institutions, systematically disempowers both women and those health care workers meant to be assisting them and protecting their lives in times of emergency. Mawingu itself was a flawed institution, struggling with competing demands and the proliferation of government-imposed bureaucratic guidelines, but it found itself in a much more broadly dysfunctional system, the country's health care sector as a whole. Within this context, the individuals at the hospital, and the hospital as an organization, sought to make do and provide care that was good enough. Guided by codified nursing ethics of compassionate, selfless caring, medical ethics of doing no harm, and morals related to the interdependence of people in the broader social community, nurses and doctors at Mawingu battled deaths that unfolded and transpired at the crossroads of constant negotiation and local norms of everyday ethics. Pervasive scarcity often undermined their efforts to improve maternal health outcomes, but until the central government prioritizes solving supply chain problems and improving the candidate pool for nursing training, for two examples, hospital birth will remain an incomplete solution to the problem of decreasing the deaths of pregnant women.

MEANINGS OF MATERNAL DEATH FOR THE REGION

I initially decided to visit the Rukwa region after reading the 2010 *Demographic and Health Survey* published in 2011, just as I was beginning graduate studies. The region, of which I had never heard, ranked in the bottom five of what were, at the time, twenty-one mainland regions on all measures related to maternal, reproductive, and child health. The statistics there provided little idea of causes behind the region's poor performance on nearly all these indicators. The numbers could tell me only that 69.6 percent of women were still giving birth outside biomedical facilities. Some 36.8 percent (13.4 percent in the 2015 report) of these were with relatives; another 31.1 percent (18.2 percent) percent with local midwives, the *wakunga wa jadi;* and a mere 29.5 percent (64.2 percent in 2015) percent with a skilled attendant—that is, in a biomedical facility.[3] While no one ever explicitly linked their employment in the region to this report, which the country (aided by outside organizations) publishes every five years, many of the medical officers (that is, the MDs) and regional officials told me they had begun their work in Rukwa in late 2011 or early 2012. For those who had had long careers in the region, these statistics and the region's relatively poor performance surely had come as no surprise.

Another legacy from the Nyerere era is that government employees have long been sent to regions other than their regions of origin. Friends have explained to me that this was Nyerere's strategy for preventing ethnic tensions and maintaining peace in the country. This system of being assigned a work location also helps to ensure that people are available to work in remote or otherwise less desirable locations. Given a choice, many people would elect to work in the main urban centers, often where they did their training. For health care workers posted to Rukwa, the region's reputation as inhospitable and as a home to witches and powerful healers intimidated many.

Every day on the hospital maternity ward, in morning meetings with the regional medical officer, and in maternal death audit meetings, the health care providers and administrators worked to advance a new image of their region and combat its old one on the national stage. For several years, the White Ribbon Alliance of Tanzania focused on the Rukwa region, drawing national-level attention to the poor quality of health care and facilities there (figure 16). The outcome was support and funding, but the region also became the face of maternal mortality and subpar services at the national level. The deaths of these women had come to represent the backwardness of the region, a region in which people, as Dr. Joseph told me on my first visit in 2012, were "still sleeping." The regional commissioner, the highest government official in the region, Engineer Stella Manyanya, also spent a great deal of time

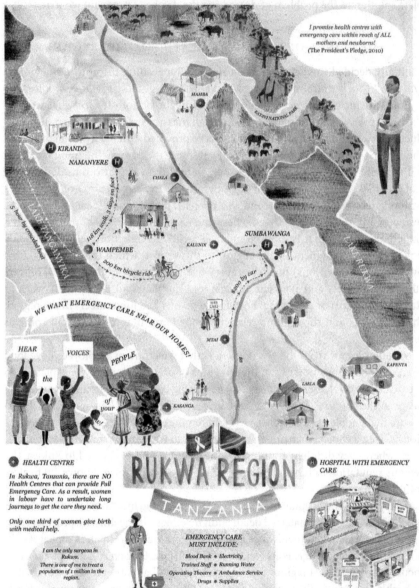

FIGURE 16. Illustration of the Rukwa region from the White Ribbon Alliance Campaign from 2013 to 2015. The figure of the doctor is saying, "I am the only surgeon in Rukwa. There is one of me to treat a population of one million in the region." Copyright White Ribbon Alliance; illustration by Hannah Bailey.

talking about and publicly committing to reducing maternal and neonatal deaths in her region. As the RMO related in the maternal death audit meeting in which he spoke of the importance of collecting accurate, timely statistics on maternal death, these numbers came to shape the reputation of the region in front of Parliament at the highest levels of national governance. Being able to cite declines in maternal deaths in the region proved to national leaders that the Rukwa region and its new administrators were making progress and were properly engaged in the transformative practices of *maendeleo,* or development, that would inevitably lead the nation to greater success as a model of progress and improvement.

MEANINGS OF MATERNAL DEATH FOR THE STATE

The promise of health care services for Tanzanian citizens originated as part of the fundamental goals of Nyerere's postindependence socialist state. In that era, the minister of health celebrated health care workers as crucial actors in the nation-building project. Writing to them in a memo dated May 18, 1964, just shy of one month after Tanganyika's unification with the island nation of Zanzibar to create the modern Tanzanian state, Minister of Health Bryceson wrote of the role of health care workers in Nyerere's first Five-Year Development Plan. He described how their formal employment in health care did not exempt them from nation-building activities such as working on a communal farm, building a road, or teaching others to read; this was their personal role. For their professional roles, Bryceson ends his memo by saying: "We are responsible for the health of the nation. The attainment of the broad aim of an increase in life expectancy is dependent upon our efforts. The very target of an improved standard of living is dependent to a large extent on the success of our teaching. I know that our medical workers, of all grades both in the Ministry and in the Voluntary Agencies, are already hard worked. Nevertheless, I am asking for more time, more effort."[4]

This rhetoric, which invokes providers as key actors in nation building, imbued them with a sense of purpose and responsibility that those currently working do not feel as strongly. The more diffuse twenty-first-century rhetoric of development and human rights simply does not resonate as strongly on the local level and therefore is not the same motivator for working hard under difficult conditions. A nurse who had started her career under Nyerere said, "Work accountability, people were really working very hard. People had respect and they had love. That is different from what you see [these days]." Some others also told me they felt that during Nyerere's time the health care facilities had been better stocked with the supplies that were available during that period and that, overall, health care providers had been more focused on providing care instead of trying to make money. Enriching oneself for personal, rather than national or community, profit was antithetical to the mission of Nyerere's Ujamaa.

In this internally facing mode, the persistent high rates of maternal deaths represent an unfulfilled promise of the Nyerere era, when the state valorized and valued health care workers. Even those Tanzanians who are too young to remember the socialist period or were born after Nyerere had already stepped down from the presidency continue to cling to the idea of state care for its citizens rooted in this era. So too, the national television stations continue to play excerpts from Nyerere's speeches every night as part of the news hour. Nyerere, Baba wa Taifa, father of the nation, still watches over every government office, peering down at workers from his portrait always given pride of place next to the current president and the office clock. The current president, John Pombe Magufuli, has very effectively drawn on elements of Nyerere's rhetoric to marshal support for contemporary state-building projects, proving that this ideology still resonates.

In a more externally facing mode, maternal mortality continues to play a role in state deservingness for aid. Paradoxically, reducing the maternal mortality ratio proves the country is doing well, complying with international guidelines and donor demands, and improving citizens' quality of life while, at the same time, suggesting a waning need for outside assistance. Stubbornly high rates, though, signal the country's ongoing status as a "developing" country dependent on aid and outside expertise. Maternal mortality continues to be a significant indicator by which countries throughout the world measure each other and relative success. Such indicators are essentially proxies for larger measures of state success, including economic and political stability, administrative acumen, and the realization of the globally recognized human right to health. Even in high-income countries, such as the United States, maternal and neonatal death rates signify inefficiencies, inequities, and imbalances.

Tanzanian national priorities, in relation to maternal health care and derived from global guidelines and recommendations, now emphasize place of birth and access to biomedical care over all other considerations, driving more and more women to these places without commensurate investment in ensuring that facilities are capable of taking on these new clients. This drive has led to overcrowding, worsening scarcity, provider burnout, and inattentive (at best) care, while also limiting women's autonomy through punitive restrictions on home births and home birth providers.[5] It is difficult not to conclude that misplaced emphasis may be prohibiting further declines in maternal deaths in places such as Tanzania, but ultimately it is far easier to tell people to go to the hospital than it is to uproot structural inequities producing maternal deaths and severe morbidity.

MEANINGS OF MATERNAL DEATH FOR THE GLOBAL COMMUNITY

Globally, defining who has a right, or the legitimacy, to make claims on care and on what quality of life has become a significant component of political agendas. Poor women in rural corners of the low-income global South have achieved recognition, biolegitimacy,[6] through their suffering. Their deaths in the universal experience of childbirth mark them as deserving of humanitarian and political attention. Yet within their own countries, for countries such as Tanzania, the deaths of pregnant women continue to present a stubborn problem. The Millennium Development Goal 5A, to reduce maternal mortality by three-quarters from the 1990 levels by the program's end date in 2015, was one of the primary remaining goals. Tanzania, and many other countries, particularly in sub-Saharan Africa, failed to meet these goals, making some progress but not enough. Even then, the numbers that policy makers and public health practitioners, statisticians and demographers used to calculate these ratios and their changes are deeply and fundamentally flawed.

The bottom line is that for every country maternal mortality remains a question, asking leaders, "Whose lives do you value, and what level of death is acceptable for marginalized women?" Fundamentally, maternal mortality on the global scale is about the value we attach to women's lives and to which women's lives. Second-wave feminism in Western countries, and the United Nations Decade for Women from 1976 to 1985, were significant drivers in the initial push to elucidate the true extent of maternal deaths, numbers that, when first published, shocked many.[7] Not until the mid-1970s did the world even have its first glimpse of the extent of the global burden of maternal mortality. In 1987, the then-director general of the World Health Organization, Halfdan Mahler, wrote, "[Maternal mortality] has been a *neglected* tragedy; and it has been neglected because those who suffer it are neglected people, with the least power and influence over how national resources shall be spent; they are the poor, the rural peasants, and, above all, women."[8] Despite the passing of more than thirty years, this statement remains just as valid today as it was then. Some countries have been able to invest significant resources in reducing maternal deaths, supported and pushed by robust political will. Many other lower-income countries continue to struggle because of extensive competing demands on their resources.

Since the 1990s, the global community has come to see maternal mortality as a human rights issue. Several groups have attempted to formulate a so-called rights-based approach to reducing maternal mortality, incorporating this language into the Sustainable Development Goals. Carla AbouZahr writes that maternal mortality does not have an easy target for eradication, like a pathogen or vector, making it a more diffuse public health challenge, but also that "failure to take action to prevent maternal death amounts to discrimination because only women face the risk."[9] Because of the necessary and absolutely normal act of biological reproduction, women will always need care during pregnancy and while giving birth; their lives will always be hanging in the balance of these care practices.

Though pregnancy is not an illness under most normal circumstances, strikingly large biobureaucracies have emerged, seeking to provide care in those times when pregnancy and childbirth deviate from the biologically determined norm.

States have employed biobureaucratic institutions for functional and idealistic ends. The expansion of these biobureaucracies has brought with it and, in fact, created scarcity through implementation of labyrinthine procedures for accessing even the supplies and expertise available. Biobureaucracy has also generated a different form of scarcity, a scarcity of affective, intersubjective caring that meets patients' expectations and desires. The space for these forms of caring has shrunk to accommodate the reams of paperwork and documentation accompanying technical care's protocols and best practices. Maternal health and death in Rukwa provide a particularly poignant perspective on the expansion and functioning of these biobureaucracies globally as policies and advocacy campaigns now tell women and their families that giving birth in biomedical facilities is the only responsible choice. The insinuation is that giving birth anywhere else, purposefully or not, not only is irresponsible but can lead directly to a woman's death; hospitals like Mawingu can save a woman so long as she knows the right way to use them. And yet, so many of these institutions globally still fail women every day.

THE INVISIBLE HANDMAIDENS OF SAFE MOTHERHOOD

Even as national and global governing bodies around the world recommit to reducing the deaths of women during pregnancy and childbirth via targets in the Sustainable Development Goals, those who are most responsible for delivering on these promises are nearly invisible. Their work environments are often chaotic and unsafe, undignified and structurally violent. Nurses diligently toil away for years without promotion, recognition, or praise, let alone access to additional training or skills maintenance programs. They improvise and improvise and improvise until the actual guidelines are a figment of the imagination, an impossibility thought up in far-off places. In the interstices, nurses and doctors themselves get married, give birth, become ill, conduct business, care for parents and relatives, and work to sustain themselves and their children. They are on the front lines of clinical and affective care, engaging in practices of care that demand everything of them unless they put up walls and barriers, walk more slowly, respond less quickly. Each and every time they step into their workplace, they must be ready to compromise or weigh their different professional values, ethics, and morals, so forcefully does their environment preclude so many standard operating procedures and clear-cut pathways to something called good care.

For the nurses and doctors working in places like Mawingu Regional Hospital, maternal mortality is also implicitly about the building and re-formation of their ethical selves in varying circumstances, negotiating values of life and communalism at odds with a biomedical system and world created by capitalism and colonialism that privilege certain lives over others. Worse, it is a system that forces individuals to make the choice about whether their own life or that of a stranger is worth more. This ethical choosing and its attendant quandaries contribute to the continuance of maternal deaths in these low-resource settings. Maternal deaths continue to occur because the system has been organized to privilege the appearance of accountability, the documentation of it, over the actual, radical change necessary for a real kind of accountability that does justice to women's lives and to their communities. Caught in the crosshairs of competing demands and systemic desires for appearance and form over substance, maternity care providers are in an impossible position—often asked by policies to choose between protecting themselves or protecting the women they serve. The benefits of serving themselves second are lost in a system that, as time moves forward, increasingly devalues their service and overall contributions to society as civil servants and guardians of the lives of others. Arrangements in which more and more work at higher and higher quality are expected with fewer and fewer resources push efficiency to its limits and beyond. The spaces left for thoughtful, compassionate care are compressed ever further until they are imperceptible even to the carers themselves, let alone to the women who rely upon them.

PUTTING THE CARE PROVIDERS BACK IN HEALTH CARE

While others have sought to put the "M" back in MCH (maternal child health) or the "mother" back in Safe Motherhood, I started from a different point entirely.[10] I have sought to put the care providers back in health care because interventions have come to target improving the skills of biomedical providers as the current key to preventing maternal deaths. These people, the biomedical providers, are the ones who "would encounter the failing pregnant, or birthing bodies."[11] But while anthropologists have been busy conducting research with women and their families, exploring the meanings of pregnancy and birth, they have inadvertently flattened out the portrayals of health care personnel. Researchers have separated these providers from their social connections and their broader political economic milieu, even while working hard to explicate these very factors and their influences in the lives of pregnant women. The direction of policy has not shifted to be more woman centered; if anything, the new Sustainable Development Goals and the new Strategies toward Ending Preventable Maternal Mortality focus even more explicitly on health care facilities, promoting systems approaches to improving care and reducing deaths.[12] Yet much work must still be done to build more comprehensive and accurate understandings of how maternal health care providers are just as embedded as women and communities in networks and systems that fundamentally affect maternal deaths. Those networks and systems shape their care practices and what they are able to offer to their patients.

In September 2016, the *Lancet* published a series on maternal mortality that focused on "the mismatch between burden [of maternal death] and coverage" of biomedical health care services for women and girls.[13] This mismatch also reveals how global health has failed to accurately understand and harness the experiences of both patients and providers, leading to a disconnect between plans and actual needs of people on the ground.[14] That, then, is what I have sought to do here by demonstrating that even though policy planners or experts at the WHO, in charge of designing recommendations for best practice, and the nurses and doctors at Mawingu Hospital share a belief in the powers of biomedicine, a wide gulf separates them. According to Lynn Freedman, who contributed to the *Lancet* series, "The point is not that global strategies, evidenced-based guidelines, or high-level monitoring and accountability initiatives are inherently wrong or unnecessary. But when they consume most of the oxygen in the room, drowning out voices and signals coming from the ground, they distort both understanding and action."[15] Here I have presented an alternative perspective that has made clear many of the forces behind deviations from WHO or Tanzanian Ministry of Health guidelines and initiatives regarding maternal deaths. It also shows that systems much larger than one hospital have, in fact, necessitated these deviations and continue to incentivize accounting for these deviations over actually improving care in significant and lasting ways.

THE COMPLEX REACH OF SCARCITY AND IMPERFECT CARE

The scarcity with which nurses and doctors struggled every day generated a perception that ideal care was nearly impossible to provide. This environment led to reduced expectations that providers and hospital administrators could solve clinical or systemic problems, constrained as they were by a system that currently, and historically, made it so difficult to do so. As providers worked in an environment of scarcity and simultaneously within a complex of demands for data collection and metrics, improvisation and the justification of deviation from guidelines became part of their everyday lives. They shifted their efforts from providing care to accounting for deviations from ideal care, which was set out in guidelines and standard operating procedures generated in other parts of the country or world. Good outcomes often happened by chance and could not be replicated, defying the bureaucratic policies and procedures in place meant to standardize, with the consequence of uneven, unpredictable results. An accounting culture, focused on justifying deviations from high-quality care or on collecting data, and undergirded by the power of a global system, worked hard to replace a caring culture, one in which both patients and hospital staff members received the types of care they needed in order to survive and thrive.

Nurses provide the vast majority of the care to pregnant women but often have minimal power within the hospital hierarchy—their efforts often were undervalued and overlooked. They used alternative means to try to gain certain outcomes or resources for their patients, drawing on informal routes to influence or social capital by manipulating documents or by other means. An institutional lack of care contributed to the continued production of nursing care that gave the appearance of lacking motivation and compassion as nurses said they were demoralized by their lack of visibility within the hospital structure. The care that nurses were able to provide and the care practices in which they engaged were also influenced by the demands of their personal lives, which they were not always able to leave behind them when they left their homes for work. Interactions with hospital administrators conditioned nurses to be secretive and self-regulatory when they made mistakes in care, further producing an environment in which staff members and administrators did not engage in open discussions about care practices and nurses' needs but produced robust forms of informal accountability.

Health care providers at all levels were forced to modify, improvise, and cut corners so that women got at least some care, care that was good enough.[16] The constraints of their work environment produced conditions that were not amenable to quick action or early intervention; the nurses and doctors came to see early, efficient intervention as a near impossibility. In some cases, global guidelines about respectful maternity care might hold nurses in violation of the idealized forms of practice—for instance, when they yelled at a woman in labor or hit her legs because she was not exerting enough effort or paying enough attention to critical instructions. But in their everyday ethics, nurses believed they were indeed caring for women, employing such practices solely for the purpose of making sure a woman's baby emerged alive in an environment with few technical alternatives: What good were kind words and comforting touches if a woman's baby was stillborn?

Sometimes, however, patients' negative interactions with nurses, which they did not always fully understand, undermined their trust in the system. Women entered the hospital setting after a lifetime of gender inequity and differential access to education, respect, and decision-making powers. They came to the ward conditioned by their own stories, and those of other women, about biomedical providers—stories that too frequently centered on cases of abuse, neglect, negligence, or corruption. Collective memory recited stories of blood being sold to families when a life was on the line, or of village nurses telling families they needed to buy gloves and then magically producing a pair for sale, or they conjured images of drivers carrying pregnant women's lifeless bodies back home, limbs strapped to limbs to keep the corpse on the back of the motorcycle.

In villages, on the hospital ward, and on the national stage, Tanzania continues to play out the battle first recorded in the colonial era: What is the proper site for childbirth—the home or the hospital? While global public health studies and interventions have disavowed the skills, knowledge, and social roles of local midwives, they have less critically accepted young, barely trained health care providers in the biomedical tradition. Because it is nearly impossible to predict who will develop a complication during an otherwise problem-free pregnancy and childbirth, the government and the global community have adopted the stance that every woman should be under the supervision of institutional biomedical care. In the colonial era, the biggest barrier to allowing all women to give birth in facilities was a lack of trained personnel and a lack of infrastructure, buildings, to accommodate so many women. Nearly eighty years later, the same problems continue to plague the Tanzanian government, whose push to send women to institutions has outpaced its recruitment and support of the necessary providers. Penalizing home birth by charging fines to those who do not manage to give birth in a health facility, whether by accident or by intent, serves no purpose other than fostering additional ill-will in communities with already strained relations between women, their families, and health care providers.

Governments and NGOs alike seem to be looking for quick fixes, for the magic bullets that will stop the more than eight thousand maternal deaths that occur in Tanzania every year and send shock waves through families and communities. Yet maternal health is a systemic problem, and when a woman dies in a health facility her death is a culmination of all the structures that have influenced her life to that point. Her death is also a product of the complex, bureaucratic, and socially tense environment of the facility itself. Sending ever-increasing numbers of women to facilities will do nothing to reduce the numbers of women dying when those facilities are poorly stocked, suffer from supply chain problems originating at the national level, have inadequate funding mechanisms due to the unequal effects of decentralization, and systematically perpetrate violence against the staff members by keeping them living in poverty, subject to abuse by superiors, denigrated on the basis of their gender, and shut out from crucial information because of poor communication, lack of transparency, and lack of respect. After all, without the supplies and skills, a hospital is just a guesthouse—full of beds and nothing else; as an environment for giving birth, it is, essentially, no better than home.

Biomedicine and biobureaucratic expansion continue to determine which pregnant bodies deserve biomedical assistance, where these same bodies should be allowed to give birth, and with access to what personnel and what resources. The bounds, limits, and acceptable forms of ethical biomedical caring for pregnant women were long ago determined and continue to produce many challenges and conflicts within both communities and biomedical institutions. Ethical care on the Mawingu maternity ward is shaped and reshaped by the community, individual patients' families, nurses' and doctors' families, individuals' religious beliefs and practices, codified professional ethics via medical ethics, the nursing association's Code of Ethics, and invocations of Florence Nightingale, paragon of nursing care, as well as by informal ethics based in the communalism of the health care professions and the interdependence at the heart of social living in Tanzania. Nurses and doctors, as well as health administrators, must balance all of these ethical forms and systems, as well as the ambiguities and personal discretion involved in each encounter, during each intersubjective negotiation or confrontation. The providers are forced to action in the provision of care on a daily basis, but they both enact and resist certain forms of care and certain forms of ethics through subtle means as they are engaged in the practices of caring. The object of resistance is variously the patient, the hospital, the hospital's administrators, the health care system at large, or even the out-of-touch global protocols structuring nearly everything but impossible to fulfill. These intersubjective ethical negotiations become vital to providing clinical care that saves women's lives or that lets others slip through the cracks and drift away into death. Policy and public health approaches to explaining the ongoing burden of maternal mortality, and solutions to address it, are utterly unequipped to capture these everyday ethics and care practices that so profoundly shape women's outcomes via the functioning of the system as enacted through the bodies and minds of health care workers.

EPILOGUE

I sat in the hall at the hospital where we normally had the morning clinical meeting. It had been transformed into a festive venue for the evening in celebration of International Nurses Day, May 12, Florence Nightingale's birthday. Brightly colored bunting and rows of plastic chairs faced the head table, which was covered with various beverages in glass bottles. In the midst of the din from the enormous speakers, I looked around at the hospital staff members, everyone dressed up in evening finery, patterns and colors filling the room. With less than a month left at Mawingu, I began to feel as if I was disembedding from the maternity ward and the hospital. I looked around at the nurses and doctors, part of the group so often demonized in the popular press in Tanzania or written about as the opposition in women's stories of interactions and experiences during pregnancy and childbirth. Through their stories, and from working alongside them, I had started to think of them more as antiheroes of a sort—unkind at times, yes; selfish, surely, as are we all. But also as possessing the strength, tenacity, resilience, and ingenuity that kept a system moving along.

The hospital staff members were undeniably human, with all the attendant needs, desires, flaws, and aspirations. These needs and desires sometimes came into conflict with their professional mandate to care and their personal aspirations to do so to the very best of their abilities. At those moments of negotiation between their needs and those of the patients, they entered into complicated, but sometimes instantaneous, calculations of care, which constituted a version of the local ethics of care at play in Mawingu and similar hospitals throughout Tanzania and other low-resource settings. A system constrained by political economic processes with deep roots shaped the health care workers' (in)ability to enact change or provide care that fulfilled the technical and emotional needs of their patients, colleagues, and subordinates all at once. Caught in this system, they worked to provide pregnant women with care that was good enough, while also maintaining some semblance of lives for themselves even as they were entangled in a global complex that expected them to continually implement new policies with little commensurate support.

I am finishing writing this book just three days into 2020, the two-hundredth anniversary of Florence Nightingale's birth and the year that the WHO has declared to be the Year of the Nurse and Midwife. In this, their year, I hope we can remember that nurses and midwives are vital for the success of health care systems the world over. But, too, we must remember that they are people who deserve workplaces that facilitate their full (technical and affective) caring potential and treat them with dignity and respect. Beyond needing their care, the world needs their innovation, resilience, tenacity, creativity, and potential for radical change; these will be some of our most necessary inputs for generating and carrying out plans to accomplish sustainable declines in maternal death.

Though the faults in the health care system in Tanzania are much more visible much more frequently than elsewhere, similar weaknesses in maternity care are present in places all over the world. In May 2017, ProPublica and National Public Radio (NPR) in the United States unveiled an investigative journalism project over a year in the making, a series of pieces that over the ensuing months provided a picture of maternal mortality and severe morbidity in the United States that was shocking to many.[1] The first paragraph of this collaborative project's second article states, "When a new or expectant mother dies, her obituary rarely mentions the circumstances. Her identity is shrouded by medical institutions, regulators and state maternal mortality review committees. Her loved ones mourn her loss in private. The lessons to be learned from her death are often lost as well."[2] While the authors are referring to the United States, the high-income country with the highest maternal mortality ratio, these words could just as easily have come from reporting in Tanzania or from this book.[3] The drivers of increasing maternal deaths in the United States certainly have specific roots, some related to stratified reproduction in a country where access to services is often determined by wealth or poverty, and to racism. Another contributor might be the growing fixation on improving neonatal outcomes to the detriment of the mothers themselves.[4] Martin and Montagne found that at the US federally funded Maternal-Fetal Medicine Units Network, the leading obstetrics research collaborative, only four of thirty-four initiatives specifically focused on mothers themselves, while twenty-four specifically focused on babies.[5] Not so different from the 1987 question "Where is the M in MCH?"[6] In the end, many of the problems appear to be the same across institutional settings.

In another point of commonality, records of maternal death and severe morbidity in the US sometimes also blame women. The blame is not necessarily for delays in reaching care during birth but for preexisting conditions or poor prenatal care that hospitals perceive to be contributors to their problems.[7] In an extensive exploration of hospital data related to maternal health outcomes, *USA Today* identified hospitals in various settings throughout the US with worse-than-usual outcomes even when such factors as poverty and the woman's racial identity were controlled for.[8] Much as in the maternal death audit meetings in Tanzania and on the ward, a lack of transparency and a fixation on locating blame with mothers obstruct improvement. At one hospital in New Orleans profiled in the *USA Today* series, it is clear that though it is located in a high-income, high-resource country, the institution is plagued by issues similar to those prevalent in Tanzania. Slow response times, poor communication with doctors, a lack of adequately skilled and supervised clinicians, and poor attention to the details of women's medical histories all create life-threatening or deadly situations.[9]

These issues are everyday realities in Tanzania, where many more women die each year because the remaining elements of the system (such as supply chains, drug availability, diagnostics, and proximity to higher levels of care) are less robust. But ultimately what I hope these examples demonstrate is that while we may imagine maternal mortality is confined to places like Tanzania, like the Mawingu Regional Hospital, these deaths still occur, and are on the rise, in one of the world's wealthiest nations. And the causes and contributing factors leading to deaths in the hospital setting in the United States are not so very different from those leading to deaths at Mawingu. In the end, it will always be the most marginalized in any society who bear the biggest burden of maternal deaths.

Overall, we must ask ourselves, as anthropologists, health care workers, policy makers, public health practitioners, community members, and humans, a critically important question. How can we appropriate biobureaucracy and technical interventions and use them to repoliticize maternal death instead of allowing current projects and interventions to continue to reduce maternal mortality to causes amenable to technical intervention? Any answer to this question will not be easy. The answers will force us to confront difficult truths about inequities. Those comfortable and enriched by current political economics are sure to meet any proffered answers and solutions with resistance. These difficult answers will be one of the most crucial components of plans for finally eliminating the deaths of pregnant women globally.

APPENDIX

Deaths Occurring during the Field Period

These deaths included all those resulting from pregnancy-related causes for women who were admitted to Mawingu Regional Hospital's maternity and gynecology wards from January 2014 through April 2015. No deaths were reported for May 2015. Missing data reflect information missing from the woman's file.

TABLE 2 Number of deaths per district

District	Number of Deaths
Sumbawanga Rural (DC)	8
Kalambo	8
Sumbawanga Urban	17
Nkasi	1

NOTE: It is possible there was a low number of deaths from Nkasi District because critical cases from that district were referred to the district hospital, in Namanyere, before ever making it to Mawingu Hospital. For several years the Namanyere hospital has had full CEmONC (comprehensive emergency obstetric and neonatal care) capabilities.

TABLE 3 Deaths at Mawingu Regional Hospital, January 2014–April 2015

Date of Death	Village/Town of Origin	Age	G	P	Cause of Death	Other Complications
2014						
1/8/14	NO DATA	—	—	—	—	—
1/13/14	Kisumba Kasote	35			APH, placental abruption	Cardiopulmonary arrest
2/7/14	Isesa	25			Dx as anemia?	
2/16/14	Kizwite	35	2	2	Malaria, pulmonary TB	HIV/AIDS stage 4

(Contd.)

TABLE 3 (Continued)

Date of Death	Village/Town of Origin	Age	G	P	Cause of Death	Other Complications
2/23/14	Samazi	21	1		Eclampsia	
2/25/14	Edeni	22	3	2	Hypovolemic shock	Incomplete abortion
2/27/14	Chanji	23	1	0	?	Heart disease? Anemia?
3/4/14	Kasekela	26	3	3	Anesthetic complications, aspiration	
3/5/14	Malangali	23	3	3	PPH, surgical complications	Anemia, blood supply
4/6/14	Mkole	23	2	2	Anemia, CCF	
4/9/14	Katusa	24	2	1	Suspected embolism	
4/19/14	Malolwa	30	5	5	PPH, retained placenta	Anemia
4/27/14	Mwimbi	34	6	5	IUFD, ruptured uterus	Late referral, DOA
5/30/14	Madibila/Ilolesha	37	10	9	Obstructed labor, IUFD	
6/5/14	Mtimbwa	30	?	?	? Suspected sepsis	Malaria suspected
6/9/14	FILE MISSING	—	—	—	—	—
6/23/14	Kifone	22			Malaria in pregnancy	
7/1/14	Chelenganya	24	3	3	Sepsis	Native drug intoxication
7/12/14	Kizwite	20	1		Embolism	
7/31/14	Katonto	20	1		PPH, eclampsia	Anemia
8/12/14	Mazwi	26			Abortion, septic shock	
8/14/14	Laela/Mshani	40	7	6	APH, PPH	Anemia, shock
9/21/14	Lowe	18	1	0	Sepsis	
9/22/14	Sumbawanga Asilia	30	7	6	Severe anemia, PV bleeding	
9/24/14*	Kizwite	35			Renal failure	
10/12/14	Lua/Maomba/ Bakwta RC	19	2	1	Malaria in pregnancy	
10/20/14	Legezamwendo	33	7	6	APH, ruptured uterus	Anemia
10/22/14**	Legezamwendo	32			Intestinal obstruction	HIV/AIDS stage 4
11/20/14	Kilimahewa	28	3	2	APH, placental abruption	HIV+
12/31/14	Sandulula	21	2	1	Embolism?	
2015						
1/26/15	Isesa	22	3	3	Septic shock	Cardiorespiratory failure?

Date of Death	Village/Town of Origin	Age	G	P	Cause of Death	Other Complications
2/22/15	Ilemba	20	2	2	Sepsis? Malaria? Pneumonia?	HIV+
2/23/15	Mpui	28	3	2	Eclampsia	Obesity
3/5/15	Mazwi	24	1	1	Embolism?	
4/15/15	FILE MISSING	?	?	?	—	—
4/15/15	Isesa	30	?	?	Hypovolemic shock	
4/17/15	Kanyezi	36	9	9	PPH, DIC	Local herbs

ABBREVIATIONS: G = gravida; P = parity; APH = antepartum hemorrhage; CCF = congestive cardiac failure; DIC = disseminated intravascular coagulopathy (causes blood to clot excessively and then leads to an inability to clot, leading to severe bleeding); Dx = diagnosis; IUFD = intrauterine fetal death; PPH = postpartum hemorrhage; PV = per vagina.

COLOR KEY: yellow = Sumbawanga Urban District; orange = Kalambo District; blue = Sumbawanga Rural District; green = Nkasi District.

* Ruled not a maternal death during the maternal death audit meeting but upon consulting an obstetric pathologist in the United States, Dr. David A. Schwartz, we determined, on the basis of the information available, that the renal failure was a result of her pregnancy, thereby qualifying her death as having a pregnancy-related cause.

** Ruled not a maternal death during the maternal death audit meeting.

We talked about

Biobureaucracy and how that

> partographs - 95

> supply + demand,

> connect w/ Packard's discussion of Cuba

→ British colonialism

> Blaming Women - 8

GLOSSARY OF MEDICAL TERMS

Active labor — The part of the first stage of labor when the woman's cervix begins to dilate more quickly and contractions become longer, stronger, and closer together, resulting in transition to the second stage of labor, when the woman starts pushing.

Active management of the third stage of labor — Used to remove the placenta instead of letting it separate from the uterus and be expelled with a contraction. The provider exerts sustained force on the umbilical cord while applying counterpressure to the woman's uterus to pull the placenta free.

Antepartum hemorrhage — Severe bleeding occurring anytime in the pregnancy before the woman gives birth; common causes could be threatened miscarriage or abnormalities of the placenta, such as placenta previa or placental abruption.

APGAR score — A point system used to measure newborns' reflexes and assess their condition and determine if they need any further medical intervention after birth.

Cesarean section (alt. C-section) — A surgical procedure to remove the baby from the mother's uterus.

Congestive cardiac failure — A chronic, progressive condition that affects the heart muscle's ability to pump effectively; the term usually refers to the stage in which fluid builds up around the heart and causes it to pump inefficiently.

Eclampsia — The onset of seizures during pregnancy (or the postpartum period) caused by the high blood pressure of preeclampsia; confirmed by protein in the urine combined with the presence of seizures.

Embolism	When a material causes a blockage inside a blood vessel, preventing blood flow in whole or in part. In pregnancy, amniotic fluid embolism is a threat and can cause sudden and unexpected death of the woman.
Fresh stillbirth	A stillbirth in which a baby has died shortly before being delivered, as opposed to a macerated stillbirth.
Hemorrhage	Extreme blood loss.
Macerated stillbirth	A stillbirth in which the baby has died prior to the delivery, as long as days or weeks before, sometimes leading to tissue necrosis as the body starts to reabsorb the fetal tissue.
Manual removal of the placenta	A procedure in which a health care provider must remove the placenta that the body has not expelled; includes using the hand to follow the umbilical cord into the woman's uterus and removing the placenta, or pieces of the placenta, that have not separated from the uterine wall.
Obstructed labor	A condition in which, though the uterus is contracting, the baby does not exit the pelvis. This can have a number of underlying causes and can result in fetal, newborn, or maternal disability or death.
Partograph	A graphical representation of a pregnant woman's progress during labor and delivery. Providers use it to record contractions, dilation, fetal heart rate, fetal descent, among other information. See figure 11.
Placental abruption	An uncommon condition in which the placenta detaches from the uterus prematurely. Can cause vaginal bleeding and can result in fetal distress, preterm delivery, and stillbirth.
Postpartum hemorrhage	Bleeding that occurs after the woman gives birth, caused, most commonly, by tears, poor uterine contraction (atony) resulting in failure of the blood vessels to close, retained pieces of the placenta, or blood clotting disorders.
Preeclampsia	A condition during pregnancy that is characterized by high blood pressure, fluid retention, and protein in the urine. If untreated, preeclampsia can lead to eclampsia and is life-threatening.
Pregnancy-induced hypertension	The development of new hypertension (high blood pressure) in a pregnant woman after twenty weeks' gestation but without the presence of protein in the urine or other signs of preeclampsia.
Primigravida	Someone in her first pregnancy.
Resuscitation	Processes of correcting physiological problems in a patient who is acutely unwell. Can include, for example, cardiopulmonary resuscitation, which is meant to restore blood flow and breathing.
Retained placenta	A condition in which the placenta fails to separate from the wall of the uterus within approximately thirty minutes after giving birth to the baby.

Sepsis A complication that arises in response to severe infection; the body's response can lead to tissue damage, organ failure, and death.

Stillbirth When a baby has died while still in utero, from known or unknown causes.

Uterine rupture Often caused by obstructed labor and sometimes attributed to the use of herbal medicines. Occurs when the baby is unable to descend and be born, commonly due to the baby's malposition, celphalopelvic disproportion, or poor dilation. The strength of the contractions causes the uterus to burst open, nearly always resulting in the death of the baby unless doctors can operate immediately. More common in women who are grand multipara because of weakened uterine muscles. The uterus can also rupture along previous C-section incision sites.

sepsis — A complication that arises in response to severe infection; the body's response can lead to tissue damage, organ failure, and death.

stillbirth — When a baby has died while still in utero, from known or unknown causes.

[illegible]

NOTES

INTRODUCTION

1. Wendland (2016, 62).

2. Williams (1994, 7).

3. TNA, Acc. No. 450, File 108/9/169C.

4. On these goals of "modernizing" women in colonial Tanganyika, see Comaroff and Comaroff (1992, 215–16); Crozier (2007, 3); Vaughan (1991).

5. Hulton et al. (2014); Oni-Orisan (2016); Storeng and Béhague (2017); WHO (2015b). Data collection extends to a much earlier time; see Adams (2016) for a brief history of the uses of statistical data in health projects.

6. WHO (2016).

7. Maine and Rosenfield (1999); Ronsmans and Graham (2006).

8. WHO (2015c).

9. Rosenfield and Maine (1985).

10. Starrs (2006); Storeng and Béhague (2016).

11. Storeng and Béhague (2016).

12. H. Campbell and Stein (1992); McHenry (1994).

13. Nyerere (1958); Biermann and Wagao (1986); McHenry (1994).

14. H. Campbell and Stein (1992); McHenry (1994).

15. WHO (1978).

16. Bech et al. (2013); Iliffe (1998, 208).

17. Iliffe (1998, 212).

18. H. Campbell and Stein (1992, 5); Iliffe (1998, 203); Jennings (2008); Lambert and Sahn (2002, 120).

19. FCI (2007, 78).

20. FCI (2007, 78–79).

21. Iliffe (1998, 203).
22. Iliffe (1998, 203).
23. FCI (2007, 76).
24. FCI (2007, 76); TMoH (1990).
25. Amooti-Kaguna and Nuwaha (2000); Danforth et al. (2009); Kyomuhendo (2003); Lubbock and Stephenson (2008); Mrisho et al. (2007).
26. Bazzano et al. (2008); Kyomuhendo (2003); Okafor and Rizzuto (1994).
27. Majoko et al. (2002); McDonagh (1996); Yuster (1995).
28. On their failure, see Starrs (2006).
29. Koblinsky et al. (2006); Ronsmans et al. (2003); Scott and Ronsmans (2009).
30. DRHR, WHO (2008). BEmONC training includes instruction on the identification of danger signs indicating serious complications, the management of normal labor and delivery, the treatment of emergencies, appropriate referral procedures, neonatal resuscitation techniques, and maintenance of necessary supplies and equipment needed for a safe and healthy delivery. Trainings also include information on postpartum care and techniques for culturally appropriate, respectful communication with clients and their family members.
31. UN (2015).
32. WHO (2015a).
33. WHO (2015a). For comparison, women in the United States have a 1 in 3,800 chance and women in the Netherlands just 1 in 8,700 chance of dying from pregnancy-related causes (WHO 2015c).
34. Geissler, Rottenburg, and Zenker (2012, 17).
35. GBD Maternal Mortality Collaborators (2016). This is compared to 26.4 deaths per 100,000 live births for women in the US and just 3.8 for women in Finland.
36. TMoHCDGEC et al. (2016, 321).
37. TMoHCDGEC (2020).
38. TMoH (2001).
39. UN (2016). There seems to be no mention of whom this global average will necessarily leave behind.
40. Kohrman (2005, 3).
41. Wolf (2012).
42. Quote from Hunt (1999, 4).
43. Adams (2016); Erikson (2012); Geurts (2015); Merry (2011).
44. Adams (2016, 37); Biruk (2018); Kingori and Gerrets (2016).
45. Storeng and Béhague (2017); Wendland (2016).
46. Allen (2004); Berry (2010); Brunson (2010); Chapman (2010); Sargent (1982, 1989); Van Hollen (2003).
47. Sumbawanga Regional Referral Hospital (2013).
48. Sumbawanga District Council (2012).
49. Smythe (2006, 22); Willis (1978, 1981).
50. Willis (1978, 146–47).
51. Willis (1978).
52. Metz (2013).
53. Clinical officers were more commonly present in lower-level health facilities.

54. This changed in 2018 when the central government moved all regional hospitals directly under the control of the Ministry of Health, Community Development, Gender, Elderly and Children, though the regionally based Health Management Teams still play a supervisory role.

55. WHO (2012).

56. Alber and Drotbohm (2015).

57. See Pols (2015).

58. Livingston (2012); McKay (2012); Mol (2002, 2008); Mol, Moser, and Pols (2010); Stevenson (2014).

59. Brodwin (2013).

60. Brodwin (2013, 12).

61. Brodwin (2013, 18).

62. Puig de la Bellacasa (2017, 6).

63. On localized forms of ethical care, see Raghuram (2016). On African moral philosophies, see Harding ([1987] 1998); Metz (2013).

64. Mol, Moser, and Pols (2010, 13).

65. Wind (2008, 84).

66. E. Campbell and Lassiter (2015); Sufrin (2015; 2017, 19); Wacquant (2011).

67. Puig de la Bellacasa (2017, 6).

68. Wendland (2010, 22). But since Wendland wrote that statement, there have been a handful of studies on the perspectives of this workforce, notably including those also from African scholars. See Heaton (2013); Kyakuwa (2009); Kyakuwa and Hardon (2012); H. Martin (2009); Mulemi (2010); Tousignant (2018).

1. THE MAWINGU REGIONAL HOSPITAL MATERNITY WARD

1. Chang and King (2011).
2. Jordan (1993, 152).
3. TNA, Acc. No. 450, File 314.
4. Exavery et al. (2013).
5. Exavery et al. (2013).
6. Bridges (1990).
7. Sumbawanga District Council (2012).
8. TNA, Acc. No. 450, File 55/255.
9. TNA, Acc. No. 450, Files 55/321 and 55/336.
10. Morrisson (2002, 121).
11. Mubyazi et al. (2006).
12. FCI (2007, 78).
13. Sikika (2011, 4).
14. *Tanzania Daily News* (2015).
15. *Citizen* (2015).
16. WHO (2014).
17. PMORALG (2015, 1).
18. Mkoka et al. (2014).

2. WORKING IN SCARCITY

Some parts of this chapter overlap with my previously published article "Working in Scarcity: Effects on Social Interactions and Biomedical Care in a Tanzanian Hospital," *Social Science and Medicine* 187 (2017): 217–24, doi: https://doi.org/10.1016/j.socscimed.2017.02.010.

1. Livingston (2012); Mkoka et al. (2014); Sullivan (2011).

2. This has become a standard part of active management of the third stage of labor (AMTSL), and oxytocin works on the smooth muscles of the uterus to help it contract, thereby causing the blood vessels to close, preventing more prolonged and serious bleeding.

3. See Marwa and Strong (2015).

4. *Citizen* (2015).

5. The extra pay could be extraduty pay (for additional shifts) or on-call pay (for shifts on which a person reported for part of the time or was placed on standby and, depending on patient load, might be called into work or not).

6. After Lipsky (2010).

7. Mechanic (1962, 352).

8. Iliffe (1998); Maestad and Mwisongo (2011).

9. White (2000).

10. Beidelman (1993, 33–35); Taylor (1992); White (1994, 2000).

11. H. Martin (2009, 128).

12. Dextrose 5% is not used to support women with fluid loss or to help support blood pressure, so it would not be useful if a woman was suffering from eclampsia or PPH.

13. Strong (2017).

14. Lewis (2006); Mwafisi (1999); Anti-Corruption Resource Center (2014). After I completed this fieldwork, John Pombe Magufuli was elected in the fall of 2015. He was elected on a platform that included strong anticorruption rhetoric, and he has proven himself to be tough on many of these activities. Initially, upon his election and in its immediate aftermath, many Tanzanians told me they enjoyed his style of leadership and strong anticorruption ways as he purged fake workers from payrolls and fired on the spot government workers who were not at their desks during working hours. Enthusiasm soon faded as people realized Magufuli's new order also severely limited more informal (i.e., corrupt) routes for business that appeared to significantly reduce people's disposable income. Starting in May 2016, friends pointed out to me the reduced number of government employees and businesspeople in Dar es Salaam bars and restaurants as a sign that people no longer had money to spend.

3. PROTOCOLS AND DEVIATIONS

1. On projectification, see Geissler, Rottenburg, and Zenker (2012, 17). On the explosion of NGOs, see Geissler (2015).

2. Misoprostol is used to control or prevent bleeding by encouraging the smooth muscles of the uterus to contract after labor. International views on the use of misoprostol have changed from recommending its universal use to now making it a second- or third-line drug for the treatment of postpartum hemorrhage. Misoprostol can also be used to induce labor and is a common abortifacient globally.

3. Hochschild ([1983] 2012).
4. Brown (2010).
5. de Klerk (2013, 2012).
6. Mol, Moser, and Pols (2010, 12).
7. Mol, Moser, and Pols (2010, 12–13).
8. Armbruster (2006).
9. Any remaining pieces of placental tissue can cause the uterus to not contract. This is one of the most common causes of postpartum hemorrhage, a leading cause of maternal death.
10. Strong (2017, 220).
11. Strong (2018).
12. Pérez D'Gregorio (2010).
13. Bohren et al. (2015, 7).
14. Chambliss (1996, 104–5).
15. Mhamela (2013).
16. Tanzania Nurses and Midwives Council (2009).
17. Mol, Moser, and Pols (2010, 12–13).
18. Chronic iron-deficient anemia can result in increased cardiac output, a condition that, when combined with the expanded blood volume of pregnancy, can lead to congestive heart failure (Cunningham et al. 1986; Hegde, Rich, and Gayomali 2006).

4. "BAD LUCK," LOST BABIES, AND THE STRUCTURING OF REALITIES

Portions of the section "The Case of Pendo's Baby" have previously appeared on my blog as part of the post entitled "Ethical Dilemmas and Medical Malpractice" (Strong 2014).

1. Brown (2010, 20, emphasis added).
2. McKay (2012).
3. A nuchal cord is simply an umbilical cord that becomes wrapped around the baby's neck. In rare cases, the cord becomes very tight, forms a knot and essentially cuts off the baby's oxygen supply or prevents the baby's descent.
4. WHO Maternal Health and Safe Motherhood Program (1994).
5. Philpott and Castle (1972).
6. Bosse, Massawe, and Jahn (2002); Umezulike, Onah and Okaro (1999); Yisma et al. (2013).
7. Berg and Bowker (1997, 529).
8. Heimer and Gazley (2012).
9. Hull (2012).
10. Heimer and Gazley (2012); Melberg et al. (2018).
11. Olivier de Sardan, Diarra, and Moha (2017, 80).
12. For a similar example of the productive capabilities of bureaucratic documents, see Hull (2012).
13. Melberg et al. (2018).
14. Biruk (2018, 5–6).
15. Street (2011, 830).

16. Cephalopelvic disproportion is a primary cause of obstructed labor and is a mismatch between the size of the baby's head and the mother's pelvic outlet, determined by the bony structures of the pelvis, making it difficult, if not impossible, for the mother to give birth vaginally.

17. Macerated stillbirths were those in which the baby had died some time prior to delivery and the tissue was often starting to break down and decay in utero, leading to the name.

18. Without knowledge of the specific facility, it is difficult to know if these providers were nurses, clinical officers, or medical attendants. Many village facilities were staffed by medical attendants who had less (or no) training in midwifery and who often struggled to appropriately diagnose complications and danger signs.

19. The idea of legal action was mostly hearsay in this region. A more likely outcome of complaints at Mawingu would have been an investigation of the provider by their national governing and licensing body, which could have resulted in the revocation of the provider's license to practice in the country. I address this issue in the next chapter.

20. Afnan-Holmes et al. (2015); McClure, Nalubamba-Phiri, and Goldenberg (2006).

21. Haws et al. (2010).

22. Haws et al. (2010).

23. On toughening, see de Klerk (2013, S483).

24. Castle (1994); Haws et al. (2010); Scheper-Hughes (1992); van der Sijpt and Notermans (2010).

25. See also Harrington (1998).

26. Erikson (2012, 370).

27. Hull (2012, 36).

28. Hetherington (2011, 77).

5. LANDSCAPES OF ACCOUNTABILITY IN CARE

1. Afnan-Holmes et al. (2015, e399).

2. In the normal mechanics of birth, the baby actually assists the mother's body in moving it through the birth canal. A dead fetus is unable to do so, and the process is often much longer in the second stage of labor—from full dilation (10 cm) to the complete emergence of the baby.

3. See, for example, Erikson (2012).

4. Geissler (2015).

5. Strong (2017).

6. Rottenburg (2009); Sullivan (2011, 2012).

7. Whyte and Siu (2015, 28).

8. Willis (1981, 181).

9. Willis (1981, 183).

10. Buguzi (2015); Harrington (1998).

11. Buguzi (2015).

12. H. Kandoro, personal communication, May 2019.

13. Harrington (1998, 2004).

14. Harrington (1998, 151).

15. Brodwin (2013, 20).
16. Vierke (2012).
17. I have intentionally left out the specifics of what he wrote in the rest of the postoperative report in order to protect him and because these details are not important for the point I am putting forth here. However, poor progress of labor was an accurate diagnosis, regardless of the ultimate cause.
18. Lambeck (2015, xi).
19. Brodwin (2013, 18).
20. Tanzania Nurses and Midwives Council (2009).

6. THE STORIES WE TELL ABOUT THE DEATHS WE SEE

1. Table 3 in the Appendix gives particulars of all the deaths that occurred while I was at the hospital in 2014 and 2015.
2. Armstrong et al. (2014); TMoHSW (2006).
3. Mills (2011, 1).
4. Danel, Graham, and Boerma (2011, 779).
5. A number of institutions and countries use this audit system, including the United Kingdom (Knight et al. 2015).
6. On the obsession with metrics, see Adams (2016, 23); Erikson (2012).
7. Adams (2016, 36).
8. Davis et al. ([2012] 2015, 1).
9. Suh (2018, 663).
10. Morgan and Roberts (2012, 243).
11. See Castro and Savage (2019); Singer (2017, 2018); Smith-Oka (2015).
12. Ferguson (1994).
13. Li (2007, 125).
14. Ferguson (1994); Li (2007, 7).
15. Armstrong et al. (2014, 1089); see also van Hamersveld et al. (2012).
16. Armstrong et al. (2014, 1089).
17. Adams (2016).
18. All the quotes from the meetings are paraphrased. Because of the confidential nature of the audit meetings, I was not allowed to record the discussions and frequently do not have verbatim quotes.
19. De Kok et al. (2017, 1089).
20. D.A. Schwartz, personal communication, August 2015.
21. Weber (1947, 215).
22. Gupta (2012, 24–25).
23. Li (2007); Wendland (2016).
24. De Kok et al. (2017); van Hamersveld et al. (2012).
25. Wendland (2016, 78).
26. Geissler, Rottenburg, and Zenker (2012, 13).
27. On the simplifications inherent in the exercise of the health care audit, see Gerrets (2012).
28. Ferguson (1994); Li (2007).

7. ALREADY DEAD

1. Mattingly and Garro (2000, 15).
2. Mattingly and Garro (2000, 16–17).
3. See Dawley (2000); Fahy (2007).
4. Allen (2004, 2); MacDonald (2019).
5. One could argue that luck, the will of God, or even witchcraft controlled the availability of supplies in this setting, but I never heard any of the nurses or doctors refer to any of these factors as the cause of stock-outs.
6. See the next chapter for extensive available literature on contributors to maternal death related to life outside the hospital.
7. Colen (1995, 78).
8. See also Spangler (2011) for an excellent analysis of embodied inequality for poor women in another region of Tanzania, demonstrating the links between stratified reproduction, social exclusion, overly general policies, state modernity projects, and maternal health.
9. Rossiter (1985, 100).
10. Public health practitioners and clinicians often include factors such as women's autonomy and status within a society, delays in deciding to seek care, failure to recognize the severity of an obstetric problem, or family issues that cause a delay in seeking care, which can also be related to delays associated with lack of transportation and poor infrastructure, as indirect causes of death (Danforth et al. 2009; Gabrysch and Campbell 2009; Mrisho et al. 2007; Pembe et al. 2008; Prevention of Maternal Mortality Network 1992).
11. Thaddeus and Maine (1994).
12. Adams (2016); Wendland (2016).

8. "PREGNANCY IS POISON"

1. Briggs (2001); Farmer (1992, 1999); Fassin (2001); Jones (2014); Scherz (2018).
2. Chemla and Keller (2017, 3).
3. As a general rule, women who were in their fifth pregnancy or beyond were called grand multipara and were immediately referred to a higher level of care to ensure that emergency care would be available. Clinically, these women were more prone to uterine rupture, prolapse, and postpartum hemorrhaging, necessitating surgical intervention and/or blood transfusions.
4. MacDonald (2019).
5. MacDonald (2019, 269).
6. Spangler (2011).
7. It is virtually impossible to extricate education from several other indicators of women's empowerment, including decision-making autonomy, access to household resources, and a broader political and social environment that supports women's access to economic opportunity and legal rights (McTavish et al. 2010).
8. Ahmed et al. (2010); McAlister and Baskett (2006).
9. McAlister and Baskett (2006).
10. A number of public health studies have suggested a lack of female autonomy in decision-making as a limiting factor in the utilization of health care services (Gage 2007; Koblinsky et al. 2006; Lubbock and Stephenson 2008; WHO 2015c).

11. Waiswa et al. (2008); Hawkins et al. (2005, 17).

12. Human Rights Watch (2017).

13. *Citizen* (2017).

14. BBC (2017).

15. Pressure from advocacy, human rights, and civil society organizations led the World Bank to withhold US$500 million from the Tanzanian government in 2018 until Tanzania reversed its stance on pregnant schoolgirls (Bhalla 2020). The Tanzanian Ministry of Education announced on April 1, 2020, that they were accepting the World Bank funds and, according to a letter from the minister of education posted on April 6, 2020, on the ministry's official Twitter account (photographed in a tweet), the funds will support secondary school students throughout the country "without discrimination, and shall include girls who drop out of school for various reasons, including pregnancy" (https://twitter.com/wizara_elimuTz/status/1247222894826065920/photo/1). Some commenters say this is a "backdoor" way of unofficially lifting the ban (Rodriguez 2020).

16. When a woman is not pregnant, yet displays all the outward signs of pregnancy, including weight gain in the abdomen, amenorrhea, and even morning sickness. The phantom pregnancy might be caused psychologically, for example from pressure or desire for a pregnancy, or by physiological abnormalities, particularly with the endocrine system.

17. Women in urban Tanzania expressed a desire for smaller family sizes in my own interviews between 2009 and 2011; see also NBS and ICF Macro (2011, 57).

18. Though it has dropped quickly (Afnan-Holmes et al. 2015).

19. WHO (1989, 67).

20. Gordon and Gordon (2007, 33).

21. Turshen (1984, 55–56).

22. WHO (1989, 68).

23. Langwick (2008, 2011).

24. Sargent and Bascopé (1997, 183).

25. Langwick (2012); Pigg (1997).

26. Cogburn (2019); Wendland (2016, 2018).

9. THE MEANINGS OF MATERNAL DEATH

1. See Whyte (1997) for Uganda.

2. Ferguson (1994).

3. NBS and ICF Macro (2011); TMoHCDGEC et al. (2016).

4. TNA, Acc. No. HE, File 1172/67.

5. Wendland (2018).

6. Fassin (2009).

7. AbouZahr (2003).

8. Mahler (1987, 668).

9. AbouZahr (2003, 18).

10. Rosenfield and Maine (1985); Berry (2010, 190).

11. Berry (2010, 192).

12. WHO (2015b).

13. Freedman (2016).

14. Freedman (2016, 4).

15. Freedman (2016, 5).
16. Mol, Moser, and Pols (2010, 12).

EPILOGUE

1. N. Martin, Cillekens, and Freitas (2017); N. Martin and Montagne (2017a); Martin and Montagne (2017b).
2. N. Martin, Cillekens, and Freitas (2017).
3. GBD 2015 Maternal Mortality Collaborators (2016); Martin and Montagne (2017b).
4. N. Martin and Montagne (2017a).
5. N. Martin and Montagne (2017a).
6. Rosenfield and Maine (1985).
7. Young, Kelly, and Schnaars (2019).
8. Kelly and Young (2019); Young, Kelly, and Schnaars (2019).
9. Young, Kelly, and Schnaars (2019).

REFERENCES

ARCHIVAL SOURCES

TNA (Tanzania National Archives), Dar es Salaam

Medical Department Files, Accession No. 450

File 55	Building of the Sumbawanga Hospital, 1936–57
File 108/9	Maternity and Child Welfare (General)
File 314	Training of Native Midwives (Certificated)

Medical Department Files, Accession No. HE

File 1172	Medical Development Plan

OTHER SOURCES

AbouZahr, Carla. 2003. "Safe Motherhood: A Brief History of the Global Movement, 1947–2002." *British Medical Bulletin* 67: 13–25. doi: https://doi.org/10.1093/bmb/ldg014.

Adams, Vincanne, ed. 2016. *Metrics: What Counts in Global Health.* Durham, NC: Duke University Press.

Afnan-Holmes, Hoviyeh, Moke Magoma, Theopista John, Francis Levira, Georgina Msemo, Corinne E. Armstrong, Melissa Martínex-Álvarez, et al. 2015. "Tanzania's Countdown to 2015: An Analysis of Two Decades of Progress and Gaps for Reproductive, Maternal, Newborn, and Child Health, to Inform Priorities for Post-2015." *Lancet* 3 (7): e396–e409. doi: https://doi.org/10.1016/S2214-109X(15)00059-5.

Ahmed, Saifuddin, Andreea A. Creanga, Duff G. Gillespie, and Amy O. Tsui. 2010. "Economic Status, Education and Empowerment: Implications for Maternal Health Service Utilization in Developing Countries." *PLoS ONE* 5 (6): e11190. doi: https://doi.org/10.1371/journal.pone.0011190.

Alber, Erdmute, and Heike Drotbohm, eds. 2015. *Anthropological Perspectives on Care: Work, Kinship, and the Life-Course.* New York: Palgrave Macmillan.

Allen, Denise Roth. 2004. *Managing Motherhood, Managing Risk: Fertility and Danger in West Central Tanzania.* Ann Arbor: University of Michigan Press.

Amooti-Kaguna, B., and F. Nuwaha. 2000. "Factors Influencing Choice of Delivery Sites in Rakai District of Uganda." *Social Science and Medicine* 50 (2): 203–13. doi: https://doi.org/10.1016/s0277-9536(99)00275-0.

Anti-Corruption Resource Center. 2014. *Overview of Corruption in Tanzania.* U4 Expert Answer. www.u4.no/publications/overview-of-corruption-in-tanzania.pdf.

Armbruster, Deborah. 2006. "Prevention of Postpartum Hemorrhage: The Role of Active Management of the Third Stage of Labor." *International Journal of Gynecology and Obstetrics* 94 (S2): S122–S123. doi: https://doi.org/10.1016/S0020-7292(06)60004-0.

Armstrong, Corinne E., Isabelle L. Lange, M. Magoma, Veronique Filippi, and C. Ronsmans. 2014. "Strengths and Weaknesses in the Implementation of Maternal and Perinatal Death Reviews in Tanzania: Perceptions, Processes and Practice." *Tropical Medicine and International Health* 19 (9): 1087–95. doi: https://doi.org/10.1111/tmi.12353.

Bazzano, Alessandra Nina, Betty Kirkwood, Charlotte Tawaih-Agyemang, Seth Owusu-Agyei, and Philip Adongo. 2008. "Social Costs of Skilled Attendance at Birth in Rural Ghana." *International Journal of Gynecology and Obstetrics* 102: 91–94. doi: https://doi.org/10.1016/j.ijgo.2008.02.004.

BBC (British Broadcasting Company). 2017. "John Magufuli's Pregnant Schoolgirl Ban Angers Tanzanian Women." June 23. www.bbc.com/news/world-africa-40379113?ocid=socialflow_twitter.

Bech, Margunn M, Yusufu Q. Lawi, Deodatus A. Massay, and Ole B. Rekdal. 2013. "Changing Policies and Their Influence on Government Health Workers in Tanzania, 1967–2009: Perspectives from Rural Mbulu District." *International Journal of African Historical Studies* 46 (1): 61–103.

Beidelman, Thomas O. 1993. *Moral Imagination in Kaguru Modes of Thought.* Washington, DC: Smithsonian Institution Press.

Berg, Marc, and Geoffrey Bowker. 1997. "The Multiple Bodies of the Medical Record: Toward a Sociology of an Artifact." *Sociological Quarterly* 38 (3): 513–37.

Berry, Nicole S. 2010. *Unsafe Motherhood: Mayan Maternal Mortality and Subjectivity in Post-war Guatemala.* Fertility, Reproduction, and Sexuality, vol. 21. New York: Berghahn Books.

Bhalla, Nita. 2020. "Tanzania Lets Pregnant Girls Attend School with World Bank Project." Thomson Reuters Foundation, April 7. www.reuters.com/article/us-tanzania-women-education-trfn/tanzania-lets-pregnant-girls-attend-school-with-world-bank-project-idUSKBN21P2WE.

Biermann, Werner, and Jumanne Wagao. 1986. "The Quest for Adjustment: Tanzania and the IMF, 1980–1986." *African Studies Review* 29 (4): 89–103.

Biruk, Crystal. 2018. *Cooking Data: Culture and Politics in an African Research World.* Durham, NC: Duke University Press.

Bohren, Meghan A., Joshua P. Vogel, Erin C. Hunter, Olha Lutsiv, Suprita K. Makh, João Paulo Souza, Carolina Aguiar, et al. 2015. "The Mistreatment of Women during

Childbirth in Health Facilities Globally: A Mixed-Methods Systematic Review." *PLOS Medicine* 12 (6): e1001847. doi: https://doi.org/10/1371/journal.pmed.1001847.

Bosse, G., S. Massawe, and A. Jahn. 2002. "The Partograph in Daily Practice: It's Quality That Matters." *International Journal of Gynecology and Obstetrics* 77: 243–44. doi: https://doi.org/10.1016/s0020-7292(02)00004-8.

Bridges, Jacqueline M. 1990. "Literature Review on the Images of the Nurse and Nursing in the Media." *Journal of Advanced Nursing* 15: 850–54. doi: https://doi.org/10.1111/j.1365-2648.1990.tb01917.x.

Briggs, Charles. 2001. "Modernity, Cultural Reasoning, and the Institutionalization of Social Inequality: Racializing Death in a Venezuelan Cholera Epidemic." *Comparative Studies in Society and History* 43 (4): 665–700.

Brodwin, Paul. 2013. *Everyday Ethics: Voices from the Front Line of Community Psychiatry.* Oakland: University of California Press.

Brown, Hannah. 2010. "'If We Sympathise with Them, They'll Relax': Fear/Respect and Medical Care in a Kenyan Hospital." *Medische Antropologie* 22 (1): 125–42.

Brunson, Jan. 2010. "Confronting Maternal Mortality, Controlling Birth in Nepal: The Gendered Politics of Receiving Biomedical Care at Birth." *Social Science and Medicine* 71: 1719–27. doi: https://doi.org/10.1016/j.socscimed.2010.06.013.

Buguzi, Syriacus. 2015. "Legal, Technology Dilemma Facing Doctors in Tanzania." *Citizen,* November 14. www.thecitizen.co.tz/news/Legal—technology-dilemma-facing-doctors-in-Tanzania/1840340-2955840-ufedex/index.html.

Campbell, Elizabeth, and Luke Eric Lassiter. 2015. *Doing Ethnography Today: Theories, Methods, Exercises.* Oxford: Wiley-Blackwell.

Campbell, Horace, and Howard Stein, eds. 1992. *Tanzania and the IMF: The Dynamics of Liberalization.* Boulder, CO: Westview Press.

Castle, Sarah E. 1994. "The (Re)negotiation of Illness Diagnoses and Responsibility for Child Death in Rural Mali." *Medical Anthropology Quarterly* 8 (3): 314–35. doi: https://doi.org/10.1525/maq.1994.8.3.02a00040.

Castro, Arachu, and Virginia Savage. 2019. "Obstetric Violence as Reproductive Governance in the Dominican Republic." *Medical Anthropology* 38 (2): 123–36. doi: https://doi.10.1080/01459740.2018.1512984.

Chambliss, Daniel F. 1996. *Beyond Caring: Hospitals, Nurses, and the Social Organization of Ethics.* Chicago: University of Chicago Press.

Chang, Jiat-Hwee, and Anthony D. King. 2011. "Towards a Genealogy of Tropical Architecture: Historical Fragments of Power-Knowledge, Built Environment and Climate in the British Colonial Territories." *Singapore Journal of Tropical Geography* 32: 283–300. doi: https://doi.org/10.1111/j.1467-9493.2011.00434.x.

Chapman, Rachel R. 2010. *Family Secrets: Risking Reproduction in Central Mozambique.* Nashville, TN: Vanderbilt University Press.

Chemla, Karine, and Evelyn Fox Keller, eds. 2017. *Cultures without Culturalism: The Making of Scientific Knowledge.* Durham, NC: Duke University Press.

Citizen. 2015. "Lawmakers Query Sh127 Billion Health Debt." June 3. www.thecitizen.co.tz/News/Lawmakers-query-Sh127-billion-health-debt/-/1840340/2738158/-/yoocypz/-/index.html.

Citizen. 2017. "JPM Closes Debate on Teen Mothers." June 23. www.thecitizen.co.tz/News/JPM-closes-debate-on-teen-mothers/1840340-3983644-s7jsbxz/index.html.

Cogburn, Megan D. 2019. "Homebirth Fines and Health Cards in Rural Tanzania: On the Push for Numbers in Maternal Health." *Social Science and Medicine*, August 23. doi: https://doi.org/10.1016/j.socscimed.2019.112508.

Colen, Shellee. 1995. "'Like a Mother to Them': Stratified Reproduction and West Indian Childcare Workers and Employers in New York." In *Conceiving the New World Order: The Global Politics of Reproduction*, edited by Faye D. Ginsburg and Rayna Rapp, 78–102. Berkeley: University of California Press.

Comaroff, John, and Jean Comaroff. 1992. *Ethnography and the Historical Imagination*. Boulder, CO: Westview Press.

Crozier, Anna. 2007. *Practising Colonial Medicine: The Colonial Medical Service in British East Africa*. London: I.B. Tauris.

Cunningham, G.F., J. Pritchard, G.D.V. Hankins, P.L. Anderson, M.J. Lucas, and K.F. Armstrong. 1986. "Peripartum Heart Failure: Idiopathic Cardiomyopathy or Compounding Cardiovascular Events?" *Obstetrics and Gynecology* 67 (2): 157–68.

Danel, Isabella, Wendy J. Graham, and Ties Boerma. 2011. "Maternal Death Surveillance and Response." *Bulletin of the World Health Organization* 89: 779–79A. doi: https://doi.org/10.2471/BLT.11.097220.

Danforth, E.J., M.E. Kruk, P.C. Rockers, G. Mbaruku, and S. Galea. 2009. "Household Decision-Making about Delivery in Health Facilities: Evidence from Tanzania." *Journal of Health, Population, and Nutrition* 27 (5): 696–703. doi: https://doi.org/10.3329/jhpn.v27i5.3781.

Davis, Kevin, Angelina Fisher, Benedict Kingsbury, and Sally Engle Merry. [2012] 2015. *Governance by Indicators: Global Power through Quantification and Rankings*. Oxford: Oxford University Press.

Dawley, Katy. 2000. "The Campaign to Eliminate the Midwife." *American Journal of Nursing* 100 (10): 50–56.

de Klerk, Josien. 2012. "The Compassion of Concealment: Silence between Older Caregivers and Dying Patients in the AIDS Era, Northwest Tanzania." *Culture, Health and Sexuality* 14 (S1): S27–S38. doi: https://doi.org/10.1080/13691058.2011.631220.

de Klerk, Josien. 2013. "Being Tough, Being Healthy: Local Forms of Counselling in Response to Adult Death in Northwest Tanzania." *Culture, Health and Sexuality* 15 (S4): S482–S494. doi: https://doi.org/10.1080/13691058.2013.809607.

de Kok, Bregje, M. Imamura, L. Kanguru, O. Owolabi, F. Okonofua, and J. Hussein. 2017. "Achieving Accountability through Maternal Death Reviews in Nigeria: A Process Analysis." *Health Policy and Planning* 32 (8): 1083–91. doi: https://doi.org/10.1093/heapol/czx012.

DRHR (Department of Reproductive Health and Research), WHO (World Health Organization). 2008. "Proportion of Births Attended by a Skilled Health Worker 2008 Updates." Factsheet. WHO/RHR/08.22. https://apps.who.int/iris/bitstream/handle/10665/69950/WHO_RHR_08.22_eng.pdf;jsessionid=2795E1F9FF91E1B74C7BA5E2C16ADF05?sequence=1.

Erikson, Susan L. 2012. "Global Health Business: The Production and Performativity of Statistics in Sierra Leone and Germany." *Medical Anthropology* 31 (4): 367–84. doi: https://doi.org/10.1080/01459740.2011.621908.

Exavery, Amon, Angelina M. Lutambi, Neema Wilson, Godfrey M. Mubyazi, Senga Pemba, and Godfrey Mbaruku. 2013. "Gender-Based Distributional Skewness of the United Republic of Tanzania's Health Workforce Cadres: A Cross-Sectional Health Facility Survey." *Human Resources for Health* 11: 28. doi: https://doi.org/10.1186/1478-4491-11-28.

Fahy, Kathleen. 2007. "An Australian History of the Subordination of Midwifery." *Women and Birth* 20: 25–29. doi: https://doi.org/10.1016/j.wombi.2006.08.003.

Farmer, Paul. 1992. *Aids and Accusation: Haiti and the Geography of Blame.* Berkeley: University of California Press.

Farmer, Paul. 1999. *Infections and Inequalities: The Modern Plagues.* Berkeley: University of California Press.

Fassin, Didier. 2001. "Culturalism as Ideology." In *Cultural Perspectives on Reproductive Health,* edited by P. Fassin, 300–317. Oxford: Oxford University Press.

Fassin, Didier. 2009. "Another Politics of Life Is Possible." *Theory, Culture and Society* 26 (5): 44–60. doi: https://doi.org/10.1177/0263276409106349.

FCI (Family Care International). 2007. *Safe Motherhood: A Review.* Family Care International. www.familycareintl.org/UserFiles/File/SM%20A%20Review_%20Full_Report_FINAL.pdf.

Ferguson, James. 1994. *The Anti-politics Machine: "Development," Depoliticization, and Bureaucratic Power in Lesotho.* Minneapolis: University of Minnesota Press.

Freedman, Lynn. 2016. "Implementation and Aspiration Gaps: Whose View Counts?" *Lancet* 388 (10056): 2068–69. doi: https://doi.org/10.1016/S0140-6736(16)31530-6.

Gabrysch, Sabine, and Oona M.R. Campbell. 2009. "Still Too Far to Walk: Literature Review of the Determinants of Delivery Service Use." *BMC Pregnancy and Childbirth* 9: 34. doi: https://doi.org/10.1186/1471-2393-9-34.

Gage, Anastasia J. 2007. "Barriers to the Utilization of Maternal Health Care in Rural Mali." *Social Science and Medicine* 65: 1666–82. doi: https://doi.org/10.1016/j.socscimed.2007.06.001.

GBD 2015 Maternal Mortality Collaborators. 2016. "Global, Regional, and National Levels of Maternal Mortality, 1990–2015: A Systematic Analysis for the Global Burden of Disease Study 2015." *Lancet* 388 (10053): 1775–1812. doi: https://doi.org/10.1016/S0140-6736(16)31470-2.

Geissler, Paul Wenzel, ed. 2015. *Para-states and Medical Science: Making African Global Health.* Durham, NC: Duke University Press.

Geissler, Paul Wenzel, Richard Rottenburg, and Julia Zenker, eds. 2012. *Rethinking Biomedicine and Governance in Africa: Contributions from Anthropology.* Bielefeld, Germany: Transcript Verlag.

Gerrets, René. 2012. "Governing Malaria: How an Old Scourge Troubles Precepts in Social Theory." In *Rethinking Biomedicine and Governance in Africa: Contributions from Anthropology,* edited by Paul Wenzel Geissler, Richard Rottenburg, and Julia Zenker, 23–42. Bielefeld, Germany: Transcript Verlag.

Geurts, Kathryn Linn. 2015. "On the Worlding of Accra's Rehabilitation Training Centre." Somatosphere.net, April 27. http://somatosphere.net/2015/04/on-the-worlding-of-accras-rehabilitation-training-centre.html#_ednref7.

Gordon, April A., and Donald L. Gordon, eds. 2007. *Understanding Contemporary Africa.* 4th ed. Boulder, CO: Lynne Rienner.

Gupta, Akhil. 2012. *Red Tape: Bureaucracy, Structural Violence, and Poverty in India.* Durham, NC: Duke University Press.

Harding, Sandra. [1987] 1998. "The Curious Coincidence of Feminine and African Moralities." In *African Philosophy: An Anthology,* edited by Emmanuel Chukwudi Eze, 360–72. Malden, MA: Blackwell. Originally published in *Women and Moral Theory,* edited by Eva Feder Kittay and Diana T. Meyers, 296–315 (Lanham, MD: Rowman and Littlefield).

Harrington, John A. 1998. "Privatizing Scarcity: Civil Liability and Health Care in Tanzania." *Journal of African Law* 42 (2): 147–71. doi: https://doi.org/10.1017/S0021855300011803.

Harrington, John A. 2004. "Medical Law and Health Care Reform in Tanzania." *Medical Law International* 6: 207–30.

Hawkins, Kristan, Karen Newman, Deborah Thomas, and Cindy Carlson. 2005. *Developing a Human Rights-Based Approach to Addressing Maternal Mortality: Desk Review.* London: Department for International Development, Health Resource Center.

Haws, Rachel A., Irene Mashasi, Mwifadhi Mrisho, Joanna Armstrong Schellenberg, Gary L. Darmstadt, and Peter J. Winch. 2010. "'These Are Not Good Things for Other People to Know': How Rural Tanzanian Women's Experiences of Pregnancy Loss and Early Neonatal Death May Impact Survey Data Quality." *Social Science and Medicine* 71: 1764–72. doi: https://doi.org/10.1016/j.socscimed.2010.03.051.

Heaton, Matthew M. 2013. *Black Skin, White Coats: Nigerian Psychiatrists, Decolonization, and the Globalization of Psychiatry.* Athens: Ohio University Press.

Hegde, Nikita, Michael W. Rich, and Charina Gayomali. 2006. "The Cardiomyopathy of Iron Deficiency." *Texas Heart Institute Journal* 33 (3): 340–44.

Heimer, Carol A., and J. Lynn Gazley. 2012. "Performing Regulation: Transcending Regulatory Ritualism in HIV Clinics." *Law and Society Review* 46 (4): 853–87. doi: https://doi.org/10.1111/j.1540-5893.2012.00519.x.

Hetherington, Kregg. 2011. *Guerrilla Auditors: The Politics of Transparency in Neoliberal Paraguay.* Durham, NC: Duke University Press.

Hochschild, Arlie Russell. [1983] 2012. *The Managed Heart: Commercialization of Human Feeling.* Berkeley: University of California Press.

Hull, Matthew S. 2012. *Government of Paper: The Materiality of Bureaucracy in Urban Pakistan.* Berkeley: University of California Press.

Hulton, Louise, Zoe Matthews, Adriane Martin-Hilber, Richard Adanu, Craig Ferla, Atnafu Getachew, Charles Makwenda, et al. 2014. "Using Evidence to Drive Action: A 'Revolution in Accountability' to Implement Quality Care for Better Maternal and Newborn Health in Africa." *International Journal of Gynecology and Obstetrics* 127: 96–101. doi: https://doi.org/10.1016/j.ijgo.2014.07.002.

Human Rights Watch. 2017. *"I Had a Dream to Finish School": Barriers to Secondary Education in Tanzania.* New York: Human Rights Watch.

Hunt, Nancy Rose. 1999. *A Colonial Lexicon: Of Birth Ritual, Medicalization, and Mobility in the Congo.* Durham, NC: Duke University Press.

Iliffe, John. 1998. *East African Doctors: A History of the Modern Profession.* Cambridge: Cambridge University Press.

Jennings, Michael. 2008. *Surrogates of the State: NGOs, Development, and Ujamaa in Tanzania.* Bloomfield, CT: Kumarian Press.

Jones, Jared. 2014. "Ebola, Emerging: The Limitations of Culturalist Discourses in Epidemiology." *Journal of Global Health,* April 1. www.ghjournal.org/ebola-emerging-the-limitations-of-culturalist-discourses-in-epidemiology/.

Jordan, Brigitte. 1993. *Birth in Four Cultures: A Cross Cultural Investigation of Childbirth in Yucatan, Holland, Sweden, and the United States.* 4th ed. Prospect Heights, IL: Waveland Press.

Kelly, John, and Alison Young. 2019. "The Secret Number Maternity Hospitals Don't Want You to Know, and Why We're Revealing It." *USA Today,* March 7. www.usatoday.com/story/news/investigations/deadly-deliveries/2019/03/07/childbirth-complication-rates-secret-heres-why-were-revealing-them/2927105002/?asdfjs.

Kingori, Patricia, and René Gerrets. 2016. "Morals, Morale and Motivations in Data Fabrication: Medical Research Fieldworkers Views and Practices in Two Sub-Saharan African Contexts." *Social Science and Medicine* 166: 150–59. doi: https://doi.org/10.1016/j.socscimed.2016.08.019.

Knight, Marian, Derek Tuffnell, Sara Kenyon, Judy Shakespeare, Ron Gray, and Jennifer J. Kurinczuk, eds. 2015. *Saving Lives, Improving Mothers' Care: Surveillance of Maternal Deaths in the UK 2011–13 and Lessons Learned to Inform Maternity Care from the UK and Ireland Confidential Enquiries into Maternal Deaths and Morbidity, 2009–13.* Oxford: National Perinatal Epidemiology Unit, University of Oxford.

Koblinsky, Marge, Zoë Matthews, Julia Hussein, Dileep Mavalankar, Malay K. Mridha, Iqbal Anwar, Endang Achadi, et al. 2006. "Going to Scale with Professional Skilled Care." *Lancet* 368 (9544): 1377–86. doi: https://doi.org/10.1016/S0140-6736(06)69382-3.

Kohrman, Michael. 2005. *Bodies of Difference: Experiences of Disability and Institutional Advocacy in the Making of Modern China.* Berkeley: University of California Press.

Kyakuwa, Margaret. 2009. "Ethnographic Experiences of HIV-Positive Nurses in Managing Stigma at a Clinic in Rural Uganda." *African Journal of AIDS Research* 8 (3): 367–78. doi: https://doi.org/10.2989/AJAR.2009.8.3.13.934.

Kyakuwa, Margaret, and Anita Hardon. 2012. "Concealment Tactics among HIV-Positive Nurses in Uganda." *Culture, Health and Sexuality* 14 (S1): S123–S133. doi: https://doi.org/10.1080/13691058.2012.716452.

Kyomuhendo, Grace Bantebya. 2003. "Low Use of Rural Maternity Services in Uganda: Impact of Women's Status, Traditional Beliefs and Limited Resources." *Reproductive Health Matters* 11 (21): 16–26. doi: https://doi.org/10.1016/s0968-8080(03)02176-1.

Lambek, Michael. 2015. *The Ethical Condition: Essays on Action, Person, and Value.* Chicago: University of Chicago Press.

Lambert, S., and D. Sahn. 2002. "Incidence of Public Spending in the Health and Education Sectors in Tanzania." In *Education and Health Expenditure and Poverty Reduction in East Africa: Madagascar and Tanzania,* edited by C. Morrisson, chap. 2. Paris: OECD Development Center.

Langwick, Stacey A. 2008. "Articulate(d) Bodies: Traditional Medicine in a Tanzanian Hospital." *American Ethnologist* 35 (3): 428–39. doi: https://doi.org/10.1111/j.1548-1425.2008.00044.x.

Langwick, Stacey A. 2011. *Bodies, Politics, and African Healing: The Matter of Maladies in Tanzania.* Bloomington: Indiana University Press.

Langwick, Stacey A. 2012. "The Choreography of Global Subjection: The Traditional Birth Attendant in Contemporary Configurations of Global Health." In *Medicine, Mobility, and Power in Global Africa: Transnational Health and Healing,* edited by H.J. Dilger, A. Kane, and S.A. Langwick, 31–59. Bloomington: Indiana University Press.

Lewis, Maureen. 2006. "Governance and Corruption in Public Health Care Systems." Center for Global Development Working Paper No. 78. http://www1.worldbank.org/publicsector/anticorrupt/Corruption%20WP_78.pdf.

Li, Tania Murray. 2007. *The Will to Improve: Governmentality, Development, and the Practice of Politics*. Durham, NC: Duke University Press.

Lipsky, Michael. 2010. *Street-Level Bureaucracy: Dilemmas of the Individual in Public Services*. 30th Anniversary expanded ed. New York: Russell Sage Foundation.

Livingston, Julie. 2012. *Improvising Medicine: An African Oncology Ward in an Emerging Cancer Epidemic*. Durham, NC: Duke University Press.

Lubbock, Lindsey Ann, and Rob B. Stephenson. 2008. "Utilization of Maternal Health Care Services in the Department of Matagalpa, Nicaragua." *Pan American Journal of Public Health* 24 (2): 75–84. doi: https://doi.org/10.1590/s1020-49892008000800001.

MacDonald, Margaret. 2019. "The Image World of Maternal Mortality: Visual Economies of Hope and Aspiration in the Global Campaigns to Reduce Maternal Mortality." *Humanity* 10 (2): 263–85. doi: https://doi.org/10.1353/hum.2019.0013.

Maestad, Ottar, and Aziza Mwisongo. 2011. "Informal Payments and the Quality of Health Care: Mechanisms Revealed by Tanzanian Health Workers." *Health Policy* 99 (2): 107–15. doi: https://doi.org/10.1016/j.healthpol.2010.07.011.

Mahler, Halfdan. 1987. "The Safe Motherhood Call to Action." *Lancet* 1 (8534): 668–70.

Maine, Deborah, and Allen Rosenfield. 1999. "The Safe Motherhood Initiative: Why Has It Stalled?" *American Journal of Public Health* 89 (4): 480–82.

Majoko, F., L. Nyström, S. Munjanja, and G. Lindmark. 2002. "Usefulness of Risk Scoring at Booking for Antenatal Care in Predicting Adverse Pregnancy Outcome in a Rural African Setting." *Journal of Obstetrics and Gynecology* 22 (6): 604–9. doi: https://doi.org/10.1080/0144361021000020358.

Martin, Helle Max. 2009. *Nursing Contradictions: Ideals and Improvisation in Uganda*. Diemen, Netherlands: AMB.

Martin, Nina, Emma Cillekens, and Alessandra Freitas. 2017. "Lost Mothers." ProPublica, July 17. www.propublica.org/article/lost-mothers-maternal-health-died-childbirth-pregnancy

Martin, Nina, and Renee Montagne. 2017a. "The Last Person You'd Expect to Die in Childbirth." NPR, May 12. www.npr.org/2017/05/12/527806002/focus-on-infants-during-childbirth-leaves-u-s-moms-in-danger.

Martin, Nina, and Renee Montagne. 2017b. "U.S. Has the Worst Rate of Maternal Death in the Developed World." NPR, May 12. www.npr.org/2017/05/12/528098789/u-s-has-the-worst-rate-of-maternal-deaths-in-the-developed-world.

Marwa, Samwel, and Adrienne Strong. 2015. "Three Case Studies and Experiences of Maternal Death at a Regional Referral Hospital in Rukwa, Tanzania." In *Maternal Mortality: Risk Factors, Anthropological Perspectives, Prevalence in Developing Countries and Preventative Strategies for Pregnancy-Related Death*, edited by David Schwartz, 197–213. New York: Nova Science.

Mattingly, Cheryl, and Linda C. Garro. 2000. *Narrative and the Cultural Construction of Illness and Healing*. Berkeley: University of California Press.

McAlister, Chryssa, and Thomas F. Baskett. 2006. "Female Education and Maternal Mortality: A Worldwide Survey." *Journal of Obstretrics and Gynecology* 28 (11): 983–90. doi: https://doi.org/10.1016/S1701-2163(16)32294-0.

McClure, Elizabeth M., Mutinta Nalubamba-Phiri, and Robert L. Goldenberg. 2006. "Stillbirth in Developing Countries." *International Journal of Gynaecology and Obstetrics* 92 (2): 82–90. doi: https://doi.org/10.1016/j.ijgo.2006.03.023.

McDonagh, Marilyn. 1996. "Is Antenatal Care Effective in Reducing Maternal Morbidity and Mortality?" *Health Policy and Planning* 11 (1): 1–15. doi: https://doi.org/10.1093/heapol/11.1.1.

McHenry, Dean E. 1994. *Limited Choices: The Political Struggle for Socialism in Tanzania.* Boulder, CO: Lynne Rienner.

McKay, Ramah. 2012. "Documentary Disorders: Managing Medical Multiplicity in Maputo, Mozambique." *American Ethnologist* 39 (3): 545–61. doi: https://doi.org/10.1111/j.1548-1425.2012.01380.x.

McTavish, Sarah, Spencer Moore, Sam Harper, and John Lynch. 2010. "National Female Literacy, Individual Socio-Economic Status, and Maternal Health Care Use in Sub-Saharan Africa." *Social Science and Medicine* 71: 1958–63. doi: https://doi.org/10.1016/j.socscimed.2010.09.007.

Mechanic, David. 1962. "Sources of Power of Lower Participants in Complex Organizations." *Administrative Science Quarterly* 7 (3): 349–64.

Melberg, Andrea, Abdoulaye Hama Diallo, Katerini T. Storeng, Thorkild Tylleskär, and Karen Marie Moland. 2018. "Policy, Paperwork, and 'Postographs': Global Indicators and Maternity Care Documentation in Rural Burkina Faso." *Social Science and Medicine* 215: 28–35. doi: https://doi.org/10.1016/j.socscimed.2018.09.001.

Merry, Sally E. 2011. "Measuring the World: Indicators, Human Rights, and Global Governance." *Current Anthropology* 52 (S3): S83–S95.

Metz, Thaddeus. 2013. "The Western Ethic of Care or an Afro-Communitarian Ethic? Specifying the Right Relational Morality." *Journal of Global Ethics* 9 (1): 77–92. doi: https://doi.org/10.1080/17449626.2012.756421.

Mhamela, Gregory. 2013. *History of Nursing in Tanzania.* Dar es Salaam: Tanzania Nursing and Midwifery Council.

Mills, Samuel. 2011. *Maternal Death Audit as a Tool Reducing Maternal Mortality.* http://siteresources.worldbank.org/INTPRH/Resources/376374-1278599377733/MaternalDeathAuditMarch22011.pdf.

Mkoka, Dickson A., Isabel Goicolea, Angwara Kiwara, Mughwira Mwangu, and Anna-Karin Hurtig. 2014. "Availability of Drugs and Medical Supplies for Emergency Obstetric Care: Experience of Health Facility Managers in a Rural District of Tanzania." *BMC Pregnancy and Childbirth* 14 (108). doi: https://doi.org/1671-2393/14/108.

Mol, Annemarie. 2002. *The Body Multiple: Ontology in Medical Practice.* Durham, NC: Duke University Press.

Mol, Annemarie. 2008. *The Logic of Care: Health and the Problem of Patient Choice.* New York: Routledge.

Mol, Annemarie, Ingunn Moser, and Jeannette Pols, eds. 2010. *Care in Practice: On Tinkering in Clinics, Homes, and Farms.* Bielefeld, Germany: Transcript Verlag.

Morgan, Lynn, and Elizabeth Roberts. 2012. "Reproductive Governance in Latin America." *Anthropology and Medicine* 19 (2): 241–54. doi: https://doi.org/10.1080/13648470.2012.675046.

Morrisson, Christian. 2002. *Education and Health Expenditure and Poverty Reduction in East Africa: Madagascar and Tanzania.* Paris: OECD Development Center.

Mrisho, Mwifadhi, Joanna A. Schellenberg, Adiel K. Mushi, Brigit Obrist, Hassan Mshinda, Marcel Tanner, and David Schellenberg. 2007. "Factors Affecting Home Delivery in Rural Tanzania." *Tropical Medicine and International Health* 12 (7): 862–72. doi: https://doi.org/10.1111/j.1365-3156.2007.01855.x.

Mubyazi, Godfrey, Julius Massaga, Mathias Kamugisha, J-Nyangoma Mubyazi, Grace C. Magogo, K-Yahya Mdira, Samuel Gesase, et al. 2006. "User Charges in Public Health Facilities in Tanzania: Effect on Revenues, Quality of Services and People's Health-Seeking Behavior for Malaria Illnesses in Korogwe District." *Health Services Management Research* 19: 23–35. doi: https://doi.org/10.1258/095148406775322061.

Mulemi, Benson. 2010. *Coping with Cancer and Adversity: Hospital Ethnography in Kenya.* Leiden, Netherlands: African Studies Centre.

Mwafisi, M.J. 1999. "Corruption in the Health Sector." Paper presented at the International Anti-corruption Conference, Durban, South Africa, October 9–15. http://9iacc.org/papers/day4/ws7/d4ws7_mjmwaffisi.html.

NBS (National Bureau of Statistics) and ICF Macro. 2011. *Tanzania Demographic and Health Survey, 2010.* Dar es Salaam, Tanzania: NBS and ICF Macro.

Nyerere, Julius K. 1968. *Ujamaa—Essays on Socialism.* London: Oxford University Press.

Okafor, Chinyelu B., and Rahna R. Rizzuto. 1994. "Women's and Health-Care Providers' Views of Maternal Practices and Services in Rural Nigeria." *Studies in Family Planning* 25 (6): 353–61. doi: https://doi.org/10.2307/2137879.

Olivier De Sardan, Jean-Pierre, Aissa Diarra, and Mahaman Moha. 2017. "Travelling Models and the Challenge of Pragmatic Contexts and Practical Norms: The Case of Maternal Health." *Health Research Policy and Systems* 15 (Suppl. 1): 71–87. doi: https://doi.org/10.1186/s12961-017-0213-9.

Oni-Orisan, Adeola. 2016. "The Obligation to Count: The Politics of Monitoring Maternal Mortality in Nigeria." In *Metrics: What Counts in Global Health,* edited by Vincanne Adams, 82–101. Durham, NC: Duke University Press.

Pembe, Andrea B., David P. Urassa, Elisabeth Darj, Anders Carlstedt, and Pia Olsson. 2008. "Qualitative Study on Maternal Referrals in Rural Tanzania: Decision Making and Acceptance of Referral Advice." *African Journal of Reproductive Health* 12 (2): 120–31. doi: https://doi.org/10.2307/25470655.

Pérez D'Gregorio, Rogelio. 2010. "Obstetric Violence: A New Legal Term Introduced in Venezuela." *International Journal of Gynecology and Obstetrics* 111: 201–2. doi: https://doi.org/10.1016/j.ijgo.2010.09.002.

Philpott, R.H., and W.M. Castle. 1972. "Cervicographs in the Management of Labour in Primigravidae." *Journal of Obstetrics and Gynaecology of the British Commonwealth* 79: 599–602. doi: https://doi.org/10.1111/j.1471-0528.1972.tb14207.x.

Pigg, Stacey L. 1997. "Authority in Translation: Finding, Knowing, Naming, and Training 'Traditional Birth Attendants' in Nepal." In *Childbirth and Authoritative Knowledge: Cross-Cultural Perspectives,* edited by Robbie E. Davis-Floyd and Carolyn F. Sargent, 233–62. Berkeley: University of California Press.

PMORALG (Prime Minister's Office of Regional Administration and Local Government). 2015. "Sumbawanga Regional Hospital Comprehensive Hospital Operations Plan." Ministry of Health and Social Welfare, Tanzania.

Pols, Jeannette. 2015. "Towards an Empirical Ethics in Care: Relations with Technologies in Health Care." *Medicine, Health Care and Philosophy* 18: 81–90. doi: https://doi.org/10.1007/s11019-014-9582-9.

Prevention of Maternal Mortality Network. 1992. "Barriers to Treatment of Obstetric Emergencies in Rural Communities of West Africa." *Studies in Family Planning* 23 (5): 279–91.

Puig de la Bellacasa, María. 2017. *Matters of Care: Speculative Ethics in More Than Human Worlds.* Minneapolis: University of Minnesota Press.

Raghuram, Parvati. 2016. "Locating Care Ethics beyond the Global North." *ACME: An International Journal for Critical Geographies* 15 (3): 511–33. https://acme-journal.org/index.php/acme/article/view/1353.

Rodriguez, Leah. 2020. "Tanzania Is Lifting Discriminatory Ban on Pregnant Schoolgirls." *Global Citizen,* April 8. www.globalcitizen.org/en/content/tanzania-lifts-pregnant-schoolgirl-ban/.

Ronsmans, C., J. F. Etard, G. Walraven, L. Høj, A. Dumont, L. de Bernis, and B. Kodio. 2003. "Maternal Mortality and Access to Obstetric Services in West Africa." *Tropical Medicine and International Health* 8 (10): 940–48.

Ronsmans, Carine, and Wendy J. Graham. 2006. "Maternal Survival 1: Maternal Mortality: Who, When, Where, and Why." *Lancet* 368: 1189–200. doi: https://doi.org/10.1016/S0140-6736(06)69380-X.

Rosenfield, Allan, and Deborah Maine. 1985. "Maternal Mortality—A Neglected Tragedy. Where Is the M in MCH?" *Lancet* 326 (8446): 83–85.

Rossiter, C.E. 1985. "12. Maternal Mortality." *BJOG: An International Journal of Obstetrics and Gynaecology* 92 (Suppl. 5): 100–115. doi: https://doi.org/10.1111/j.1471-0528.1985.tb15876.x.

Rottenburg, Richard. 2009. "Social and Public Experiments and New Figurations of Science and Politics in Postcolonial Africa." *Postcolonial Studies* 12 (4): 423–40.

Sargent, Carolyn Fishel. 1982. *The Cultural Context of Therapeutic Choice: Obstetrical Care Decisions among the Bariba of Benin.* Culture, Illness, and Healing, vol. 3. Dordrecht: Boston.

Sargent, Carolyn Fishel. 1989. *Maternity, Medicine, and Power: Reproductive Decisions in Urban Benin.* Comparative Studies of Health Systems and Medical Care. Berkeley: University of California Press.

Sargent, Carolyn, and Grace Bascopé. 1997. "Ways of Knowing about Birth in Three Cultures." In *Childbirth and Authoritative Knowledge: Cross-Cultural Perspectives,* edited by Robbie E. Davis-Floyd and Carolyn F. Sargent, 183–208. Berkeley: University of California Press.

Scheper-Hughes, Nancy. 1992. *Death without Weeping: The Violence of Everyday Life in Brazil.* Berkeley: University of California Press.

Scherz, China. 2018. "Stuck in the Clinic: Vernacular Healing and Medical Anthropology in Contemporary Sub-Saharan Africa." *Medical Anthropology Quarterly* 32 (4): 539–55. doi: https://doi.org/10.1111/maq.12467.

Scott, S., and C. Ronsmans. 2009. "The Relationship between Birth with a Health Professional and Maternal Mortality in Observational Studies: A Review of the Literature." *Tropical Medicine and International Health* 14 (12): 1523–33.

Sikika. 2011. "Medicines and Supplies Availability Report." Retrieved from http://sikika.or.tz/images/content/mp3/medicines%20and%20medical%20and%20supply%20availability%20report.pdf.

Singer, Elyse. 2017. "From Reproductive Rights to Responsibilization: Fashioning Liberal Subjects in Mexico City's New Public Sector Abortion Program." *Medical Anthropology Quarterly* 31 (4): 445–63. doi: https://doi.org/10.1111/maq.12321.

Singer, Elyse. 2018. "Lawful Sinners: Reproductive Governance and Moral Agency around Abortion in Mexico." *Culture, Medicine, and Psychiatry* 42: 11–31. doi: https://doi.org/10.1007/s11013-017-9550-y.

Smith-Oka, Vania. 2015. "Microaggressions and the Reproduction of Social Inequalities in Medical Encounters in Mexico." *Social Science and Medicine* 143: 9–16. doi: https://doi.org/10.1016/j.socscimed.2015.08.039.

Smythe, Karen R. 2006. *Fipa Families: Reproduction and Catholic Evangelization in Nkansi, Ufipa, 1880–1960*. Portsmouth, NH: Heineman.

Spangler, Sydney A. 2011. "'To Open Oneself Is a Poor Woman's Trouble': Embodied Inequality and Childbirth in South-Central Tanzania." *Medical Anthropology Quarterly* 25 (4): 479–98. doi: https://doi.org/10.1111/j.1548-1387.2011.01181.x.

Starrs, Ann M. 2006. "Safe Motherhood Initiative: 20 Years and Counting." *Lancet* 368: 1130–32. doi: https://doi.org/10.1016/S0140-6736(06)69385-9.

Stevenson, Lisa. 2014. *Life beside Itself: Imagining Care in the Canadian Arctic*. Berkeley: University of California Press.

Storeng, Katerini T., and Dominique P. Béhague. 2016. "'Lives in the Balance': The Politics of Integration in the Partnership for Maternal, Newborn, and Child Health." *Health Policy and Planning* 31: 992–1000. doi: https://doi.org/10.1093/heapol/czw023.

Storeng, Katerini T., and Dominique P. Béhague. 2017. "'Guilty until Proven Innocent': The Contested Use of Maternal Mortality Indicators in Global Health." *Critical Public Health* 27 (2): 163–76. doi: https://doi.org/10.1080/09581596.2016.1259459.

Street, Alice. 2011. "Artefacts of Not-Knowing: The Medical Record, the Diagnosis and the Production of Uncertainty in Papua New Guinean Biomedicine." *Social Studies of Science* 41 (6): 815–34. doi: https://doi.org/10.1177/0306312711419974.

Strong, Adrienne E. 2014. "Ethical Dilemmas and Medical Malpractice." *Blog: From the Field*, May 2. https://adrienne-strong.com/blog-from-the-field/2014/5/2/ethical-dilemmas-and-medical-malpractice.

Strong, Adrienne E. 2017. "Working in Scarcity: Effects on Social Interactions and Biomedical Care in a Tanzanian Hospital." *Social Science and Medicine* 187: 217–24. doi: https://doi.org/10.1016/j.socscimed.2017.02.010.

Strong, Adrienne E. 2018. "Causes and Effects of Occupational Risk for Healthcare Workers on the Maternity Ward of a Tanzanian Hospital." *Human Organization* 77 (3): 273–86.

Sufrin, Carolyn. 2015. "'Doctor, Why Didn't You Adopt *My* Baby?' Observant Participation, Care, and the Simultaneous Practice of Medicine and Anthropology." *Culture, Medicine, and Psychiatry* 39: 614–33. doi: https://doi.org/10.1007/s11013-015-9435-x.

Sufrin, Carolyn. 2017. *Jailcare: Finding the Safety Net for Women behind Bars*. Berkeley: University of California Press.

Suh, Siri. 2018. "Accounting for Abortion: Accomplishing Transnational Reproductive Governance through Post-abortion Care in Senegal." *Global Public Health* 13 (6): 662–79. doi: https://doi.org/10.1080/17441692.2017.1301513.

Sullivan, Noelle. 2011. "Mediating Abundance and Scarcity: Implementing an HIV/AIDS-Targeted Project within a Government Hospital in Tanzania." *Medical Anthropology* 30 (2): 202–21. doi: https://doi.org/10.1080/01459740.2011.552453.

Sullivan, Noelle. 2012. "Enacting Spaces of Inequality: Placing Global/State Governance within a Tanzanian Hospital." *Space and Culture* 15 (1): 57–67. doi: https://doi.org/10.1177/1206331211426057.

Sumbawanga District Council. 2012. "District Profile." www.rukwa.go.tz/sumbawangadc.html.

Sumbawanga Regional Referral Hospital. 2013. *Rukwa Region Comprehensive Hospital Operational Plan (CHOP)*. United Republic of Tanzania Prime Minister, Office of Regional Administration and Local Government.

Tanzania Daily News. 2015. "Tanzania: MSD Might Collapse if Debt Not Paid, State Told." July 4. http://allafrica.com/stories/201507060702.html.

Tanzania Nurses and Midwives Council. 2009. *Nursing Ethics: A Manual for Nurses*. Dar es Salaam: Tanzania Nurses and Midwives Council.

Taylor, Christopher C. 1992. *Milk, Honey, and Money: Changing Concepts in Rwandan Healing*. Washington, DC: Smithsonian Institution Press.

Thaddeus, Sereen, and Deborah Maine. 1994. "Too Far to Walk: Maternal Mortality in Context." *Social Science and Medicine* 38 (8): 1091–1110.

TMoH (Tanzania Ministry of Health). 1990. *National Health Policy*. Dar es Salaam: United Republic of Tanzania Ministry of Health.

TMoH (Tanzania Ministry of Health). 2001. "Progress in Safe Motherhood in Tanzania during the 1990s: Findings Based on NSS/AMMP Monitoring." Working Paper No. 1. Ministry of Health, Dar es Salaam.

TMoHCDGEC (Tanzania Ministry of Health, Community Development, Gender, Elderly and Children). 2020. "Reproductive Health." Tanzania National Health Portal. https://hmisportal.moh.go.tz/hmisportal/#/themes/rch.

TMoHCDGEC (Tanzania Ministry of Health, Community Development, Gender, Elderly and Children), TMoH (Tanzania Ministry of Health), Zanzibar, NBS (National Bureau of Statistics), Office of Chief Government Statistician, and ICF. 2016. *Tanzania Demographic and Health Survey and Malaria Indicator Survey, 2015–2016*. Dar es Salaam: Tanzania Ministry of Health.

TMoHSW (Tanzania Ministry of Health and Social Welfare). 2006. *Guidelines for Maternal and Perinatal Death Reviews*. Dar es Salaam: Tanzania Ministry of Health and Social Welfare.

Tousignant, Noémi. 2018. *Edges of Exposure: Toxicology and the Problem of Capacity in Postcolonial Senegal*. Durham, NC: Duke University Press.

Turshen, Meredeth. 1984. *The Political Ecology of Disease in Tanzania*. New Brunswick, NJ: Rutgers University Press.

Umezulike, A.C., H.E. Onah, and J.M. Okaro. 1999. "Use of the Partograph among Medical Personnel in Enugu, Nigeria." *International Journal of Gynecology and Obstetrics* 65: 203–5. doi: https://doi.org/10.1016/s0020-7292(98)00168-4.

UN (United Nations). 2015. *The Millennium Development Goals Report 2015*. New York: United Nations.

UN (United Nations). 2016. "Sustainable Development Goals: 17 Goals to Transform Our World." www.un.org/sustainabledevelopment/sustainable-development-goals/.

van der Sijpt, Erica, and Catrien Notermans. 2010. "Perils to Pregnancies: On Social Sorrows and Strategies Surrounding Pregnancy Loss in Cameroon." *Medical Anthropology Quarterly* 24 (3): 381–98. doi: https://doi.org/10.1111/j.1548-1387.2010.01110.x.

van Hamersveld, Koen T., Emil den Bakker, Angelo S. Nyamtema, Thomas van den Akker, Elirehema H. Mfinanga, Marianne van Elteren, and Jos van Roosmalen. 2012. "Barriers to Conducting Effective Obstetric Audit in Ifakara: A Qualitative Assessment in an Under-resourced Setting in Tanzania." *Tropical Medicine and International Health* 17 (5): 652–57. doi: https://doi.org/10.1111/j.1365-3156.2012.02972.x.

Van Hollen, Cecilia. 2003. *Birth on the Threshold: Childbirth and Modernity in South India.* Berkeley: University of California Press.

Vaughan, Megan. 1991. *Curing Their Ills: Colonial Power and African Illness.* Stanford, CA: Stanford University Press.

Vierke, Clarissa. 2012. "Mafumbo: Considering the Functions of Metaphorical Speech in Swahili Context." In *Selected Proceedings of the 42nd Annual Conference on African Linguistics: African Languages in Context,* edited by M.R. Marlo, N.B. Adams, C.R. Green, M. Morrison, and T.M. Purvis, 278–90. Somerville, MA: Cascadilla Proceedings Project.

Wacquant, Loïc. 2011. "Habitus as Topic and Tool: Reflections on Becoming a Prizefighter." *Qualitative Research in Psychology* 8 (1): 81–92. doi: https://doi.org/10.1080/14780887.2010.544176.

Waiswa, Peter, Margaret Kemigisa, Juliet Kiguli, Sarah Naikoba, George W. Pariyo, and Stefan Peterson. 2008. "Acceptability of Evidence-Based Neonatal Care Practices in Rural Uganda: Implications for Programming." *BMC Pregnancy and Childbirth* 8 (21). doi: https://doi.org/10.1186/1471-2393-8-21.

Weber, Max. 1947. *From Max Weber: Essays in Sociology.* Edited and translated by H.H. Gerth and C.W. Mills. London: Kegan Paul, Tranch, Trubner.

Wendland, Claire. 2010. *A Heart for the Work: Journeys through an African Medical School.* Chicago: University of Chicago Press.

Wendland, Claire. 2016. "Estimating Death: A Close Reading of Maternal Mortality Metrics in Malawi." In *Metrics: What Counts in Global Health,* edited by Vincanne Adams, 57–81. Durham, NC: Duke University Press.

Wendland, Claire. 2018. "Who Counts? What Counts? Place and the Limits of Perinatal Mortality Measures." *AMA Journal of Ethics* 20 (3): 278–87. doi: https://doi.org/10.1001/journalofethics.2018.20.3.pfor2-1803.

White, Luise. 1994. "Blood Brotherhood Revisited: Kinship, Relationship, and the Body in East and Central Africa." *Africa: Journal of the International African Institute* 64 (3): 359–72.

White, Luise. 2000. *Speaking with Vampires: Rumor and History in Colonial Africa.* Berkeley: University of California Press.

WHO (World Health Organization). 1978. "Alma Ata Declaration." www.who.int/publications/almaata_declaration_en.pdf.

WHO (World Health Organization). 1989. "The Status of Women and Maternal Mortality." http://whqlibdoc.who.int/publications/1989.9241561289_chap4_eng.pdf.

WHO (World Health Organization). 2012. *Maternal Mortality, Factsheet.* Retrieved October 27. www.who.int/mediacentre/factsheets/fs348/en/.

WHO (World Health Organization). 2014. "Health Expenditure Tables Database." http://apps.who.int/nha/database/ViewData/Indicators/en.

WHO (World Health Organization). 2015a. "Maternal Deaths Fell 44% since 1990—UN." News release, November 12. www.who.int/news-room/detail/12-11-2015-maternal-deaths-fell-44-since-1990-un.

WHO (World Health Organization). 2015b. *Strategies toward Ending Preventable Maternal Mortality.* Geneva: World Health Organization.

WHO (World Health Organization). 2015c. *Trends in Maternal Mortality, 1990–2015.* Geneva: World Health Organization Press.

WHO (World Health Organization). 2016. "Pregnant Women Must Be Able to Access the Right Care at the Right Time, Says WHO." News release, November 7. www.who.int/news-room/detail/07-11-2016-pregnant-women-must-be-able-to-access-the-right-care-at-the-right-time-says-who.

WHO (World Health Organization) Maternal Health and Safe Motherhood Program. 1994. "World Health Organization Partograph in Management of Labour." *Lancet* 343:1399–1404.

Whyte, Susan Reynolds. 1997. *Questioning Misfortune: The Pragmatics of Uncertainty in Eastern Uganda.* Cambridge: Cambridge University Press.

Whyte, Susan Reynolds, and G.E. Siu. 2015. "Contingency: Interpersonal and Historical Dependencies in HIV Care." In *Ethnographies of Uncertainty in Africa,* edited by E. Cooper and D. Pratten, 19–34. New York: Palgrave MacMillan.

Williams, Robert G. 1994. *States and Social Evolution: Coffee and the Rise of National Governments in Central America.* Chapel Hill: University of North Carolina Press.

Willis, Roy G. 1978. "Magic and Medicine in Ufipa." In *Culture and Curing: Anthropological Perspectives on Traditional Medical Beliefs and Practices,* edited by P. Morley and R. Wallis, 139–51. Pittsburgh, PA: University of Pittsburgh Press.

Willis, Roy G. 1981. *A State in the Making: Myth, History, and Social Transformation in Pre-Colonial Ufipa.* Bloomington: Indiana University Press.

Wind, Gitte. 2008. "Negotiated Interactive Observation: Doing Fieldwork in Hospital Settings." *Anthropology and Medicine* 15 (2): 79–89. doi: https://doi.org/10.1080/13648470802127098.

Wolf, Angelika. 2012. "Health Security on the Move: Biobureaucracy, Solidarity, and the Transfer of Health Insurance to Senegal." In *Medicine, Mobility, and Power in Global Africa: Transnational Health and Healing,* edited by Hansjörg Dilger, Aboudlaye Kane, and Stacey A. Langwick, 92–114. Bloomington: Indiana University Press.

Yisma, Engida, Berhanu Dessalegn, Ayalew Astatkie, and Nabreed Fesseha. 2013. "Knowledge and Utilization of Partograph among Obstetric Care Givers in Public Health Institutions of Addis Ababa, Ethiopia." *BMC Pregnancy and Childbirth* 13 (17). doi: https://doi.org/10.1186/1471-2393-13-17.

Young, Alison, John Kelly, and Christopher Schnaars. 2019. "Hospitals Blame Moms When Childbirth Goes Wrong. Secret Data Suggest It's Not That Simple." *USA Today,* March 9. www.usatoday.com/in-depth/news/investigations/deadly-deliveries/2019/03/07/maternal-death-rates-secret-hospital-safety-records-childbirth-deaths/2953224002/?fbclid=IwAR09MBarXEVC2qV6W9_PmjV5CS6PU9SdRxIXkwECD_cnvEdtvPRRZY-souQQ.

Yuster, E.A. 1995. "Rethinking the Role of the Risk Approach and Antenatal Care in Maternal Mortality Reduction." *International Journal of Gynecology and Obstetrics* 50 (Suppl. 2): S59–S61.

INDEX

Founded in 1893,
UNIVERSITY OF CALIFORNIA PRESS
publishes bold, progressive books and journals on topics in the arts, humanities, social sciences, and natural sciences—with a focus on social justice issues—that inspire thought and action among readers worldwide.

The UC PRESS FOUNDATION
raises funds to uphold the press's vital role as an independent, nonprofit publisher, and receives philanthropic support from a wide range of individuals and institutions—and from committed readers like you. To learn more, visit ucpress.edu/supportus.